1985

BUILDING
CLASSROOM
DISCIPLINE

BUILDING CLASSROOM DISCIPLINE

From Models to Practice

Second Edition

C. M. Charles

San Diego State University

Collaboration by Karen Blaine

Longman
New York & London

BUILDING CLASSROOM DISCIPLINE
From Models to Practice

Longman Inc., 1560 Broadway, New York, N.Y. 10036
Associated companies, branches, and representatives
throughout the world.

Developmental Editor: Lane Akers
Editorial Supervisor: Thomas Bacher
Interior Design: Thomas Bacher
Production/Manufacturing: Ferne Y. Kawahara

Library of Congress Cataloging in Publication Data

Charles, C. M.
    Building classroom discipline.

    Includes bibliographies and index.
    1. School discipline. I. Title.
LB3012.C46   1984   371.5   84-4765
ISBN 0-582-28532-1

Manufactured in the United States of America
Printing: 9 8 7 6 5 4 3 2 1   Year: 92 91 90 89 88 87 86 85 84

CONTENTS

● Introduction ●

DISCIPLINE

Problems and Promises

Each year since 1970 the Gallup poll has conducted a survey of the nation's attitudes toward the public schools. One question on the survey asks: "What do you think are the biggest problems with which the *public* schools in this community must deal?" Year after year, the respondents have placed the same concern at the head of the list. That concern has to do with discipline, or, specifically, with the lack thereof. This concern has held the prime spot in the public's mind even though the media have given much more attention to integration, busing, declining test scores, and the use of drugs by teenage students. Indeed, no other concern has been close to that of discipline, although the 1983 report of The National Commission on Excellence in Education *(A Nation at Risk),* asserting that poor schooling was becoming a danger to the security of the nation, aroused great concern about standards, quality teaching, and the need for increased financial support for education.

Public opinion can be suspect because sometimes it does not rest on solid fact and is subject to influences of the sensational, such as physical attacks on teachers and school vandalism and arson. In the case of discipline, however, one hears little disagreement with the view held by the public. Numerous reports have shown that teachers place discipline at the head of their concerns about teaching, and that even the students themselves see it as the main problem. According to the 1981 Nationwide Teacher Opinion Poll, conducted by the National Education Association, 9 teachers in 10 said that student misbehavior interferes with their teaching, and 25% of them said it interferes greatly. That report revealed that 110,000 teachers suffered physical attack from students during the previous 12 months, most of them in the classroom. In one-third of the cases, no action was taken against the offending student. Reportedly, one-third of all teachers were sometimes or often afraid of personal attack from students.

Although none of the 110,000 reported attacks caused serious physical injury, the emotional trauma associated with them no doubt contributed greatly to the intense levels of stress now noted among teachers. A study by the International Labor Office identified stress as the main health and safety problem for teachers. Its attendant symptoms include exhaustion, frustration, tension, hypertension, severe depression, and alcoholism. Violence is a major cause of stress, and while it occurs most frequently in North American classrooms it is becoming more common in Europe. In Latin America violence has resulted in the kidnapping and even killing of teachers. (*Today's Education,* 1981b).

While teachers may have a generalized fear of physical attack, only a small percentage ever experience anything of a serious nature. Usually, they have verbal encounters with hostile, defiant students. Research in hundreds of classrooms has shown that even serious verbal confrontations occur only rarely. Teachers may fear them, and rightfully so, but discipline problems for teachers consist overwhelmingly of what are, by comparison, innocuous behaviors such as students talking without permission, daydreaming, wandering about the room, or otherwise not doing what they have been directed to do. These types of behaviors, according to research done by Jones (1979), make up around 99% of the discipline problems typically encountered by teachers.

If Jones is correct in noting that over 99% of all student misbehavior is simply amiable talking and goofing off, can one objectively conclude that discipline is a genuine problem for teachers? From information available, the answer appears to be convincingly affirmative. There is no discounting the exceptionally high levels of stress known to persist in teachers. It is reasonable to assume that this stress results partly from having to contend with occasionally defiant or disrespectful students and partly from the need to deal endlessly with those mild misbehaviors that disrupt teaching and learning. Cruickshank (1981) and his colleagues studied teacher "problems" for 15 years, with problems identified as those things that interfere with teachers' reaching their instructional goals. Five problem areas were identified, one of which Cruickshank called "control": "Teachers want pupils to behave appropriately—to be relatively quiet, orderly, and courteous. They also expect students to be honest and to show respect for others and for property" (p. 403). When they must deal with students who are noisy, disorderly, discourteous, dishonest, and disrespectful, and when those behaviors interfere with the ongoing instructional program, a genuine problem exists for teachers.

WHY DO BEHAVIOR PROBLEMS PERSIST?

If teachers, administrators, parents, and students know that behavior problems are a main concern and that they interfere with teaching and learning, one would think that this problem would be remedied. Why then does it continue? There seem to be three reasons for the persistence of behavior problems. The first is that students are, in some ways, more difficult to deal with than ever before. They are less willing than previously to defer to teacher authority, to do what the teacher says. This is related to a marked decline in recent years of respect for "one's elders" (i.e., granting them authority simply because they are older). Children of the past few decades have been reared in a more permissive and more child-centered milieu in which their interests have been given greater attention and more emphasis has been put on their rights and their self-expression. This condition originates in the family and carries over to school where it receives further support from teachers, except when it causes trouble in the classroom. As children's autonomy has increased, so has parents' inclination to take the child's side in conflicts with the school. In former years parents automatically supported the teacher when informed that their child was misbehaving. Increasingly they now support the child and put the onus on the teacher.

A second reason for the persistence of discipline problems is that until recently teachers had no systematic means for dealing effectively with classroom misbehavior. Teachers developed their own bags of tricks, some of which worked and some of which did not. Most of those tricks were based on sternness and authoritarian postures, out of line with newer views of humane methods of working with children and young people. They became, therefore, less prized as well as less effective, and teachers lost much of their power in controlling misbehavior. This unfortunate condition can now be remedied, rather easily and effectively, because powerful techniques have been developed during the past 15 years that allow teachers to control misbehavior while at the same time maintaining positive personal relations. Explaining these techniques and how they are used is the main purpose of this book.

A third reason for the ongoing difficulties with classroom discipline has to do with a general acquiesence, a giving-in by teachers and administrators, because the travail of struggling with discipline has slowly worn them down. Some teachers turn bitter and adopt the attitude that kids are basically rotten— "there is not much you can do about it," "it is us against them," and "please, dear heaven, let me get through each day with as little trouble as possible." This attitude festers when schools do not make a concerted, positive attempt to establish and maintain discipline that is effective and humane. Total-school attempts at discipline can and have turned schools around, have restored conditions that permit teaching and learning, and have improved immeasureably the attitudes of students, teachers, administrators, and parents. Describing how effective programs can be implemented on a schoolwide basis is another purpose of this book.

WHAT IS DISCIPLINE?

The word discipline has several different definitions, but here it is used to mean the steps taken by school personnel to ensure that students behave acceptably while in school. Usually, the term is used to refer to what an individual teacher does to maintain proper student behavior in the classroom. There are many effective steps and procedures, and some of them are formed into systematic approaches that can be used easily, consistently, and impartially. The models of discipline discussed in subsequent chapters describe several of these approaches. Before examining those models, however, it will be helpful to explore what sort of behavior teachers wish to maintain in their classrooms. This leads to a brief consideration of behavior and misbehavior.

Behavior and Misbehavior

One understands misbehavior in relation to behavior. Behavior includes all the physical and mental acts that humans are capable of performing. The total of such acts would be incredibly large. It is evident that some of those behaviors are conducive to the goals of education. Many are neutral or irrelevant to educational progress, and still others can impede that progress. Teachers know that educational progress occurs more easily and enjoyably for everyone concerned when conducive behaviors are encouraged and obstructive behaviors suppressed.

Those behaviors that willingly and knowingly obstruct educational progress represent *misbehavior*. While the word behavior has a psychological definition—*actions performed*—the word misbehavior has only a semantic definition—*improper behavior*. What makes it improper is simply that someone has designated it as such. Sometimes, a behavior is judged by society to be inappropriate, as in the case of stealing and lying. But is talking a misbehavior? Sometimes it is, if done at inappropriate times in the classroom. This example underscores the core meaning of classroom misbehavior. *It is behavior that the teacher judges to be inappropriate for a given place or time.* The teacher decides.

Thus, discipline is tied directly to misbehavior. It is intended to suppress, control, and redirect behavior that obstructs learning. There is much agreement among educators as to what constitutes misbehavior. All teachers know that students sometimes behave in ways considered to be sweet, kind, gentle, considerate, helpful, and honest. They approve of those behaviors. They also know that students sometimes behave in ways considered hostile, abusive, disinterested, cruel, and disrespectful. They do not approve of those behaviors which they call misbehavior. Most teachers, then, use disciplinary techniques to thwart or stifle student misbehavior that disrupts, destroys, defies, hurts, or infringes on others' rights. Such misbehavior includes specific acts of cruelty, disrespect, boisterousness, cheating, fighting, name calling, sarcasm, defiance, and apathy. These behavoirs reduce effectiveness of and pleasure in teaching and learning.

But what is discipline, this set of teacher acts that control and suppress student misbehavior? Again, discipline can mean different things to different people. To some it means cracking the whip, making students toe the mark. To some it means counseling students, guiding and persuading them toward desired behavior. To some it means melding student self-control with responsibility. To some it means good manners, to some absolute quiet, to some purposeful activity with attendant noise. To all it means that students do as they are directed and do not defy the teacher.

These views seem diverse, even contradictory. Yet common threads run through them. When those threads are traced one finds the following common elements: Within a system of good discipline students (1) remain on-task, (2) behave responsibly, and (3) show good human relations. Let us explore briefly the meanings of these three elements.

On-Task

On-task means that students are doing at the designated time what they are supposed to do. Generally this means that they are working at activities assigned to them or that they have selected with the consent of the teacher. They are paying attention, not daydreaming, doodling, wandering, or bothering others.

The percentage of assigned time that students actually spend on task is known to influence the amount they learn. That is important to teachers of course, but equally important is the fact that on-task students seldom misbehave. They don't waste time or disrupt learning for others, and they don't add to teacher distress.

For teachers, the goal is to keep students on task. They must use planning and guile to make activities interesting and challenging, but not too difficult. Unless the activity is especially interesting, students profit from new input or changes of pace every 10 to 15 minutes. Since all activities cannot be spellbinding—some important ones are in truth rather dull—teachers must use techniques that assist students in paying attention to task. Injected humor, eye contact, reinforcement, pep talks, and personal attention all make their contributions. They are worth the effort since the value of attention to task can hardly be overemphasized in maintaining good classroom discipline.

Responsible Behavior

Responsibly behaving students do what they are supposed to do, even when the teacher is not looking or not present. This means they adhere to task, show self-control, respect others' rights, are nondisruptive, and show regard for their physical surroundings.

Students who exercise control are in conscious control of their own behavior. Reins are kept on emotions such as anger and exhilaration that can produce disruptive boisterousness, hostility, aggression, and defiance of authority. Students develop resistance to easy influence from others inclined toward misbehavior, they show composure and calm deliberation, and they refrain from doing silly things on the spur of the moment that can cause trouble for themselves and others.

Students who respect others' rights (1) recognize that every member of the class is entitled to peace, belongingness, freedom from threat, and the right to hold and voice their own opinions, and (2) are unwilling to interfere with the rights and privileges to which each individual is entitled. Thus, students who respect rights do not threaten, interfere, thwart, or suppress the acceptable activities of others, even when they do not agree with them.

Nondisruptive students refrain from acts that disturb the learning of others in the class. They do not laugh and talk during quiet times, pick at others, or act silly during work times.

Students who show regard for their physical surroundings do not damage or deface facilities, equipment, and materials. Neither do they leave them in disarray when they have finished using them.

Good Human Relations

Good human relations implies living by the golden rule, that is, treating others as one would like to be treated in return. Most people like friendliness, attention, help, support, and appreciation. Friendly people smile. They greet you and talk nicely. They don't act aloof or disinterested. They don't threaten or harm. Attention is peculiar in that people want it and will go out of their way to obtain it, but they want it in different forms depending on the circumstances. Most of us like to be noticed regularly, every day. We like to be greeted personally. Most, but not all of us, like to be remembered on birthdays and at other times of personal significance. Some of us like to share experiences and receive attention in return. We all want to be noticed, but most of us do not want to be noticed too much. We all want to appear special, but we don't want to appear too different. Help and support are very important to all of us. Students and teachers surely need each others' help, and they need each others' support. To help means to give direct assistance with a task, to work, and to facilitate. To support means to condone and express approval publicly.

Appreciation is needed in abundance, but it is usually given only sporadically. Appreciation is affirmation of worth, finding value in a person or in what they have done. All of us want to be valued for ourselves and for our work. We want others to say that we are fine, neat, super. We want them to laud our efforts, privately and publicly, through speech, writing, and awards.

These four golden rule elements are things we all want, and that means they are things we should give others. Many teachers strive to help students realize this fact, to teach students how to give attention, assistance, and recognition to each other. They consider that kind of behavior to be part of good discipline.

WHY IS DISCIPLINE NECESSARY?

To ask why classrooms need discipline is almost like asking why communities need law enforcement. The answer is simply that without it there are always a few people who make trouble, infringe on others' rights, and generally spoil things for the well-intentioned. The main reason for discipline, then, is to keep order in the school. But order, however desirable, is not an end in itself. One must press further to see why order in the classroom is desirable, and in so doing one finds that order secured through good discipline (1) facilitates learning; (2) fosters socialization; (3) permits democracy; (4) fills a psychological need; and (5) promotes a sense of joy in learning. Some of these conclusions may at first appear strange and, therefore, are explained in the following paragraphs.

Facilitates Learning

Humans have an incredible capacity for learning. They can learn under almost any circumstances at any time; in fact, it is virtually impossible to keep them from learning. This is not to say, however, that learning is unaffected by the conditions within which it occurs. Many kinds of learning, for instance, require that the individual work without interruptions while paying very close attention. Much school learning requires such conditions—tranquility that permits reflection. These conditions cannot be maintained in the classroom without adequate discipline, for otherwise the disruptions become frequent, noise approaches the threshold of pain, and students desert their difficult tasks to find easier and more enjoyable things to do.

Fosters Socialization

Socialization is the process of acquiring the values, beliefs, and behaviors of the societal groups to which one belongs. It includes learning the important skills that promote good human relations. Discussed previously, the key elements are friendliness, giving attention, helping and supporting, and showing appreciation. These human relations are codified to some degree in etiquette and manners. Though etiquette and manners may sometimes seem ludicrous, they are among the most important things students can learn. They provide security in knowing approved ways of acting, and they help convey the best impressions. Without discipline, the finer aspects of human relations tend to go by the board because there always seem to be people who without externally imposed restraint think largely of their own interests and are more than willing to trample on the rights of others.

Permits Democracy

Democracy is both a form of government and a way of life. It has allowed certain societies to enjoy great freedom and prosperity. It allows individual people to participate in making decisions about their own lives. It gives everyone equal status under the law and at the polls. In exchange for these benefits, democracy requires that all opinions be heard, that everyone have equal opportunity, and that everyone live by the same code or law.

John Dewey, the great American philosopher, believed that the schools had unique potential as training grounds for democracy. He thought they provided the best opportunity to practice equality, free exchange of ideas, initiative, responsibility, leadership, followership, and group endeavor. Many people later misunderstood Dewey's intentions, believing that he advocated allowing students to do as they pleased. While he did want students to show initiative, he stressed that it must be tied to responsibility, which in turn meant abiding by group rules.

Teachers continually rediscover what Dewey admonished: adherence to group rules is essential for effective group endeavor. Individualism is fine; it is to be prized. However, it must not allow one person to infringe on the rights of others. Discipline helps allow individual excellence within group law—the hallmark of American democracy.

Fills a Psychological Need

Psychologists and sociologists have discovered that people need discipline for their own personal sense of well-being. Most juvenile offenders agree that they secretly, sometimes even openly, wanted someone who cared enough about them to lay down the law and make it stick. True, they wanted warmth, compassion, and understanding, but they needed the basic boundaries of right and wrong to be designated and enforced.

Discipline provides those boundaries for school students by enforcing compliance with reasonable rules. It brings about a sense of security that comes with a firm knowledge of standards, a reduction of threat, and a recognition that others expect the best of each other. Thus, while all of us seek personal freedom and latitude of action, we at the same time need to know the lines beyond which we must not go. We need to know that someone cares enough about us to help us stay on the proper side of the line. Discipline provides that for students.

Promotes a Sense of Joy in Learning

Perhaps it seems contradictory to say that discipline brings a sense of joy. After all, how can we be happy when someone makes us do what we don't want to do? As with the case of psychological need, here is another interesting fact of human nature. Many of us, much of the time, need to have someone force us to do what we really wish we would do by ourselves. Does this sound paradoxical? Consider a few examples:

1. Being able to play a piano well brings great pleasure, and yet most of us won't practice enough on our own to become truly accomplished. Somebody has to make us do so; later, we are grateful indeed.

2. Most of us keenly wish we could speak a foreign language fluently. We enroll in classes and excitedly do the first few lessons. Before long we begin to lose enthusiasm and stop doing the sessions unless someone drives us. Later, if some of us do acquire language fluency, we are joyfully proud of our ability.

3. Most people yearn for greater self-direction, better organization, and increased work output. Few of us are satisfied with ourselves in these regards. We can improve ourselves, but someone has to urge us, show us how to set our sights in accord with our abilities, help us to organize, and spur us on to attain those things which make us proud of achieving. Once these habits are acquired, they bring the joy of self-control and productivity.

These three examples illustrate how discipline brings joy. The paradoxes of joy through discipline are:

Greater freedom that comes from increased ability and self-direction results from the restriction of freedom through discipline;

Acting in ways that we admire results from being forced to behave as we should;

Doing what we truly want to do requires at times, forceful direction from others;

Being who we truly want to be requires in part having to be made so.

WHY IS DISCIPLINE A DIFFICULT MATTER FOR TEACHERS?

There is consensus about the need for school discipline, and its implementation is known to produce valuable results in education. Despite these facts, discipline continues to be a difficult matter for most teachers. As indicated previously, discipline problems persist for two reasons: first, today's children are raised in a relatively permissive atmosphere with decreased deference for authority; and second, teachers have not until recently had available effective discipline procedures that could be implemented systematically. Improvement is fortunately occurring in both areas. There seems to be a swing away from permissiveness in child rearing, and certainly teachers now have access to effective systems of discipline. Other problems remain, however. The paradoxes inherent in our needing coercion to learn what we want to learn and become what we want to become will continue. In addition there are four other facts of human nature that cause teachers concern regarding discipline.

Facts of Nature

Discipline remains an item of difficulty for teachers because of four inescapable facts of human nature:

1. *We resist doing what others try to make us do.* It does not matter how good the intentions, how laudable the goals, how big the ultimate payoff. Even when it is something we like to do, such as play golf, read, or walk the dog, our hackles rise a bit if we are made to do it. Discipline forces students to do certain things and behave in certain ways. Everyone knows it is important. But since discipline involves coercion, the built-in human resistance rises against it.

2. *It remains eternally fashionable to denigrate authority.* People in positions of power take for granted that their names will be sullied. Think how we talk about the presidents of our country, at least while they are in office. Lincoln was reviled by great numbers of people during his tenure. Think how teachers talk about their administrators, how college students refer to their professors. Discipline and control interweave inextricably with authority. The disenchantment with figures of authority adds to the burden of discipline.

3. *Individuals have differing needs, values, interests, and abilities.* They come from backgrounds that reflect markedly different views of authority. These differences are highly significant. They make it impossible to implement any system of discipline that comes close to pleasing every student. Nor can discipline be individualized to any significant degree, as can instruction. If there is anything students insist on, it is that teachers treat every student in the same manner. They do not want to see anyone be the favorite, get too much special attention, or get away with breaking rules. They do not care about other students' special needs. They want everybody to be treated alike, unless of course they themselves are receiving the special treatment.

4. *As students grow older, they must undergo psychological weaning.* Everybody knows that children begin to act differently toward adults when they move into adolescence. Hero worship and passionate crushes abound, but so do love-hate relationships with parents, siblings, and teachers. This perfectly

natural and normal process distresses parents greatly and bothers teachers too. The young have to establish their psychological independence sooner or later. They cannot be dependent on adults forever. But the transition is a rocky one, characterized by storm and strife. Students seem to develop split personalities: They look up to adults, admire them, depend on them, love them, and imitate them, but at the same time they reject them, spurn their values, disengage from their control, defy them, and often disappoint them greatly. This rejection of adults naturally affects discipline; adults impose discipline and students reject the two of them together. Some do so secretly. Others do so blatantly. Most adolescent students still comply with rules of class control. Some do so willingly, others grudgingly, and few not at all.

While these factors of human nature continue to make discipline difficult, teachers should not be dismayed. They are simply natural phenomena with which to contend. They have, moreover, their silver linings, because student machinations and manifestations to the contrary not withstanding, students as a group need and want order, security, and justice. That is another way of saying that they need and want discipline.

WHAT TEACHERS KNOW ABOUT
BEHAVIOR AND DISCIPLINE

Experts, such as those who have furnished the models of discipline, make a great contribution to education by describing aspects of human behavior and some of the means by which it can be shaped. But practicing teachers know a good deal about human nature, too. One can't work with students day after day without learning a surprising amount about how they think, feel, and act; without learning what pleases and displeases, excites and bores, thrills and frustrates them; without learning much about the needs, defenses, aspirations, and growth patterns that motivate their behavior.

Teacher knowledge about student behavior can best be described in conjunction with age levels of students in school. Patterns of behavior change in accord with those levels. The following sections present brief descriptions of behavior traits evident to teachers of students at the primary, intermediate, junior high, high school, and adult levels.

Primary Grade Level (Ages 4 to 9)

Many kindergarten children come to school when they are 4 years old. They are still babies in many ways. They parallel play, talking and playing individually while alongside other students. They tire easily, get fussy, cry, and need to rest. They fall, sprawl, and crawl about the floor. They make little distinction between work and play, and they require close supervision and special attention. Some play well together; others are spoiled, and expect to have their own way.

Teacher discipline at this level stresses two or three rules, and students break those rules regularly. They must be reminded of the rules, continually and patiently. Students respond very well to personal attention and praise. They accept adult authority without question, although they often seek to circumvent it.

This pattern continues into Grades 1 and 2. Increasingly, students become socialized to schools, to raising hands, standing in lines and following rules. They continue to respond well to praise, affection, and various forms of behavior modification that include the personal touch.

Intermediate Grade Level (Ages 9 to 12)

As students move into Grade 4 they are becoming much more independent. They still like the attention and affection of teachers. Hugging may no longer be so eagerly sought; holding hands with the teacher may take its place. At the same time, discipline can occur effectively without the emotional involvement of the teacher.

Students recognize the logic of rules, their necessity, and their enforcement. They recognize and accept sensible consequences as the natural result of breaking rules. They can help establish the rules and should discuss their value and enforcement frequently.

Intermediate students continue to respond well to behavior modification programs. Now, however, the reinforcers can be marks and tangible objects, in addition to teacher approval and compliments, pats on the back, and recognition for their good efforts.

These students no longer blindly accept teacher authority. They may talk back and drag their heels. They will insist that both rules and punishments be sensible and they will raise a fuss if the rules and consequences are not administered consistently and impartially.

Junior High Grades (Ages 12 to 15)

Discipline is difficult with students in their junior high years. It takes a special person to be able to maintain control, teach the students, and retain personal mental health all at the time.

Teaching junior high students is difficult for six reasons:

1. Students are entering the storm and strife years of adolescence.
2. Mysterious things are happening to their bodies, things that worry, perplex, excite, and otherwise fill their minds.
3. Excitement about members of the opposite sex is beginning to erupt.

4. The process of psychological weaning from adult dependence is under way.
5. Experimentation with numerous role models and life experiences has accelerated.
6. New curriculum, class organization, and teaching styles require significant adjustments.

These six factors combine to fill students' minds to the bursting point and they provide devastating competition against English, math, and history. Students show increasing rebelliousness; their awe for teacher authority has waned. Students poke defiantly at the outer boundaries of rules, to see how far they will stretch and what will happen if they are broken just a bit. At this level good discipline requires rules that are reasonable in every way. Those rules must be enforced or else chaos will result. Teachers have to use a combination of humor, grim demeanor, behavior modification, and authority to keep order. It is essential that order be kept, otherwise students lose respect for authority, and the climate for learning is destroyed.

High School Grades (Ages 15 to 18)

The high school years mark a time of settling down for most students. The majority begin to find themselves. They reach a truce with their bodily and emotional changes, and they begin to get a tentative fix on the future. Those who become further alienated from the mainstream of personalities, customs, and institutions tend to leave school and reach out in other directions.

A new level of relationship with adults emerges. As adolescents gain increased independence, the love-hate syndrome begins to fade. They come more to respect adults as significant people in their lives and recognize their dependence on them. But the dependence is now quasilegal; that is, formalized, recognized, understood, and accepted. It is not the utterly personal, authoritative dependency of former years.

These changes call for a style of discipline that approaches an adult-to-adult relationship. This relationship does not imply an egalitarian system where teacher and students have equal status. The teacher is still boss, makes the rules, enforces them, apprehends transgressors, and doles out punishment. But the entire process is built on clear, rational grounds, and students can be talked with as adults.

Adult Level (Ages 18 and Up)

Discipline at the college and adult school level takes a noticeably different turn. Students are mature. Often some of them are older than their instructors. They expect to be treated as adults and talked to as adults. Their respect for authority, which reached a low point during the junior high years, has risen again and is of two kinds. First, there is respect for the position of instructor regardless of who fills its. Second, there is initial respect for the person who fills the position. That respect can grow greatly if the instructor is knowledge-able, skilled in teaching, and adroit in human relations. It can shrink to zero if the instructor lacks those qualities.

Adult students, unfortunately, require discipline, too. You might not think they would since they are in class by choice. No one makes them attend, and presumably they are there to learn as much as possible. But ideals are not always matched by realities. In the majority of cases, college-age adults attend required classes necessary for obtaining the degree they seek. But even when in classes they truly want to take, adults rarely give it their all without some coercion from the instructor. We all want to take the easier way sometimes. We want to talk with others instead of listening to the teacher, and would rather watch television than complete our assignments. That is adult human nature.

Adults, however, are easier to control than younger students. Requests from the instructor usually suffice, or an occasional stern lecture may help. Serious private talks are the most drastic acceptable steps. Some instructors badger student and ridicule them publicly. That practice is unacceptable under any circumstances. Students who do not perform to minimum expectancies simply suffer the consequences, which are usually lowered grades.

WHAT TEACHERS SHOULD REMEMBER

This chapter contains numerous intimations of student misbehavior and of dire teacher reactions. It is of course necessary to remember how students behave, and how poor behavior can be forestalled, guided, and corrected. But concentrating solely on misbehavior tends unfairly to make students look bad and teachers inept.

There are several positive things teachers should remember. Keeping these points uppermost in mind helps produce a positive attitude, a feeling of correctness about working with learners, a sense of being in charge, and a self-assurance that one's efforts are leading in positive directions. Here are some such points:

1. Most students want to learn, even when they pretend they do not.
2. Most students truly appreciate, admire, and like teachers who are kind and who try to help them.
3. Most students have positive attitudes toward school. (Sometimes they consider it sophisticated to pretend they do not.)
4. Most students need and want an adult to be in charge of their learning.

5. Almost all students want fair, reasonable, and consistently enforced rules in the classroom.
6. Most students resent class troublemakers (but may pay attention to them, laugh, and otherwise reinforce the misbehavior).
7. All parents want their children to learn.
8. Most parents are strongly on the side of teachers.
9. Most parents think fairly strict discipline is desirable.
10. A large majority of adults who have children in school think teachers are doing a fine job.

These facts help put discipline in proper perspective. They show that the discipline necessary for best learning is needed and wanted by students and parents. They show that students and parents appreciate teachers' efforts in setting the tone for and maintaining class discipline. They show that parents and students will support reasonable systems of discipline.

These positive aspects of discipline are not always easy to keep in mind, especially when unpleasant situations arise. Occasional reminders help, such as positive slogans posted in the room and discussions with the class about fair rules and good behavior. Student practice in complimenting and helping other students is valuable, too. These kinds of reminders keep teachers and student on an even keel. They help everyone realize that teachers and students are working toward the same end—the best learning, accomplished within the most pleasant circumstances possible.

REFERENCES

CUICKSHANK, D. "What We Know about Teachers' Problems." *Educational Leadership* 38 (February 1981) 402-405.
JONES, F. "The Gentle Art of Classroom Discipline." *National Elementary Principal* 58: (June 1979) 26-32.
"Opinion Poll: Disruptive Behavior." *Today's Education* 70 (November–December 1981a) 10.
"Trends: Teachers Suffer Stress Around the World." *Today's Education* 70 (November Education (November–December 1981b) 6.

For further reading about the traits and behaviors of individuals at different age levels and in different cultural groups, the following are recommended:

DAVIS, A. *Social Class Influence upon Learning.* Cambridge, Mass.: Harvard University Press, 1948.
DEWEY, J. *Democracy and Education.* New York: MacMillan, 1916.
ERIKSON, E. *Childhood and Society.* New York: Norton, 1950.

FREUD, S. *The Ego and the Mechanisms of Defense.* New York: International Universities Press, 1946.

HAVIGHURST, R. *Developmental Tasks and Education.* New York: David McKay, 1952.

MEAD, M. *Sex and Temperament in Three Primitive Societies.* New York: New American Library, 1935.

PIAGET, J. *Science of Education and the Psychology of the Child.* New York: Orion Press, 1970.

ROGERS, C. *Freedom to Learn.* Columbus, Ohio: Charles E. Merrill, 1969.

SKINNER, B. F. *Science and Human Behavior.* New York: Macmillan, 1953.

ZINTZ, M. *Education across Cultures.* (2nd ed.) Dubuque, Iowa: Kendall/Hunt, 1969.

SEVEN MODELS OF DISCIPLINE

1. The Kounin Model: *Withitness, Alerting, and Group Management*
2. The Neo-Skinnerian Model: *Shaping Desired Behavior*
3. The Ginott Model: *Addressing the Situation with Sane Messages*
4. The Glasser Model: *Good Behavior Comes from Good Choices*
5. The Dreikurs Model: *Confronting Mistaken Goals*
6. The Jones Model: *Body Language, Incentive Systems, and Providing Efficient Help*
7. The Canter Model: *Assertively Taking Charge*

·1·

THE KOUNIN MODEL
Withitness, Alerting, and Group Management

KOUNIN BIOGRAPHICAL SKETCH

Jacob Kounin was born in Cleveland, Ohio, on January 17, 1912. He received his master's degree in 1936 from Western Reserve University and his doctorate in 1939 from Iowa State University. In 1946 he was appointed to a professorship at Wayne State University, and since that time he has served there in the area of educational psychology. Dr. Kounin has made numerous presentations to the American Psychological Association, the American Educational Research Association, and many other organizations. He has served often as a consultant and visiting professor at several universities.

Dr. Kounin is best known for his work, *Discipline and Group Management in Classrooms* (1977), a book that grew out of two decades of research. In the earlier years, his studies focused on group management, with emphasis on how handling the misbehavior of one student affected other students. Kounin observed that a general effect occurred in the group, which he called the *ripple effect*.

From ripple effect studies came subsequent research on disciplinary and group management techniques. This research involved videotapes made in 80 elementary school classrooms. Kounin analyzed these thousands of hours of tape and discovered several dimensions of group management that promoted student work involvement and reduced the amount of misbehavior. The most significant of those dimensions are examined in the sections that follow.

KOUNIN'S KEY IDEAS

1. When teachers correct misbehavior in one student, it often influences the behavior of nearby students. This is known as the ripple effect.

2. Teachers should know what is going on in all parts of the classroom at all times. Kounin calls this awareness, withitness.

3. The ability to provide smooth transitions between activities and to maintain consistent momentum within activities is crucial to effective group management.

4. Teachers should strive to maintain group alertness and to hold every group member accountable for the content of a lesson, which allows optimal learning to take place.

5. Student satiation (boredom) can be avoided by providing a feeling of progress and by adding variety to curriculum and classroom environment.

Let's see what Kounin has to say about each of these key ideas.

THE RIPPLE EFFECT

Kounin's research on the ripple effect started innocently one day when a college student was reprimanded for reading a newspaper during a lecture. Immediately afterward, there occurred a difference in the behavior of students who had not been targets of the reprimand. They reacted by sitting up straighter, paying closer attention, and refraining from deviant behavior. This observation led Kounin to believe that the way in which teachers issue desists (remarks intended to suppress misbehavior) influences behavior in students who witness the desist. The effect of the desist ripples from the target student outward to others.

Kounin tested the ripple effect in four settings—college, kindergarten, high school, and summer camp. In the college study he set up an experiment to test the effect of a supportive desist (offering help to correct the deviant behavior) versus a threatening desist (chastising the deviant). Both produced a ripple effect. In the kindergarten study, Kounin again tried to find whether the quality of the desist influenced the degree of conforming behavior. The three qualities of desists were:

1. *Clarity.* The desist carried information that named the deviant, specified the behavior that was unacceptable, and listed the reasons for the desist.
2. *Firmness.* An "I mean it" attitude was projected with follow-through until the child stopped the misbehavior.
3. *Roughness.* The desist included anger, threats, physical handling, and punishment.

Kounin found that increased clarity tended to increase conforming behavior in students who witnessed the desist. Firmness in the desist increased conformity only in students who were themselves misbehaving at the time. Roughness did not improve behavior; it simply upset the audience children, making them anxious, confused, and restless. It was also noted that the ripple effect was very pronounced on the first day of school but tended to diminish as the year wore on.

In the summer camp study, Kounin attempted to measure the ripple effect with children from 7 to 13 years of age. He could find no measurable effect and decided that this was due to the fact that misconduct at camp was considered more trivial than misbehavior at home or school, and it resulted in fewer consequences. Children in summer camps did not take desists seriously.

In the high school study, Kounin found that the type of desist had no effect on the amount of misbehavior exhibited by the audience students. He found that an extremely angry outburst caused some emotional discomfort for students witnessing the desist. What did influence behavior in high school was the degree to which the teacher was liked. High regard for the teacher coupled with high motivation to learn created maximum work involvement and minimum misbehavior among students.

From these studies one can conclude that the ripple effect, in itself, is powerful at the elementary level. It becomes weaker at the secondary and college levels where it depends on the popularity or prestige of the teacher.

WITHITNESS

Kounin coined the term *withitness* to describe the trait of teachers having eyes in the back of their heads. This trait conveys to students that the teacher knows what is going on in all areas of the classroom at all times. Kounin felt that this trait was communicated more effectively by teachers' behaviors than by their words. Further, it was effective only if students were convinced that the teacher really knew what was going on.

Kounin found two elements of withitness that contributed to effectiveness. The first is the ability to select the correct student for a desist. Suppose Bob and Bill are teasing Mary while the teacher is directing a small group. Mary finally says in a loud voice, "Stop that you two!" The teacher tells Mary to go sit alone and ignores the instigators of the incident. This tells the students that the teacher does not know what is going on. The second element is attending to the more serious deviancy when two are occurring simultaneously. Here is an illustration: Jill is playing with a toy at her desk. Meanwhile James and Eric are pushing each other violently around the drinking fountain. The teacher looks up and says, "Jill, bring that toy up to me and then get back to work." The teacher failed to take any action against the fight at the drinking fountain. If mistakes like these occur often, students begin to get the idea that the teacher is not truly aware. This encourages them to engage in misbehavior without fear of getting caught.

Timing also influences withitness. A major mistake in timing is to wait until the misbehavior spreads before taking action. A student throws a paper ball at the wastebasket. Another student sees this and decides to try it. Three or four others join in until there is a virtual basketball game in progress. Scenes like this do not occur if teachers display withitness. They correct misbehavior as soon as it occurs. This action shows students that the teacher knows exactly what is going on and will not tolerate misbehavior.

Another timing mistake is to allow the misbehavior to increase in seriousness before stopping it. Let's return to the example of the two boys at the drinking fountain. James went there to get a drink. Eric pushed his way in front of James. James pushed him out of the way claiming he was there first.

Eric hit James. James hit back. They scuffled. The teacher waited too long to intervene. If she had been aware of what was happening, she could have spoken to Eric when he first butted in. In this way, she would have conveyed her withitness to the students.

Kounin found that if children perceive that teachers are with it (in that they choose the right culprit and correct misbehavior at once), they are less likely to misbehave. Withitness was found to induce more work involvement and less misbehavior, especially in teacher-directed lessons. Handling the correct deviant on time was more important to classroom control than was the firmness or clarity of a desist.

OVERLAPPING

In his videotape studies, Kounin became aware of a group-management technique that he labeled overlapping. *Overlapping* is the ability to attend to two issues at the same time. Here is an example. A teacher is meeting with a small group and notices that two students at their seats are playing cards instead of attending to an assignment. The teacher could:

1. Stop the small-group activity, walk over to the card players, stand there until they are back on task, and then attempt to reestablish the lesson in the small group.
2. Have the small group continue while addressing the card players from where the small group is sitting and continue to monitor the students at their seats while conducting the small-group lesson.

Teachers are interrupted often while they are working with a group. A student might approach with a paper that must be looked at before the student can continue with his work. Teachers skilled in overlapping can check the paper while glancing at the small group and adding encouraging remarks such as "Go on," or "That's correct." Thus, the teacher has attended to two issues simultaneously.

Not surprisingly Kounin found that teachers who were adept at overlapping were also aware of the broader scope of happenings in the classroom. They were more with it. Overlapping loses its effectiveness if the teacher does not also demonstrate withitness. If students working independently know that the teacher is aware of them and able to deal with them, they are more likely to remain on task.

MOVEMENT MANAGEMENT

Kounin's research revealed an important relationship between student behavior and *movement* within and between lessons. He did not mean physical movement of students or teachers. He meant lesson *pace, momentum,* and *transitions.* Teachers' ability to move smoothly from one activity to the next and to maintain momentum within an activity has a great deal to do with their effectiveness in controlling behavior in the classroom. In smooth transitions, student attention is turned easily from one activity to another. Student concentration is kept on the task at hand.

Kounin discovered two transition mistakes—*jerkiness* and *slowdowns*— both of which encourage student misbehavior.

Jerkiness

When activities do not flow smoothly from one into the other, the transition is called jerky. Kounin identified four causes of jerkiness. A first cause of jerky transitions is a teacher behavior called *thrusts.* Thrusts occur with the teacher suddenly bursts into an activity with a statement or directions, but the group is not ready to receive the message. For example suppose students are working on an art project. The teacher is doing desk work. Without looking up to see if the group is ready to receive a message, the teacher says, "Put your supplies away and get ready for reading." Half of the class does not hear and the other half starts to move around in confusion. Their attention was not directd to the teacher who thrust a message onto the group without assessing their readiness to follow directions, causing confusion and noconformance.

A second cause of jerky transitions is a behavior called *dangles.* Kounin described dangles as the practice of leaving one activity dangling in midair to start another activity and then returning to the first activity. For example, the class has just begun a math lesson. The teacher calls on three students to go to the board. On their way up she suddenly asks, "How many of you brought your money for the field trip?" She then counts the raised hands, goes to her desk, and writes the number down. The class is distracted from the math lesson. Many students are now talking about the field trip. It is difficult at this point to bring them back to the business at hand.

A third cause of jerkiness is *truncations,* the same behavior as dangles except that the teacher never returns to the first activity. Let's say a teacher asks the class to get out their literature books. As they begin, he says, "Did we practice the Thanksgiving skit yesterday? No? Oh dear, we need to do that right now." Literature is forgotten, left dangling, and there is never time during the period to return to the lesson.

A fourth cause of jerkiness is *flip-flops,* another variation of dangling. When a flip-flop occurs, teachers have terminated one activity, begun a second, and then returned to the first. Mrs. Smith has the students put away their math assignment and get out their library books. After a few minutes she interrupts their reading and asks, "How many of you got to number 10 on your math assignment today?" She proceeds to check them one by one, never returning to the reading.

Jerky transitions interrupt smooth flowing from one activity to another. They cause confusion, unnecessary activity, noise, and nonconformance. They provide an opportunity to misbehave. It is difficult for students to turn their attention from one task to another. It is even more difficult for them to get down to work and concentrate on the new task. Smooth transitions help them direct their attention appropriately and keep it focused.

Slowdowns

If jerkiness is at one end of the transition continuum, slowdowns are at the other end and are just as detrimental to effective teaching. Slowdowns are delays, and they waste time between activities. They occur because of two phenomena: *overdwelling* and *fragmentation,* both of which impede progress and allow friction to occur.

Overdwelling, according to Kounin, is the major cause of slowdowns. It takes the form of spending too much time giving directions and explanations. Teachers often begin a task with elaborate directions and long, drawnout explanations, going far beyond what is required for understanding how to proceed. Some teachers also have a tendency to overdwell on student behavior. To correct misbehavior, these teachers lecture on and on, as a means of conveying their displeasure. Students soon turn off this sort of nagging and begin thinking of other things while the teacher contines to talk.

Kounin labeled another type of overdwelling *actone overdwelling,* which occurs when teachers concentrate more on details than on the main idea of the lesson. Suppose Miss Anderson is doing a math lesson with the class. She writes some problems on the board for the students to copy. As they are copying, she stops them saying, "Make sure there is a one-inch margin on your paper. Skip lines between problems. Number each problem. Don't put more than three problems on a line. Put a box around the answer." The teacher has drawn attention away from the concepts being taught by focusing attention on details. This slowed the activity and caused students to lose sight of the main focus of the lesson.

Related to actone overdwelling is *prop overdwelling.* This happens when teachers devote more time and attention to physical props than to the lesson. Let's look at an art lesson. After the materials are passed out Mr. Crisp says, "Everyone hold up your paint container. Do you have one-fourth of a cup? Now everyone should have two brushes. Is there anyone who doesn't have a big and a little brush? Measure the area on which you are going to paint. It should be exactly 8 inches by 11 inches. Put your paint on your right, your brushes on your left, and the paper in the middle. Be sure to hold your brush exactly like this." By the time Mr. Crisp gets around to the activity, the students have begun to lose interest. The sooner the students can involve themselves in activity, the less time they have to be doing something they should not.

You can see how overdwelling causes students to lose interest in the main idea of the activity. They begin to feel that they already know the information the teacher is passing on. They quit listening and find something else to do, often something inappropriate. Teachers should practice giving the minimum amount of instructions necessary for the lesson.

Fragmentation was identified by Kounin as another major cause of slow-downs. Fragmentation occurs when teachers break an activity down into several unnecessary steps when it could be more easily handled as a whole. During a science lesson the teacher began, "Row 1 may get up and get their beakers. Row 2 may get theirs. Now Row 3. Now, Row 1 may line up to put some bicarbonate of soda in their beakers. Row 2 may follow them," and so forth. When each row had obtained their bicarbonate of soda the teacher had them go row by row to add water. This left the remainder of the class sitting at their desks with no direction, doing nothing or else beginning to find something with which to entertain themselves.

Another type of fragmentation was evident in the science lesson. Kounin called it *group fragmentation*. After every student had the necessary substances in their beakers the teacher proceeded: "Okay Roy, now pour in the vinegar while we watch. Good. Now Susie, it's your turn. Patti, you're next." The teacher had individuals doing the activity when it would have made more sense to have the class do it together. It is always better to involve as many students as possible in an activity. This helps focus attention and decreases the possibility of boredom and misbehavior.

Transitions may seem at first to be a relatively minor concern, but Kounin concluded from his investigations that *teachers' ability to manage smooth transitions and maintain momentum was more important to work involvement and classroom control than any other behavior-management technique.*

GROUP FOCUS

Teachers have few opportunities to work exclusively with one student. Mostly they work with groups, sometimes the entire class, and sometimes several smaller groups working concurrently. Kounin found that the ability to maintain a concerted group focus is essential to a productive, efficient classroom. Teachers are better able to maintain group focus when they take into careful account (1) *group format*, (2) *degree of accountability* of each student for the content of the lesson, and (3) effective focus of group *attention*.

Group Format

Group format refers to grouping students in such a manner that maximum active participation is encouraged. Generally speaking, maximum participation is obtained through working with larger, rather than smaller groups. At times, individual students or very small groups are needed for achieving the objectives of the lesson. Where possible, however, larger groups should be used as a means of ensuring greater participation. This allows teachers to call on many different students instead of a few. When responses are called for, the teacher may ask the group to respond in unison, or one student may be asked to do an activity at the chalkboard while the remaining members of the group follow by doing the activity at their seats. Having everyone involved in an activity eliminates the group waiting for one member to perform.

Accountability

Accountability refers to each student in the group being responsible for learning each of the steps or concepts being taught in a lesson. It is enhanced when teachers show awareness of how each student is progressing. Kounin recommends several techniques for holding all members of a group accountable. Some of them are:

1. All students hold up response props for the teacher to see.
2. The teacher asks all members to observe and check on accuracy while one member performs.
3. The teacher asks all members to write the answer and then at random calls on several students to respond.
4. The teacher circulates and observes the responses of nonreciters.
5. The teacher calls for a unison response and then checks individuals at random.

Group accountability has much in common with overlapping. The teacher is able to deal with the entire group and yet have individuals show accountability for their progress. When students perceive that the teacher will definitely and immediately hold them accountable for the content of the lesson, they are more likely to pay attention and remain involved in the activity.

Attention

Attention is a third element in group focus. Group alerting involves focusing the attention of all group members on the activity at all times. Kounin advocates the following for maintaining attentive group focus.

1. The teacher attracts attention by looking around the group in a suspenseful manner, or saying, "Let's see who can . . . "
2. The teacher keeps in suspense who will be called on next and avoids a predictable pattern of response.
3. The teacher varies unison responses with individual responses.
4. Nonreciters are alerted that they may be called on in connection with a reciter's response. ("Listen to Jim as he reads and see if you can guess who took the crystal ball.")

All of these practices draw the attention of the group to the lesson. Every member of the group is alerted. The teacher tries hard to keep the group on their toes.

Kounin also examined some common mistakes that contribute to non-attention within the group. Examples of such mistakes are:

1. The teacher focuses on one student at a time and excludes the other members from the lesson.
2. The teacher chooses a reciter before asking a question, causing others to stop listening because they know they won't have to respond.
3. The teacher calls on students to respond in a predictable sequence, such as going clockwise around a circle. Students then only need to be ready to respond after their neighbor. This allows them an opportunity to focus their attention elsewhere if it is not their turn to respond. (It may be interesting to note that recent research casts some doubt on Examples 2 and 3.)

Of the three elements of group focus, Kounin found the ability to maintain group attention the most important. Teachers who held the attention of every member throughout the lesson were more successful at inducing work involvement and preventing misbehavior. When students pay attention and know that they may at any time be held accountable for the information presented in a lesson, they have little time to engage in inappropriate activity. As one might suspect, group accountability and attention accompany each other, and both come into play to a greater extent in teacher-directed lessons than in lessons where students work independently.

AVOIDING SATIATION

Satiation means getting filled up with something, getting enough of it, getting bored. Kounin uses the term to describe a change in the dynamics of an activity due to repetition. He found that repetition often causes less involvement in and liking for an activity. As students become increasingly satiated, certain behavior changes result. For instance, students may introduce spontaneous variations into the activity. If made to write multiplication facts 10 times each they may after a time start writing the top line of the problem across the paper, then add the multiplication sign, then add the bottom digits, and so forth, rather than writing each problem separately.

Satiation causes careless work that results in increased errors. Students begin to do the work mechanically, devoting little thought to the process. The result is a breakdown in meaning. When students break up an activity in a different way to add variety, they may also lose their grasp on the process or concept being learned. Satiated students tend to become less involved with an activity, or they may try to escape from it. This is often shown in behaviors such as looking out the window, tying shoes, poking a neighbor, or sharpening a pencil. They look for anything to initiate some new type of stimulation. Teachers can eliminate these effects by providing progress, challenge, and variety.

Progress

Kounin studied many different classrooms to determine why some teachers induced more satiation than did others. One element found effective in slowing the rate of satiation was a feeling of progress. Students who felt they were making definite progress took longer to become satiated. Those who did the same task over and over, without any feeling of progress, satiated quickly.

Challenge

Kounin also noticed that teachers who offered challenges throughout a lesson prevented satiation. One of the many ways they provided challenges was to show enthusiasm for the lesson with remarks like, "I have a special magical math formula to teach you today." Another way was to elicit positive feelings about the lesson by saying something like, "I know you'll all get the answer to the next one!" Teachers might make comments such as, "Don't be fooled by this one. It's tricky!" These techniques work if the teacher is genuinely enthusiastic and positive—students pick up on genuine teacher interest and follow its cues.

Variety

Variety is the spice of life and is the spice of most lessons. Kounin feels that variety plays a crucial role in reducing satiation. The first thing teachers can do is vary the content of classroom activities. Elementary teachers might have a quiet reading time, followed by an active physical education session, followed by math, and then a spelling game. Students may become satiated, when activities are not varied, simply because they have to sit and work quietly for extended periods of time. Secondary teachers should consider changing the daily class routine from time to time.

Within a lesson, teachers may wish to change the level of intellectual challenge. Sometimes students may simply listen. At other times they may practice a skill or demonstrate comprehension of a concept. The teacher may challenge them by having them engage in abstract thinking or exhibit some sort of creativity. All of these require a different level of intellectual functioning.

Teachers should also vary the way they present lessons. They can demonstrate, direct an activity, ask questions for discussion, or have students solve problems on their own. While monitoring the students they may circulate among them or participate in the activities. Students enjoy variety in styles of presentation as well as variety among lessons, even when covering the same material.

Variety can also be provided in the materials used to enhance or extend learning. Some activities call for the usual pencil and paper, but others can make excellent use of slides, tape recorders, or such unusual things as a live snake or a real musician.

Finally, regrouping can add much variety. One may start a lesson with the entire class, break into small groups for close interaction, and then reconvene into the whole class. The focus changes from teacher to students and back to teacher. Variety is provided through movement and different kinds of interacting and thinking.

CONCLUSION

The techniques presented in this chapter are advocated by Kounin to create an effective classroom environment and promote optimal learning. None of them requires a punishing attitude or harsh actions from the teacher. All of them require effective and efficient group management techniques.

Teachers must be able to deal with the entire class, subgroups, pairs of students, and individuals, often at the same time. Kounin does not feel that teachers' personality traits are particularly important in their effectiveness in classroom control. What is important, he says, is teacher's ability to manage groups. To do this they must:

1. Know what is happening in every area of the classroom at all times and communicate that fact to the students;
2. Be able to deal with more than one issue at the same time;
3. Correct the appropriate target before misbehavior escalates;
4. Be able to use the ripple effect advantageously;
5. Initiate and maintain smooth and consistent momentum;
6. Maintain group focus through alerting and accountability;

7. Provide nonsatiating learning programs by including progress, challenge, and variety.

REFERENCES

KOUNIN, J. *Discipline and Group Management in Classrooms.* New York: Holt, Rinehart and Winston, 1977.

KOUNIN, J., and L. SHERMAN. "School Environments as Behavior Settings." *Theory into Practice* 18 (June 1979) :145–51.

·2·

THE NEO-SKINNERIAN MODEL

Shaping Desired Behavior

SKINNER'S BIOGRAPHICAL SKETCH

B. F. Skinner is recognized as one of the greatest living psychologists. Many consider him the greatest psychologist of all time. His work has had prodigious influence in both psychology and education.

Skinner was born in Pennsylvania in 1904. He earned his Ph.D. in psychology at Harvard University in 1931. Most of his subsequent career was spent at Harvard. There, he conducted his experimental studies in learning, working mostly with rats and pigeons, but sometimes with humans. Earlier behaviorism was concerned with stimulus–response connections in learning. Skinner looked at the learning process in the opposite way, investigating the effects on learning of stimuli provided *after* an act was performed. He found that given certain stimuli the organism repeated a given act more frequently. He called those stimuli *reinforcers*. Providing reinforcers in a systematic way was called reinforcement, and the process through which behavior was shaped in desired directions was called behavior shaping.

Skinner became widely recognized for using the process of behavior shaping to teach pigeons to do complicated acts. This teaching was often done inside a glass-walled enclosure that came to be known as a Skinner box.

Skinner's work was not confined to laboratory animals. He drew worldwide attention for his ideas about raising infants inside glass enclosures called air cribs where the child was kept dry, warm, and comfortable, with all needs satisfied. He raised his own daughter in an air crib.

Skinner drew much attention, too, with the publication of his novel *Walden Two* (1948), which described the workings of a utopian community built on principles of reinforcement. It is still widely read and has served as a model for communes in various places.

In 1971, Skinner's book *Beyond Freedom and Dignity* was published, and again world attention turned to him. He challenged traditional concepts of freedom and dignity as inadequate, insisting they are outmoded, useless, and incorrect. We are not free to choose, he asserted. Our choices are made, instead, on the basis of what has happened to us in the past; that is, on the reinforcements we have received for prior actions. Instead of concentrating on free choice, we should turn our efforts to providing conditions that improve human behavior in general.

Teachers have benefited most from Skinner's fundamental work in reinforcement as a means of controlling and motivating student behavior. Skinner's work has been enlarged, extended, and modified by numerous psychologists and educators. Its various applications to classroom practice are commonly called *behavior modification*, a technique that has been refined during the past two decades. Most teachers consider it to be one of the most valuable tools available for improving the learning and behavior of school students.

SKINNER'S KEY IDEAS

The model presented in this chapter is called neo-Skinnerian to indicate that it is made up of newer applications of Skinner's basic ideas. Skinner himself never proposed a model of school discipline. Other writers have taken his ideas on learning and adapted them to controlling the behavior of students in school. The following ideas reveal the essence of the neo-Skinnerian model:

1. Behavior is shaped by its consequences, by what happens to the individual after performing an act.

2. Behavior is strengthened if followed immediately by reinforcers. Technically, a reinforcer is a stimulus that increases the likelihood that the individual will repeat the act. We commonly think of reinforcers as rewards.

3. Strengthened behaviors are those that have become more likely to be repeated.

4. Behavior is weakened if it is not followed by reinforcement.

5. Weakened behaviors are those that have become less likely than before to be repeated.

6. Behavior is also weakened if followed by punishment. Punishment is *not* the same thing as negative reinforcement.

7. Systematic use of reinforcement (rewards) can shape individual's behavior in desired directions.

8. In the early stages of learning, constant reinforcement produces the best results. Constant means that the behavior is reinforced every time it occurs.

9. Once learning has reached the desired level, it is best maintained through intermittent reinforcement, reinforcement that is provided only occasionally, on an unpredictable schedule.

10. When applied to classroom learning and discipline, this process of behavior shaping through reinforcement is called behavior modification.

11. Behavior modification is one of the most powerful tools available to teachers for strengthening desired classroom learning and behavior.

12. Behavior modification is applied in these two ways:

    a. The teacher observes the student perform a desired act; the teacher rewards the student; the student tends to repeat the act.

    b. The teacher observes the student perform an undesired act; the teacher either ignores the act or punishes the student, then praises a student who is behaving correctly; the misbehaving student becomes less likely than before to repeat the act.

13. Behavior modification successfully uses various kinds of reinforcers. They include social reinforcers, such as verbal comments, facial expressions, and gestures; graphic reinforcers, such as marks and stars; activity reinforcers, such as free time, free reading, and collaborating with a friend; and tangible reinforcers, such as food, prizes, and printed awards.

Remember that the model of discipline described in this chapter was not proposed by B. F. Skinner, but rather is a composite of findings and ideas from many people following in Skinner's footsteps. It is a powerful model for classroom teachers, one that can be easily modified and implemented with students of all ages and backgrounds. The model will be examined by providing: (1) a general description; (2) beneficial aspects of the model; (3) dangers of punishment; (4) types of reinforcers; (5) systems of behavior modification; (6) formulation of a plan of behavior modification; and (7) implementation of a plan of behavior modification.

THE NEO-SKINNERIAN MODEL

The neo-Skinnerian model of discipline makes systematic application of the scientific principles of reinforcement for improvement of behavior and learning among school students. These principles of reinforcement apply equally well to students of all ages, from all backgrounds. Some of the specific . reinforcers, as well as ways of applying reinforcement, have to be modified in accord with the ages and interests of students. The basic principles, however, apply consistently.

Skinner established precise definitions of terms he used, such as operant behavior, reinforcing stimuli, schedules of reinforcement, successive approximations, positive reinforcement, and negative reinforcement. These terms are necessary to acquire an understanding of the model. We need not be overly concerned, however, about the exact wording of the definitions. Teachers can use the model just as well if they keep these fundamental concepts in mind.

Operant behavior is simply behavior that the student produces. It comes not as a reflex or reaction but as purposeful, voluntary action. These behaviors are any of the immense variety of actions that individuals are able to perform in voluntary ways.

Reinforcing stimuli are stimuli that the individual receives immediately after performing an operant behavior. We can think of reinforcers as rewards. When we see a student exhibit any behavior (operant) that we think especially worthy of attention we can immediately give that individual a reward. Receiving the reward pleases the student, who will likely repeat the behavior in hopes of getting further reward. The process of supplying these rewards is called reinforcement.

Schedules of reinforcement were important in Skinner's experimental work. Different schedules were shown to produce different effects. Constant reinforcement, provided every time a desired act is seen, is most effective in establishing new learnings. The individual works hard and fast to earn rewards. Once new learning is acquired it can be maintained indefinitely by using intermittent reinforcement, in which reward is supplied only occasionally. The individual knows that reward will come sooner or later and keeps on trying.

Succesive approximations simply means actions that come closer and closer to a pre-set goal. Teachers have to work toward many learnings and behaviors in gradual ways, taking one small step at a time. Successive approximations are small-step improvements leading to the overall learning. Teachers reinforce the small improvements to help the student progress more rapidly.

Positive reinforcement is the process of supplying a reward that the student wants, something that will spur greater effort. For classroom purposes we need not confuse ourselves about positive and negative reinforcement. We can simply call all rewards reinforcement.

Negative reinforcement is a term that is misunderstood (and used incorrectly) by most classroom teachers. They think of negative reinforcement as meaning harsh punishment that will suppress behavior. Negative reinforcement, however, increases the likelihood of behavior, just as positive reinforcement does. Negative means taking away something that the student doesn't like. That, in turn, increases learning and good behavior. It is easy to use negative reinforcement in the experimental laboratory with rats, but not as easy to use it in school settings. Tauber (1982) advocates its use in limited ways as illustrated in the following examples: "If you score 80 percent or higher on the exam you do not have to turn in a final paper." And, "If you get all of your assignments in on time . . . you will be able to drop your lowest grade" (p. 66). Both examples show how negative reinforcement is provided through the removal of an "aversive"—the final paper or the lowest grade.

BENEFICIAL ASPECTS OF BEHAVIOR MODIFICATION

Since the beginning of human history, parents and teachers have used punishment to motivate learning in the young. Learners did what they were supposed to do or suffered harsh lectures or even beatings from their teachers. This punitive system of motivation has persisted to the present day and is still evident in some classrooms.

Skinner found in his experiments with learning that animals worked harder and learned more quickly if given rewards for doing something right than if given punishment for doing wrong. This made sense for rats and pigeons because there was no way to tell them what we wanted them to do. Punishment didn't help them because it didn't give them guidance.

When the notion of providing rewards for doing something right was applied to school students an interesting fact came to light. Students, like rats and pigeons, responded better to positive rewards than they did to punishment. There were, and are, exceptions, but generally speaking, rewards spurred interest and effort. Moreover, they helped clarify what was expected.

Behavior modification is based almost entirely on rewards. It gives teachers power to work with students in positive ways. It lets them get away from harshness and punishment, which neither students nor teachers like. It allows them to maintain control within classroom environments that are warm, supportive, and positive, instead of cold, harsh, and punitive. This coincides with a growing trend toward humaneness in all walks of life.

Behavior modification then is good for speeding the learning of academic material as well as enhancing good personal behavior. It has the advantage of allowing the teacher to work in warm, supportive ways, emphasizing the positive and reducing the negative. It also helps students build behavior that grows in small steps. A little reward for each step accomplished helps spur interest and work output.

THE DANGERS OF PUNISHMENT

We should acknowledge that punishment is effective for stopping undesired behavior. Positive reinforcement can be too slow and ineffective when, for example, students are engaged in a fight. Life and limb cannot be adequately protected by finding a student who is sitting quietly and saying to that student, "Thank you, Susan, for sitting quietly and not fighting." Instead we must do whatever is necessary to stop the fight and hopefully suppress the students' inclination to fight, even if that means punishing the offenders.

On the other hand, we have found that while punishment suppresses unwanted behavior, it produces side effects that sometimes override our best educational intents. If students sees punishment as unwarranted, malicious, or excessive, bad feelings that are very hard to overcome result toward teachers, schools, and classmates. Those feelings may produce counterattacks or sometimes withdrawal. Always, they teach that "might makes right," that muscle is more important than mind.

For those reasons teachers are advised to use punishment as little as possible and to try the positive approach first. At the same time, one must be realistic. Positive reinforcement does not tell a person what he is doing wrong. The first step in correcting misbehavior is to be sure that students know what they are doing wrong. The second step is to be sure they know how to do it right.

Punishment depicted as logical consequences is an effective middle ground between harsh punishment and positive reinforcement. Students are punished for misbehavior, but only after they have been fully informed of what is expected of them. They know how to behave acceptably and know what will happen to them if they choose not to behave as desired. Then the punishment is seen as a logical consequence of inappropriate behavior that the student voluntarily chooses.

TYPES OF REINFORCERS

Bear in mind that reinforcers or rewards can be anything that an individual wants badly enough to do something to earn them. They can range from such mundane things as a breath of fresh air to such rarities as Pulitzer prizes. Many of the things that students want cannot be dispensed in school, and while that puts limitations on what teachers can use as reinforcers, they still have a powerful arsenal at their disposal. Reinforcers commonly used in schools fall into four categories: social, graphic, activity, and tangible.

Social reinforcers consist of words, gestures, and facial expressions. Many students work diligently just to get a smile, pat, or kind word from the teacher. How rewarding those winks can be, those nods, agreements, and "thank yous." Some examples are:

– *Verbal*
OK. Wow! Excellent. Nice going. Exactly. Right. Thank you. I like that. Would you share that? Good for you.

– *Nonverbal*
Smiles, winks, eye contact, nods, thumbs up, touches, pats, walk beside, stand near, shake hands.

Graphic reinforcers include marks of various kinds, such as numerals, checks, happy faces, and special symbols. Teachers make these marks with felt pens and rubber stamps. They may enter them on charts. They may punch holes in cards kept by the students. They may attach stars or stick-ons that are available in quantity and variety.

Acitivity reinforcers include those activities that students prefer in school. Any school activity can be used as a reinforcer if students prefer it to another. Examples of activities that usually reinforce academic learning are:

– *For younger students*
Being a monitor, sitting near the teacher, choosing the song, caring for the pet, sharing a pet or toy.

– *For middle students*
Playing a game, free reading, decorating the classroom, having extra recess time, going to an assembly.

– *For older students*
Working with a friend, being excused from a test, working on a special project, being excused from homework.

Tangible reinforcers are real objects that students can earn as rewards for desired behavior and are more powerful for some students than other types of reinforcers. They are widely used with students who have special behavior problems. Many elementary teachers use tangible reinforcers regularly. Examples of inexpensive reinforcers are: fruit, popcorn, peanuts, raisins, stapled notebooks, chalk, crayons, felt pens, pencils, badges, decals, pennants, used books, old magazines, stationery, posters, rubber stamps, certificates, notes, letters, and plastic tokens.

SYSTEMS OF BEHAVIOR MODIFICATION

Behavior modification is best approached in a systematic way. Even if it is done in a sporadic manner, it works, but less effectively. A random approach has been used for decades, based on teachers' praising students for doing good work. That fact caused many teachers to say, when behavior modification was first being introduced, "But I've always done that." In truth, however, few teachers systematically reinforced as a means of shaping desired behavior. They used praise on a hit-or-miss basis. Behavior modification is maximally effective when used in an organized, systematic, and consistent way.

Systems of behavior modification are legion. Every teacher adds a personal twist. Such flexibility is a strength because it allows teachers to apply reinforcement in ways that match their personalities and those of their students. The multitude of systems fit roughly into five catagories: (1) informal "catch 'em being good"; (2) rules–ignore–praise (RIP); (3) rules–reward–punishment (RRP); (4) contingency management; and (5) contracting.

Catch 'em Being Good

This approach rests solely on rewarding students who are doing what is expected. The teacher says, "Class, take out your math books." Several students get their books at once. Others waste time talking. The teacher picks out students who acted as directed and says: "Thank you, Helen, for being ready." "Thank you, Ted." "I like the way Ramon got his book immediately." This strategy offers two benefits. First, it reinforces the proper behavior of Helen, Ted, and Ramon, and second, it shapes behavior of other students. They quickly get out their books and are ready for math.

The "catch-'em-being-good" approach is highly effective in primary grades. Through third grade, teachers use it intensely. In intermediate grades it begins to lose effectiveness, and by junior high, students find it laughable. Other systems of behavior modification must be used at higher grade levels.

Rules–Ignore–Praise (RIP)

The RIP approach is used as follows. The teacher, perhaps in collaboration with the students, formulates a set of rules for class behavior. Those rules are made very clear and understandable to the students. They may be written on a chart and posted at the front of the room. This list is kept short—five or six rules. Students, with practice and reminder, can keep a short list in mind.

Once the rules are established the teacher watches for people who are following them. Students who do so receive praise, and every student is praised as often as possible. Student behavior that breaks the rules is ignored. That is, no direct attention is given to that student. No reinforcement comes from the teacher. Instead the teacher immediately finds a student who is following the rules and praises that student.

This system works fairly well at the elementary level, but it is not good at the secondary level. Students speak derisively of peers who are receiving public praise, calling them pets and kiss-ups. Moreover, secondary students when misbehaving are not shaped well through praise given to others. They are already getting enough positive reinforcement in the form of peer attention, teacher attention, and laughter.

Rules–Reward–Punishment (RRP)

The RRP approach builds limits and consequences into behavior modification. As with RIP, RRP begins with rules and emphasizes rewards, but it does not ignore inappropriate behavior. The added factor of limits and consequences makes this approach especially effective with older students and with students who have behavior problems.

The rules phase is the same as described earlier. Rules, as few in number as possible, are established, understood, and put on written display. The teacher becomes very directive about compliance. Students who follow the rules will be rewarded in various ways. They will receive praise, if appropriate. They will receive laudatory notes to take home to their parents. They will earn points that count toward a larger reward, either for the individual or for the class as a whole.

Students are clearly informed about what will happen if the rules are broken. They realize that it is their prerogative to break the rules. But if they do so, they simultaneously choose the consequences that follow and punishment is invoked immediately in accord with procedures described fully and carefully to the class. Thus, in a sense, the teacher does not punish misbehavior; students punish themselves. They have chosen to behave in ways that bring undesired consequences.

This system is very effective with older students. It clearly sets expectations, rewards, and punishments. Students know they choose what they will receive and that the responsibility for good behavior rests directly on their shoulders.

Contingency Mangement

Contingency management involves an elaborate system of tangible reinforcers. It is especially effective with behavior-problem students and with the mentally retarded.

Often referred to as "token economies," contingency management systems use tokens that students earn for desired behaviors such as staying in their seats, raising their hands, finishing their work, improving over their past performance, and so forth. The tokens may be exchanged for tokens of higher value. They may be cashed in for prizes such as food, toys, comic books, magazines, badges, privileges, and activities. In actual practice the tokens often become sufficiently reinforcing in and of themselves. Students have no desire to cash them in, preferring simply to have the tokens in their possession. Plastic discs and poker chips are often used for tokens. Discs of different colors are assigned different values. Some teachers print up play money in different denominations and special certificates of value.

Teachers who use token economies must be sure to award the tokens fairly and consistently. They must have an adequate supply of tokens, provide a manageable way for students to keep their tokens, and be sure that counterfeiting and extortion do not occur. They must set aside a time every few weeks for students to cash in their tokens. Students can buy "white elephants" that other students have brought from home, the teacher can obtain free materials from various shops and stores, and vouchers can be made available for special activities and privileges. Each object and voucher has its price in tokens. Some teachers like to have auctions in which students bid for the items available.

This plan should be explained carefully to the principal, the parents, and the students before it is put into practice. The explanation ensures that everyone approves and understands what is taking place, thus preventing problems that otherwise might occur.

Contracting

The use of contracts has been quite successful, especially at the intermediate and secondary levels. Contracts specify work to be done or behavior to be established, with deadlines for completion. They indicate what the payoff will be for successful accomplishment. They tell what input the teacher will give.

They lend an air of legality, promise, and responsibility. Student and teacher both sign the agreement. Sometimes parents cosign with the student.

Contract forms can be drawn on duplicating masters and quantities can be reproduced for future use. For older students quasi-legal terminology adds a pleasing touch, as do filigree and official stamps of gold foil or contact paper. While contracts are fun to use, they must be seen as serious commitments, the terms of which must be lived up to by all who have signed.

PLANNING AND IMPLEMENTING
BEHAVIOR MODIFICATION

Teachers who intend to use behavior modification should spend some time planning in advance. This planning requires two things: (1) analysis of the behaviors one wants to change, and (2) implementing a specific plan for changing those behaviors. *Analysis* consists of identifying the behaviors to be changed or improved, deciding what is wrong with them at present, and determining what they should be in the future. Analysis should include consideration of *antecedents*, conditions in the classroom that encourage mis-behavior, and *consequences*, the sytem of rewards and punishments that will be used to motivate and guide student behavior. Antecedents include such factors as distractions, boredom, poor models, awkward transitions from lesson to lesson, and so forth. Consequences include, as reinforcers, any of the many factors already described in this chapter as well as the *logical-consequence* punishers that serve to suppress misbehavior. This analysis may at first appear to be a complicated process, but in fact it can be done adequately within a few minutes time.

Implementation refers to formulating the behavior modification plan and putting it into practice. The plan follows from the analysis of behavior and the identification of desired reinforcers and punishers. It may be written in outline form, providing reminders of specific things to be done, and it can be used jointly by teachers and students.

Target behaviors are the new behaviors that one wishes to see exhibited by students. Systematic reinforcement shapes classroom behavior in the direction of those targets. If a target behavior is to prevent students from talking out in class without permission, the teacher might reward people who raise their hands and wait to be called on before they speak. Verbal praise can be used for reinforcement, such as, "Thank you, Maria, for raising your hand." If the target behavior is to stay on task for the entire work period, reinforcements are given for that behavior. Reinforcement is given very frequently at first, and as the behavior improves rewards are given less frequently.

The implementation plan calls for correcting antecedent conditions that might be contributing to poor behavior, things such as uncertainty about rules, forgetfulness, poor peer models, inadequate teacher models, awkward times between lessons, poor lesson pacing, boredom, frustration, and lack of interesting activities for students. Removal of such conditions gives the behavior modification plan a much greater change of strong success.

Students who chronically misbehave do so in part because their misbehavior is bringing them some type of reinforcement. These reinforcers might include teacher and peer attention, laughter, sense of power, getting one's own way, and so forth. This pattern must be changed so that misbehavior brings negative consequences rather than positive ones. Negative consequences range from ignoring (by both teacher and student) to isolation from the group. Positive consequences meanwhile must be supplied for desired behavior. Teachers can always find someone doing what they are supposed to do, even by accident. Teachers reinforce that person verbally, stating what it is they have done right.

An example of this would be the following. "John, you got right to work. Good going." Then, as the chronicaly misbehaving person begins to show the first improvement, you make a point of reinforcing the behavior: "Thank you, Sammy, for remembering to get right to work." Ordinarily teachers supply the reinforcers that shape desired behavior, but students can learn to reinforce each other. This occurs most easily when group effort is being rewarded by the teacher, which often brings to bear peer pressure and group approval.

Students can also learn to reinforce themselves, a tactic that can be quite powerful. Suggestions for self-reward have been put forth by several authorities, including Ogden Lindsley, Michael Mahoney, and Carl Thoresen. Lindsley (1971) has described a technique called "precision teaching" that involves graphing student performance, whether academic or personal behavior. While the graph documents the performance, it has a great additional advantage in the positive reinforcement that comes from the graphic evidence. As students see themselves improving, they strive to improve further, trying hard to surpass their previous achievements.

Older students can graph their own performances. In this way they are providing their own rewards, reinforcing their own behavior. Students often outdo themselves to have the chance to chart improvements. They are proud to keep the graphs and show them to their parents.

Mahoney and Thoresen (1972) have described a system in which students set up their own systems of reward and punishment, which they apply as consequences to their own behavior. Kindergarten students who finish their art work may go on their own to the play area. Fifth graders who have not disrupted for the entire math period may go to the reinforcement area and pick up a permit for 10 minutes of free reading. Secondary students who complete assignments accurately before they are due allow themselves to work together with a friend.

Self-rewarding is of course subject to misuse. Students will not always earn the reinforcement they select. In this event, teachers must first inspect the student's work or behavior, then signal an okay for the reinforcement. The student then selects the reinforcer.

BEHAVIOR MOD FOREVER

Teachers who begin using behavior modification in a systematic way rarely stop. They love its powerful results. They come to see it not as manipulating students but as freeing them to behave in ways that bring success and positive recognition. Systematic attention and reinforcing become natural parts of the teaching act, occurring automatically—after a while teachers do not even have to think of them. That natural spotaneity makes reinforcement even more effective. Students feel that the teacher is simply kind, considerate, and friendly, not designing or manipulative.

Teachers like what works; behavior modification works. It helps students and it makes teaching easier and more enjoyable. If you asked teachers to name the single most valuable technique for controlling and shaping student behavior, many would certainly say, "Behavior mod. Give me behavior mod forever."

REFERENCES

AXELROD, S. *Behavior Modification for the Classroom Teacher.* New York: McGraw-Hill, 1977.

BECKER,W. et al. *Teaching 1: Classroom Management.* Chicago: Science Research Associates, 1975.

LADOUCER, R., and J. ARMSTRONG. "Evaluation of a Behavioral Program for the Improvement of Grades among High School Students." *Journal of Counseling Psychology*30 (January 1983) :100–103.

MAHONEY, M., and C. THORENSEN. "Behavioral Self-Control—Power to the Person." *Educational Researcher*1 (1972) :5–7, "Precision Teaching in Perspective: An Interview with Ogden R. Lindsley," *Teaching Exceptional Children*3 (Spring 1971) :114–119.

SKINNER, B.F. *Walden Two.* New York: Macmillan, 1948.

———. *The Technology of Teaching.* New York: Appleton-Century-Crofts, 1968.

———. *Beyond Freedom and Dignity.* New York: Knopf, 1971.

TAUBER, R. "Negative Reinforcement: A Positive Strategy in Classroom Management." *Clearing House*56 (October 1982) :64–67.

·3·

THE GINOTT MODEL
Addressing the Situation with Sane Messsages

GINOTT BIOGRAPHICAL SKETCH

Haim G. Ginott is best known for his book *Between Parent and Child* (1965). In that book and in a sequel, *Between Parent and Teenager* (1969), he offered solutions to communication breakdowns that occur between parents and their offspring. Ginott believed that adults vitally impact children's self-esteem through the messages they send. In an attempt to make that impact positive, he developed specific skills for dealing with parent–child conflicts. As a fundamental principle, Ginott emphasized addressing the situation while avoiding attacks on the child's character, such as, "I like you, but I don't like what you are doing."

In a later book, *Teacher and Child* (1971), Ginott showed how those ideas could be extended to the classroom. Teachers, like parents, hold the power to make or break a child's self-concept. *Teacher and Child* deals with methods of communication that maintain a secure, humanitarian, and productive classroom environment.

Haim Ginott was born in Tel Aviv in 1922. He received his doctorate in education from Columbia University in 1952, and went on to become a professor of psychology at New York University Graduate School and a professor of psychotherapy at Adelphi University. He also served in Israel as a UNESCO consultant, was a resident psychologist on television's "Today Show," and wrote a weekly syndicated column, entitled "Between Us," that dealt with interpersonal communication. Dr. Ginott died November 4, 1973.

GINOTT'S KEY IDEAS

The following is a list of key ideas advocated in Ginott's model of discipline. The remainder of the chapter elaborates on these concepts.

1. Discipline is a series of little victories.
2. The most important ingredient in discipline is the teacher's own self-discipline.
3. The second more important ingredient is using sane messages when correcting misbehaving students. Sane messages are messages that address the situation and do not attack children's characters.
4. Teachers at their best use congruent communication, communication that is harmonious with students' own feelings about situations and themselves.
5. Teachers at their worst attack and label students' characters.
6. Teachers should model the behavior they hope to see in their students.
7. Inviting cooperation from students is vastly preferable to demanding it.
8. Teachers should express anger but in appropriate (sane) ways.

9. Labeling students disables them.

10. Sarcasm *is* and praise *often is* dangerous. Use both with great care.

11. Apologies from students should be accepted with the understanding that they intend to improve.

12. The best teachers help students to build their own self-esteem and to trust their own experience.

THE GINOTT MODEL OF DISCIPLINE

Teachers are a decisive, powerful element in the classroom. They create and maintain its environment. They have the power to humanize or dehumanize their students. Their effectiveness depends on their ability to establish an emotional climate that promotes optimal learning. Children who are in constant emotional turmoil cannot learn. To reduce this turmoil, Ginott advocates using *congruent communication,* a way of talking that is harmonious and authentic in which teacher messages to students match the students' feelings about situations and themselves. Ginott claims that the principle of congruent communication is the crucial factor in classroom climate. Teachers must constantly endeavor to use it. When they do so, they convey an attitude of helpfulness and acceptance and are continually aware of the impact of their messages on student's self-esteem. Congruent communication incorporates many different elements that we see expressed in Ginott's descriptions of teachers at their best and at their worst.

Teachers at Their Best and Worst

Ginott writes at length about teachers at their best and at their worst. At their best, they use congruent communication; at their worst, they do not. At their best, teachers strive to:

1. Send sane messages, addressing the situation rather than the child's character;

2. Express anger appropriately;

3. Invite cooperation;

4. Accept and acknowledge student feelings;

5. Avoid labeling (it is disabling);

6. Correct students by directing them appropriately;

7. Avoid the perils of praise;

8. Be brief when correcting students;

9. Be models of humane behavior.

At their worst, teachers:

1. Are caustic and sarcastic;
2. Attack children's characters;
3. Demand cooperation;
4. Deny feelings;
5. Label students as lazy, stupid, and so forth;
6. Give long and unnecessary lectures;
7. Lose their tempers;
8. Use praise to manipulate students;
9. Are poor models of humane behavior.

Let us look at some of Ginott's suggestions for helping teachers function at their best.

Sane Messages

Sane messages address situations rather than student's characters. They *accept* and acknowledge how students feel. Sanity, according to Ginott, depends on people's ability to trust their own perception of reality. Too often, adults send insane messages, telling children to distrust or deny their feelings or inner reality. They blame, preach, command, accuse, belittle, and threaten. In doing, so, they tell children to deny their feelings about themselves and to rely on others for judgement of their self-worth.

Ginott repeatedly reiterates his cardinal principle of the sane message: When a child gets in trouble the teacher should always address the situation and never judge a child's character or personality. By simply describing the scene of concern, teachers allow students to appraise the situation, consider what is right and wrong, and decide how they feel about themselves.

Here is an example of a sane message. Two children are talking during a quiet time, violating class rules. The teacher says, "This is a quiet time. It needs to be absolutely silent." An insane message, according to Ginott, would be, "You two are being very rude. You have no consideration for others."

The way teachers respond to students shows how they feel about them. Responding can build or destroy self-concept. Poor teacher responses can contradict a student's perception of himself. Good teacher responses simply state the facts, letting children decide for themselves if their behavior is in keeping with their self-images.

Expressing Anger

Teaching is a touch job. Fatigue, frustration, and conflict make teacher anger inevitable. Most people, adults and students alike, expect teachers to be saints.

This expectation, says Ginott, is wrong and self-defeating. Teachers should never deny human feelings, either their students' or their own. Their behaviors should always be genuine. That includes how they talk, behave, and respond to students. However, they need to learn to express anger, even displeasure, without damaging the student's character.

When situations arise that cause teachers to feel angry, they should simply (and sanely) describe what they see. They address the situation and tell how they feel about it. When telling how they feel, Ginott encourages the use of *I-messages*. "I am angry." "I am disappointed." These I-messages are much more appropriate expressions of anger than are *you-messages*. "You are not good." "You are lazy and messy." "You never think of anyone but yourself." I-messages tell how the teacher feels about the situation. You-messages attack the student.

When angry, good teachers state their demands clearly and firmly, avoiding language that insults or humiliates. Their messages are as brief as possible. It is important that they be good models of civilized behavior. When tempted to explode with wrath, they should ask themselves, "Am I dealing with anger in the same way I expect my students to? Am I modeling behavior I want to see replicated in my classroom?"

One last item about expressing anger. Ginott points out that an anger situation is one of those times when teachers have the full attention of students. They afford an opportunity to enrich vocabulary by expressing anger in eloquent terms, such as, "I am appalled, indignant, chagrined. I see inexcusable and intolerable behavior. I wish to terminate the situation at once." The teacher conveys two messages, one about the students' behavior and another about the power of descriptive language. Ginott notes that using words that students understand only vaguely increases the shock value of teacher expressions of anger.

Inviting Cooperation

We all depend on others, but if that dependency is too strong it creates problems. This is true when students are made too dependent on teachers. They often become lethargic and indecisive, even resentful and hostile. Ginott recommends reducing dependency problems by providing many opportunities for students to behave independently. One of the various ways Ginott suggests to promote independence is to present students with several solutions to a problem and let them decide on the one they want to adopt. This helps them feel they have some control over happenings in the classroom. They can also decide how they want to proceed in applying the solution they have chosen. Given these opportunities to make decisions they come to depend less on the teacher for motivation and direction. Also, they are more likely to live up to standards of behavior they have set for themselves.

Ginott urges teachers to invite cooperation rather than demand it. One of the ways to issue the invitation is to decide with the class before an activity is started what kinds of personal behavior are required during the activity. Another is to stop an activity that has gotten out of control and say, "We can watch the movie in silence, or we can do another math assignment. You decide." If the students continue to disrupt the activity, the teacher must follow through with the alternative, making it clear that it was the students' decision.

Teachers who do not invite cooperation must use ordering, bossing, and commanding. Ginott stresses the need to avoid direct commands, which almost always induce hostility. Again, Ginott says to describe the situation and let the students decide on their own what their course of action should be. Too often, teachers use long, drawn-out directions or explanations such as, "Close your library books. Put them in your desks. Get out your math book. Get out a pencil. Turn to page 60. Start on the assignment." Ginott suggests a simple declaration such as, "It is now math time. The assignment is on page 60." With those kinds of messages, teachers show that they respect students' ability to behave autonomously. They invite cooperation, promote self-choice, and foster responsibility. Self-image increases with independent choice of productive behavior.

Accepting and Acknowledging Feelings

Students are in an awkward position in that they recognize that they have their own feelings about themselves and about situations, but at the same time are also told how they *should* feel by adults. Ginott sees teachers in a crucial position for helping students sort out feelings. Ginott would like to see teachers minimize student confusion by withholding their own opinions and merely acting as sounding boards for students with problems.

Young children's perceptions of reality are much different from that of adults. Youngsters routinely exaggerate the truth, and their opinions often have no basis in reality. Teachers should not argue with children's perceptions, even when they are wrong. This only causes feelings of belittlement and rejection. Instead, teachers should strive to acknowledge and understand children's feelings.

Here is an example. Suppose Juan comes running in from the playground crying, "Jose threw a ball at me and hit me in the head on purpose. Everyone started laughing at me. No one likes me." The teacher could argue with the child's experience and deny his feelings, saying, "That's silly. I'm sure it was an accident. The others were laughing at something else." Or she could respond with sympathy and understanding, offering no judgment of the situation. She could say, "You seem very upset. You feel that no one likes you. Your feelings are hurt when others laugh at you." In this way, the child's feelings are acknowledged and respected. He is not put on the defensive or told how he should feel.

Ginott suggests that the teachers add another comment to such situations: "How can I help you?" This provides an opportunity for the child to come up with a solution to the problem and reveals the teacher's confidence in the child's ability to cope. By acknowledging feelings and offering to be helpful the teacher does not deny feelings, reject opinions, attack a child's character, or argue with a child's experience. Children must have an opportunity to decide how they feel and what they are going to do about it.

Children's fears are another matter that should be treated carefully. Adults have the tendency to make light of them. When they do this, they tell children that their feelings are not real. Adults also may cause them to believe that people are not supposed to feel that way. Ginott says to avoid the standard adult phrase, "There is nothing to be afraid of," which only makes children feel worse. They are now stuck with both the original fear and a new fear of showing fear. Telling children not to be afraid, angry, or sad does not dispel those emotions, but it does cause them to doubt their own inner feelings. It causes them to doubt the teacher's ability to understand and teaches them that adults are not to be trusted during times of trouble.

Labeling is Disabling

By now you realize that Ginott is adamant about there being no place in the classroom for labels, diagnoses, or prognoses of students' character. Frequently, teachers are heard delivering statements such as, "You're lazy, irresponsible, and sloppy. You'll never amount to anything, if you don't change."

Labeling is disabling, Ginott avows, because it tells students how to think about themselves. When subjected to these messages often enough they begin to believe. them. They start to live up to a negative self-image. This is especially true when adults attempt to predict a student's future. When teachers tell students to forget about going to college they may do just that. The very art of teaching demands that teachers open vistas, encourage growth and achievement, provide enlightenment, and stimulate imagination. Labeling and diagnosing a student's character only limits visions of the self and the future.

In difficult situations, teachers can avoid labeling while striving to be helpful and encouraging. They can offer statements like, "Your grades are low, but I know if we work together we can improve them." "You want to be a veterinarian? Did you know there is a career information section in our media center?" Statements such as these do not tell students what you think they can or cannot do. They encourage students to set goals for themselves and they assure them that the teacher will support and assist in the attainment of those goals. When teachers believe in students, the students begin to believe in themselves.

Correction is Direction

Throughout every day, situations arise in the classroom that require correcting comments from the teacher. Tim and Mary may throw erasers. A group of boys may discuss baseball at the listening table. Bryan is staring out of the window instead of doing his math. In these situations Ginott would recommend directing as a method of correcting. Teachers would describe the situation and then offer acceptable, alternative behavior. Often students simply need to be told what they could be doing differently. In the case of Tim and Mary the teacher might say, "Erasers are not for throwing. This is spelling time," or, "There is too much conversation at the listening table. If you are finished there, return to your seat and take out a library book."

When correcting misbehavior, teachers should avoid attacking a students' character. They should not rant and rave about what they dislike in it. When teachers tell what they see and suggest acceptable alternatives, students know how the teacher feels about the current behavior and exactly how they are supposed to behave differently. They become more likely to follow the teacher's suggestions and correct behavior on their own.

Sarcasm

Ginott has a word of advice for teachers who are tempted to use sarcasm in the classroom—do not. Many adults use sarcasm as a form of wit. Teachers often do so with students intending only to be clever and witty. More often than not, however, their sarcasm sounds clever only to themselves and not to the students receiving the comments. Too often sarcasm produces hurt feelings and damage self-esteem. Students seldom understand sarcasm and feel that they are being made fun of or belittled. It is better to avoid sarcasm altogether than to risk hurting feelings.

The Perils of Praise

Who would ever think that praise could damage a student's self concept? We all need to be told we are great, terrific, valuable. Ginott makes some provocative observations about praise. He does not deny its value, but he sees a danger there, too. The danger is that teachers can use it to manipulate student's feelings about themselves. As with negative comments, praise can have detrimental effects on forming a positive self-image. Ginott warns teachers about the use of judgmental praise—that is, praise that makes judgments about a student's character. Statements such as "You're a good boy" or "You're terrific," create a dependence on others for approval and validation of self-worth.

Again, Ginott is emphatic about the importance of describing the circumstances and letting a student decide what behavior is appropriate. When praising, teachers need to concentrate on applauding specific acts without including adjectives about the personality.

An example of Ginott's point is seen in these comments that Mrs. Richards, a teacher, wrote on a student's paper: "This is an exceptional description of human emotions. This paper truly has poetic qualities." She did not make the mistake of attributing qualities of the paper to the student's personality. In that way she allows students to come to their own conclusions about themselves from the remarks on their papers.

Another way teachers use praise inappropriately is by telling students that they are good because they know the correct answer. A logical conclusion could then be drawn by other students—that they are bad because they don't know the answer. Ginott says: "Knowledge does not make one good. The lack of it does not make one bad." Appropriate responses for correct answers are "fine," "exactly," or "that's correct." These comments carry no evaluation of the student's personality.

Praising good behavior has its drawbacks, too. When teachers praise students for behavior they are supposed to show, it may appear that they are surprised by good behavior. This implies that they expect poor behavior. Sometimes, children decide to live up to negative expectations. Teachers should express their feelings of appreciation without words that evaluate the students' behavior. Ginott would have the teacher say, "Thank you for entering quietly," or "I enjoyed working with you in art today." He would not want them to say, "You were so good at the assembly," or "You can really behave if you want to." Ginott insists that evaluative praise inevitably puts teachers in a judgmental position. It causes them to appear condescending. Persons on a higher status level are at liberty to praise those on a lower level, but not vice versa. Students would seem disrespectful if they said, "You're doing a fine job, Mr. Green. Keep it up." Since teachers are in a position of authority their value judgments carry much weight.

This evaluative praise can be used to manipulate student behavior. When teachers give profuse praise they are trying to assure repetition of a desired behavior. Students, especially older ones, sometimes resist such obvious manipulation. They feel that the praise is not sincere, but is only delivered to coerce them into desired behavior.

Praise is not a villain—used correctly, it can be productive. Such is the case when teachers describe their own feelings or describe the efforts of students.

They honestly recognize them without making value judgments about their personalities. Thus, praise should recognize and show appreciation for students' efforts yet let the students make their own evaluations about themselves. The function of praise is to support, motivate, and encourage, not to judge.

Discipline

Ginott describes discipline as "a series of little victories." It is not one thing that a teacher does one time. It is small step, ongoing, never ending. Ultimately it produces student concern, self-direction, and responsibility.

Teachers can influence behavior with threats and punishment, which generate ill will, rebellion, and subversive behavior. Or, they can influence behavior through compassion and understanding, which can turn volatile situations into victories for teachers and students alike. Students often misbehave in order to get reactions from adults. These negative reactions support students' negative opinions of themselves and also their opinions of adults. Good teachers choose words that do not confirm negative expectations.

Ginott states that the most important ingredient of effective discipline is the teacher's own self-discipline. Teachers do not lose their tempers, insult others, or resort to name calling. They are not rude, sadistic, or unreasonable. Instead, teachers strive to model the behavior they expect of students in their classrooms. They are polite, helpful, and respectful. They handle conflicts in a calm and a productive manner. In the face of crisis, good teachers show reasonable behavior, not uncivilized responses. Children always wait and watch to see how adults handle difficult situations. You can bet that they will imitate the teacher's behavior.

Ginott presents many vignettes on discipline that describe disciplinary methods that are inappropariate as well as those that are appropriate. Teachers using inappropriate discipline:

1. Lose their tempers. (*Example:* Resort to shouting, slamming books, and using verbal abuse.)
2. Resort to name calling. (*Example:* "You are like pigs!" "Clean that up!")
3. Insult students' characters. (*Example:* "Johnny, you are nothing but lazy!")
4. Demonstrate rude behavior. (*Example:* "Sit down and shut up!")
5. Overreact. (*Example:* "Mary accidentally drops a sheaf of papers she is handing out. Teacher: "Oh for heaven's sake! Can't you do anything right?")
6. Display cruelty. (*Example:* "Watch carefully on your way home from school, Jack. You're a little bit short on brains.")

7. Punish all for the sins of one. (*Example:* "Since certain people couldn't listen during the assembly, we will have to miss the next one.")

8. Threaten. (*Example:* "If I hear one more voice, we will all stay in at recess.")

9. Deliver long lectures. (*Example:* "It has come to my attention that several students think the trash can is a basketball hoop. We can throw things on the playground. In the classroom . . .")

10. Back students into a corner. (*Example:* "What are you doing? Why are you doing that? Don't you know any better? Apologize at once!")

11. Make arbitrary rules. (*Example:* Rules that involve no student discussion or input.)

Teachers using appropriate discipline:

1. Recognize feelings. (*Example:* "I can see that you are angry because you have to stay after school.")

2. Describe the situation. (*Example:* "I can see coats all over the closet floor. They need to be hung up.")

3. Invite cooperation. (*Example:* "Let's all help to be quiet, so we can go to the puppet show.")

4. Are brief. (*Example:* "We do not throw paper.")

5. Do not argue. (*Example:* They stick to a decision, but remain flexible enough to change it if they are wrong. Arguing is always a losing proposition.)

6. Model appropriate behavior. (*Example:* They always show through example how they want students to behave.)

7. Discourage physical violence. (*Example:* "In our class we talk about our problems. We do not hit, kick, or pull hair.")

8. Do not criticize, call names, or insult. (*Example:* A child interrupts the teacher's conversation. Teacher: "Excuse me. I will be with you as soon as I finish this conversation.")

9. Focus on solutions. (*Example:* "I am seeing unsportsmanlike conduct on the playground. What can we do about that?")

10. Allow face-saving exits. (*Example:* "You may remain at your desk and quietly do spelling, or you may sit by yourself in the back of the room.")

11. Allow children to set their own standards. (*Example:* "What do we need to remember when we are using paint?")

12. Are helpful. (*Example:* Matthew: "Roger and Joe are teasing me!" Teacher: "You sound upset. What would you like me to do?")

13. De-escalate conflicts. (*Example:* Student (*crumpling a paper*): "I'm not going to do this assignment. It's too hard!" Teacher: "You feel this assignment is too difficult. Would you like me to go over a few problems with you?")

SUMMARY OF GINOTT'S VIEWS

It is a teacher's job to provide an environment conducive to optimal learning. An important part of this environment is the social-emotional atmosphere in the classroom. Teachers must be aware of student's feelings. Teachers must realize that their messages have strong impact on students' feelings and self-esteem.

Ginott believes teachers can be most effective if they strive to use congruent communication—language that fits situations and feelings. When teachers learn to address a situation instead of attacking a child's character, they communicate (1) that they know what is happening, (2) that they know what they want changed, and (3) that they are aware of the student's feelings. They do not tell children how to feel about themselves or the situation.

Teachers should always be aware of emotions, both in themselves and in their students. When angry, they should express their anger, but in a calm and productive manner. By doing so they teach children how to handle their own anger. When children express emotions, they should never be denigrated or punished. Teachers should simply describe the emotions they see with statements like, "I know that you are upset," or "Sometimes your feelings get hurt when others are thoughtless." When teachers recognize emotions in themselves and in their students, they teach students to recognize and deal with their emotions in a constructive way.

Teachers should keep in mind that students are people, too. Being bossed or labeled gives students justification for being rebellious or hostile. Teachers should provide choices, ask for cooperation rather than demand it, and always offer to be helpful. They should think to themselves, "How do I want my students to relate to me and each other?" Teachers should always be the best model of behavior in their classrooms.

REFERENCES

GINOTT, H. *Between Parent and Child.* New York: Avon, 1965.
———. *Between Parent and Teenager.* New York: Macmillan, 1969.
———. *Teacher and Child.* New York: Macmillan, 1971.
———. "I am Angry! I am Appalled! I am Furious!" *Today's Education* 61 (November 1972) :23–24.
———. "Driving Children Sane." *Today's Education* 62 (November 1973) :20–25.

·4·

THE GLASSER MODEL

Good Behavior Comes from
Good Choices

GLASSER BIOGRAPHICAL SKETCH

William Glasser, a Los Angeles psychiatrist, has received national acclaim in both psychiatry and education. His book *Reality Therapy: A New Approach to Psychiatry* (1965) shifted a long-standing focus in treating behavior problems. Instead of seeking to uncover the conditions in one's past that contributed to inappropriate behavior (the psychoanalytic approach), Glasser attends to the present, to the reality of the situation. He believes that it is what one does right now that matters and that this present reality is what psychiatrists should concern themselves with.

Glasser extended his ideas from reality therapy to the school arena. His work with juvenile offenders further convinced him that teachers could help students make better choices about their school behavior. Glasser insisted that teachers should never excuse bad student behavior. Poor background or undesirable living conditions do not exempt students from their responsibility to learn and behave properly in school. This point of view together with practical advice for carrying it out forms the core of Glasser's book *Schools without Failure* (1969), acknowledged to be one of the most influential educational books of this century.

William Glasser was born in Cleveland, Ohio, in 1925. He first became a chemical engineer, but later turned to psychology and then to psychiatry. Since 1957 he has been in private practice in California, where he has assisted in correctional agencies, helped develop programs for school districts, and lectured widely about his ideas for working with school students.

GLASSER'S KEY IDEAS

The following points are keys to understanding Glasser's views on classroom discipline, which are elaborated in the remainder of the chapter.

1. Students are rational beings. They can control their behavior.
2. Good choices produce good behavior. Bad choices produce bad behavior.
3. Teachers must forever try to help students make good choices.
4. Teachers who truly care about their students accept no excuses for bad behavior.
5. Reasonable consequences should always follow student behavior, good or bad.
6. Class rules are essential, and they must be enforced.
7. Classroom meetings are effective vehicles for attending to matters of class rules, behavior, and discipline.

THE GLASSER MODEL

Glasser's views about discipline are simple but powerful. Behavior is a matter of choice: Good behavior results from good choices and bad behavior results from bad choices. A student's duty is to make good choices. A teacher's duty is to help students make those good choices.

Many educators, psychologists, and psychiatrists look into peoples' backgrounds for underlying causes of inappropriate behavior. Psychoanalysts delve far back into infancy and early childhood. Psychologists and educators look into the social environments within which people live. They search there for conditions that cause people to behave inappropriately in school.

Often one hears teachers say, "What can you expect? Sammy comes from a broken home," or, "Sara was an abused child," or, "Edmund's family lives in poverty." Glasser does not deny that such conditions exist or that they influence behavior. He simply says that humans, unlike dogs and parakeets, have rational minds and can make rational choices. They can understand what acceptable school behavior is and can choose to behave in acceptable ways.

But to make good choices students must come to see the results of those choices as desirable. If bad behavior choices get them what they want, they will make bad choices. That is where the teacher comes in—helping students see that they are choosing to act in the ways they do. The teacher forces them to acknowledge their behavior and make value judgments about it. The teacher refuses to accept excuses for bad behavior, always directing attention instead to what would be more acceptable.

Glasser's model of discipline is built around these basic ideas: (1) Behavior is a matter of choice; (2) background and poor upbringing do not make poor behavior acceptable. Students choose to act the way they do, and teachers can help students make better choices. The essence of discipline is helping students make good choices.

WHAT SCHOOL OFFERS

School offers students a chance to be successful and to be recognized for that success. It offers many students the only chance they have for genuine esteem and love, resulting in the feeling of self-worth. Self-worth produces *success identity*, which mitigates deviant behavior. The road to success identity begins with a good relationship with people who care. For students who come from atrocious backgrounds, school may be the only place to find a person genuinely interested in them.

Yet students often resist entering into quality relationships. They may fear teachers, distrust adults in general, or obtain peer rewards by disdaining teachers. Teachers, therefore, must be very persistent. They must never desist in their efforts to help students, which is how they best show that they care. Glasser repeatedly points out that students cannot begin to make better, more responsible choices until they become deeply involved emotionally with people who can, with people such as teachers.

WHAT TEACHERS SHOULD DO

Glasser sees a teacher's role in discipline as:

1. Stressing student responsibility continually;
2. Establishing rules that lead to class and individual success;
3. Accepting no excuses for bad behavior;
4. Calling on students when they misbehave to make value judgments about their behavior;
5. Identifying suitable alternatives to bad behavior;
6. Ensuring that reasonable consequences naturally follow whatever behavior a student chooses;
7. Persisting at all times; never giving up;
8. Continually reviewing rules, responsibilities, and problems in classroom meetings.

Let us examine what Glasser advises within each of these role elements.

Stress Student Responsibility

Since good behavior comes from good choices and since students ultimately must live with the choices they make, their responsibility for their own behavior is always kept in the forefront.

Discussions in which this responsibility is explored and clarified occur in classroom meetings. These meetings occur as regular parts of the curriculum. Students sit in a tight circle with the teacher and discuss matters that concern the class.

Throughout the school day the teacher calls attention directly and indirectly to the responsibilities discussed in the classroom meeting. This continual attention to student responsibility accomplishes two things, both of which are essential to Glasser's view of good discipline. First, attention emphasizes that good behavior is a good choice that students can and should make. Second, attention cements the caring bond between teacher and student. Bit by bit the message gets through that the teacher truly cares about students and their good behavior.

Establish Rules that Lead to Success

Glasser considers class rules to be essential. He writes disparagingly of programs and classes that attempt to operate without rules, in the mistaken belief that rules stifle initiative, responsibility, and self-direction. He stresses that rules are essential especially for students who have done poorly in school. Permissiveness for them tends to be destructive. It fosters antagonism, ridicule, and lack of respect for teachers and others.

Rules should be established by teachers and students together and should facilitate personal and group achievement. Rules should be adapted to the age, ability, and other realities of the students. One thing is essential: Rules must always reinforce the basic idea that students are in school to study and learn. Furthermore, rules should constantly be evaluated to see whether they are useful. When no longer useful, they should be discarded or changed. So long as they are retained, however, they must be enforced.

Accept No Excuses

For discipline to be successful, Glasser says, teachers must accept no excuses. He uses this "no excuse" dictum in two areas. The first has to do with conditions outside the school. What goes on there does not excuse bad behavior in school. Those conditions may, indeed, cause bad behavior, but that does not make it acceptable. The teacher must never say, "We can excuse Bill's behavior today because he has had trouble at home. It's okay if he yells and hits."

The second area in which Glasser says teachers should accept no excuses concerns student commitment. Once a student has decided on a course of good behavior and has made a commitment to it, the teacher must never accept excuses for the student's failing to live up to that commitment. A teacher who accepts an excuse says, in effect, that it is all right to break a commitment, that it is all right for students to harm themselves. Teachers who care, Glasser says, accept no excuses.

Call for Value Judgments

When students exhibit inappropriate behavior, teachers should have them make value judgments about it. Glasser suggests the following procedure when a student is misbehaving:

TEACHER: "What are you doing?" *(Asked in warm, personal, unthreatening voice.)*
STUDENT: *(Will usually give an honest answer if not threatened.)*
TEACHER: "Is that helping you or the class?"
STUDENT: "No."
TEACHER: "What could you do that would help?"
STUDENT: *(Names better behavior; if can think of none, teacher suggests appropriate alternatives and lets student choose.)*

By following this procedure consistently, teachers can cause students to doubt the value of their misbehavior, make responsible and better choices, and thus gradually make a commitment to choosing behaviors that bring personal success instead of failure.

Suggest Suitable Alternatives

Misbehaving students will sometimes be unable to think of appropriate behaviors they might select. The teacher should then suggest two or three acceptable alternatives. The student chooses one and reinforces the notion of choice and responsibility. The student is then expected to abide by the choice made. The teacher accepts no excuses for not doing so, although if the choice proves untenable the student is allowed to make another choice.

Invoke Reasonable Consequences

Glasser stresses that reasonable consequences must follow whatever behavior the student chooses. These consequences will be desirable if good behavior is chosen and undesirable if poor behavior is chosen. Never, says Glasser, should teachers manipulate events so that these reasonable consequences do not occur as a natural course of events. If the student consciously selects an inappropriate behavior that calls for, let us say, isolation from the group, then isolation should occur promptly without exception. Natural and reasonable consequences of bad behavior should not be physically punishing, nor should they employ caustic language, ridicule, or sarcasm. They must be undesirable, however, something unpleasant to the student. On the other hand, consequences of good behavior should be pleasant or personally satisfying in some way.

The knowledge that behavior always brings consequences and that individuals can largely choose behavior that brings pleasant as opposed to unpleasant consequences builds the sense that people are in charge of their own lives and in control of their own behavior.

Be Persistent

Caring teachers work toward one major goal—getting students to commit themselves to desirable courses of behavior. Commitment means constancy, doing something repeatedly, intentionally, and making sure that it is right. It does not mean doing that thing part of the time and not doing it part of the time.

To convey this idea and help implant it in students, teachers themselves must be constant. They must always help students make choices and have them make value judgements about their bad choices. They must always see tomorrow as a new day and be willing to start again. In short, caring teachers never give up in helping their students toward self-discipline. Even when progress is slow, they persevere because they know it is the student's best hope for ultimately gaining maturity, respect, and an identity of success.

Carry Out Continual Review

At the heart of his views about discipline Glasser places what he calls the classroom meeting. A *classroom meeting* is a discussion of topics relevant to the students by the entire class. It explores problems and suggests solutions; it does not place blame. It is carried out with students and teacher seated in a closed circle, an arrangement that has come to be known as the Glasser circle.

Glasser advocates three types of classroom meetings. He would have them all be as regular a part of the curriculum as English or math. The three types of classroom meetings are *social problem solving, educational diagnostic,* and *open ended.* The first type attempts to solve problems that arise among people living and working within the school setting. It is a natural place to consider matters related to discipline. The second type has to do with problems of curriculum, instructional activities, and learning. The third deals with any topic of concern to the students.

Discussions in classroom meetings deal with two things only—identifying the problem and seeking plausible solutions. Students are never allowed to find fault with, place blame on, or seek to punish others. Students are encouraged to make judgements about the matters under consideration. The teacher stays in the background, giving opinions sparingly and participating in a way that reflects student attitudes back to the group for examination. Glasser stresses that the meetings require practice in order to be successful, and that unless they are openly focused on finding solutions, they will not produce the desired effect.

GLASSER REVISITED

Up to this point, the ideas presented in Glasser's model of discipline were all put forth in *Schools without Failure.* Since many years have passed since its publication, and several shifts in public opinion about discipline have occurred, one wonders whether Glasser's views have remained constant.

Through 1977, at least, Glasser had changed his views little if any. He summarized them succinctly in his 1977 article, "10 Steps to Good Discipline," which appeared in *Today's Education.*

In that article Glasser made the point that his suggestions work only in school situations within which students choose to be. That is, they do not work well if students are being held against their wills. Given a group of students who are not actively struggling against being in school, teachers have a good chance to establish excellent discipline. Glasser says teachers must begin by striving to make school a good place to be where they provide, support, and promote the following conditions:

1. *People are courteous.* Adults have the main responsibility for establishing this tone by practicing the best in human relations and insisting that students do the same.

2. *The sounds of joy are heard.* These sounds come not from frivolity, but from the excitement and pleasure of significant learning and purposeful working together.

3. *Helpful communication is practiced.* People talk with each other, instead of at each other.

4. *Reasonable rules, which are unanimously agreed on, exist.* These rules make group work effective and enjoyable. They are flexible and everyone has a say in their formulation.

5. *School administrators actively participate in a system of discipline that teaches self-responsibility.* They themselves model desired behavior. They support efforts of teachers and always try to help students take responsibility for their own behavior.

Glasser reiterates specific duties of teachers in fostering "good places" and student self-responsibility. He reminds teachers to:

- *Be personal:* Care enough to get involved.
- *Refer to present behavior:* The past does not count.
- *Stress value judgements:* Have students evaluate their behavior.
- *Plan alternatives:* Work with students to develop better behaviors and allow them time to prove themselves.
- *Be committed:* Follow up; check back; pay attention and reinforce.
- *Do not accept excuses:* Do not allow students to make excuses; instead, help them replan their behavior.
- *Do not punish:* Make students be responsible. Punishment lifts responsibility from them. Students should make restitution and replan their behavior.
- *Never give up:* Hang in there longer than students expect you to. Achieving firm results takes about one or two months.

These principles constitute a general way of dealing with students, but Glasser in his 1977 article goes into greater detail about how teachers should deal with misbehavior. Previously, teachers were left wondering what to do if students defied them when asked to make value judgments about their behavior. Glasser explains further:

1. Student is misbehaving.

TEACHER: What are you doing? Is it against the rules? What should you be doing?
STUDENT: *(Responds in negative rather than positive way.)*
TEACHER: *I would like to talk with you privately at (specifies time).*

2. Private conference between teacher and student.

TEACHER: *(Repeats)* What are you doing? Was it against the rules? What should you have been doing?
STUDENT: *(Agrees to proper course of behavior.)*

3. Student later repeats the misbehavior. Teacher calls for another private conference.

TEACHER: We have to work this out. What kind of plan can you make so that you can follow the rules?
STUDENT: I'll stop doing it.
TEACHER: No, we need a plan that says exactly what you *will do*. Let's make a simple plan that you can follow. I'll help you.

4. Student later repeats misbehavior; does not abide by own plan.

> Teacher assigns "time out." This is isolation from the group. Student is not allowed to participate with group again until making a commitment to the teacher to adhere to the plan. If student disrupts during time out, he is excluded from the classroom. (A contingency plan should be set up in advance with the principal.)

5. Student, after returning to class, disrupts again.

TEACHER: Things are not working out here for you and me. We have tried hard. You must leave the class. As soon as you have a plan you are sure will allow you to follow the rules of the class, let me know. We can try again. But for now, please report to principal's office. *(Principal was informed in advance of this possibility.)*

6. If student is out of control, principal notifies parents and asks them to pick up student at school, immediately.

7. Students who are repeatedly sent home are referred to a special school or class, or to a different community agency.

Throughout, Glasser's confrontation plan stresses these elements: (1) positive approach, (2) simple plan of student behavior, (3) responsibility placed on student, and (4) teacher's willingness to help. At the same time, teachers do not accept excuses for misbehavior, nor do they cave in to disruptive pressure from students.

In short, teachers do their best to help students behave successfully. But when their efforts fail, the misbehaving student should be removed from the class. Learning must not be disrupted for anyone. This emphasis on helping, together with the acknowledgment that a large part of discipline is the student's responsibility, makes Glasser's model of discipline an attractive one for teachers.

REFERENCES

GLASSER, W. *Reality Therapy: A New Approach to Psychiatry.* New York: Harper and Row, 1965.

_____. *Schools without Failure.* New York: Harper and Row, 1965.

_____. "10 Steps to Good Discipline." *Today's Education*66 (November–December 1977) :60–3.

_____ . "Disorders in Our Schools: Causes and Remedies," *Phi Delta Kappan*59 (January 1978) :331–333.

LIPMAN, V. "Mr. Glasser's Gentle Rod." *American Education*14 (August–September 1978) :28–31.

·5·

THE DREIKURS MODEL
Confronting Mistaken Goals

DREIKURS BIOGRAPHICAL SKETCH

Rudolf Dreikurs was born in Vienna, February 8, 1897. After receiving his medical degree from the University of Vienna he began a long association with the renowned psychiatrist, Alfred Adler. Their studies dealt with family and child counseling. Dreikurs came to the United States in 1937 and eventually became director of the Alfred Adler Institute in Chicago. He was also a professor of psychiatry at Chicago Medical School. He continued to focus on family–child counseling throughout his career. Dreikurs became known as an expert in the field of classroom behavior through his books *Psychology in the Classroom* (1968), *Maintaining Sanity in the Classroom* (1982), and *Discipline without Tears* (1972). These books are valuable to teachers for their explanations of motivation behind student behavior. They also provide information for dealing with student behavior. Dr. Dreikurs died on May 31, 1972.

DREIKURS' KEY IDEAS

1. Discipline is not punishment. It is teaching students to impose limits on themselves.

2. Democratic teachers provide firm guidance and leadership. They allow students to have a say in establishing rules and consequences.

3. All students want to belong. They want status and recognition. All of their behaviors indicate efforts to belong.

4. Misbehavior reflects the mistaken belief that it will gain students the recognition they want.

5. Misbehavior is associated with four mistaken goals: attention getting, power seeking, revenge, and displaying inadequacy.

6. Teachers should identify mistaken goals and then act in ways that do not reinforce them.

7. Teachers should strive to encourage students' efforts, but avoid praising their work or character.

8. Teachers should teach students that unpleasant consequences will always follow inappropriate behavior.

THE NATURE OF DISCIPLINE

Discipline is essential to smooth functioning in schools and society. Too often, adults have an either–or concept of discipline—*either* children behave *or* they walk all over you. Most people think of discipline as punishing actions used against children in times of conflict or misbehavior.

Children form stereotyped ideas about discipline, too. Generally, they see it as arbitrary rules set up by adults to show who is in charge. They may view discipline as a complex game with rules they do not understand. Some see it as punishment given without reason. These children soon decide that being punished justifies retaliation, rebellion, and hostility.

Discipline is not punishment. Punishment is physical pain, humiliation, isolation, and revenge; it is a force imposed on one from an outside source. Dreikurs claims that "it teaches what not to do, but fails to teach what to do."

Discipline requires freedom of choice and the understanding of consequences. It is not imposed by authority figures, but rather on individuals by themselves. By choosing to behave in certain ways individuals learn to gain acceptance from others and, consequently, acceptance of themselves.

Discipline in the classroom means setting limits for students until they are able to set limits for themselves. It involves allowing students freedom to choose their own behavior. They can do this because they understand exactly what consequences will follow any behavior chosen. Good behavior brings rewards. Poor behavior *always* brings undesired consequences. When teachers teach this concept to students they are teaching students to behave in ways that are acceptable to society. This helps students promote their own welfare in all situations.

Teaching self-discipline requires a positive, accepting atmosphere. Students must feel the teacher likes and respects them. They must understand that the teacher wants what is best for them. Students must also be allowed input into establishing rules and consequences. They should always understand the reasons for rules because this allows a sense of personal commitment and involvement. It provides recognition of the need for limits.

Dreikurs believes that establishing discipline in the classroom must involve teaching the following concepts:

1. Students are responsible for their own actions.
2. Students must respect themselves and others.
3. Students have the responsibility to influence others to behave appropriately.
4. Students are responsible for knowing what the rules and consequences are in their classroom.

Dreikurs also believes that teachers who are most effective in establishing discipline are those who teach democratically. Let us explore the qualitites of different types of teachers.

TYPES OF TEACHERS

Autocratic teachers force their will on students to prove they have control of the class. They motivate students with outside pressure instead of stimulating motivation from within. They need to feel powerful and sense superiority over students. This attitude and approach tend to perpetuate problem behavior. More and more, students are rejecting authority figures. They seek a democratic atmosphere in which they are treated as human beings and react with hostility to the autocratic teacher.

Permissive teachers are equally ineffective. They, too, generate problem behavior because the atmosphere they allow is not based on everyday reality. Students in a permissive classroom do not learn that living in society requires following rules. They do not learn that failure to follow rules results in consequences. They do not learn that acceptable behavior requires self-discipline. They are confused because they believe that they can do whatever they want, and yet things do not go smoothly for them.

Discipline and control must be present in classrooms if learning is to occur. Students *want* guidance and leadership. They are willing to accept guidance if it is not forced on them and if they believe they are being heard. This does not mean that they want to run the show.

Democratic teachers are neither permissive nor autocratic. They provide firm guidance and leadership by establishing rules and consequences. They motivate students from within. They maintain order and, at the same time, they allow students to participate in decision making. Democratic teachers teach that freedom is tied to responsibility. They allow students freedom to choose their own behavior. They also teach students that they must suffer the consequences if they choose to misbehave. In this way, students learn to behave in ways that get them what they want.

Students who fail to develop self-discipline limit their choices. They choose inappropriate behavior because they do not understand that it always brings negative consequences. Freedom grows from discipline. If students understand that consequences follow behavior they are freer to choose behavior that will get them what they want. Discipline involves teaching students to establish inner controls that allow them to choose behavior compatible with their best interests. Teaching self-discipline eliminates the need for constant corrective actions by the teacher.

The following are key elements established by Dreikurs to foster a democratic classroom. Democracy requires:

1. Order.
2. Limits.
3. Firmness and kindness. Firmness from teachers shows they respect themselves. Kindness shows they respect others.
4. Student involvement in establishing and maintaining rules.
5. Leadership from the teacher.

6. Inviting cooperation—eliminating competition.

7. A sense of belonging to a group.

8. Freedom to explore, discover, and choose acceptable behavior through understanding the responsibilities and consequences associated with it.

Remember: Autocratic teachers motivate from without. Democratic teachers motivate from within.

MISTAKEN GOALS

Dreikurs makes three very strong points in his writings. First, students are social beings who want to belong. All of their actions reflect their attempts to be significant and gain acceptance. Second, students can choose to behave or misbehave. Their behavior is not outside their control. Putting these two beliefs together, Dreikurs makes his third point: Students choose to misbehave because they are under the mistaken belief that it will get them the recognition they seek. Dreikurs calls these beliefs mistaken goals.

All people want to belong, to have a place. They try all kinds of behavior to see if it gets them status and recognition. If they do not receive recognition through socially acceptable means they turn to mistaken goals, which produce antisocial behavior. Antisocial behavior reflects the mistaken belief that misbehavior is the only way to receive recognition.

Dreikurs identified four mistaken goals: *attention getting, power seeking, revenge seeking,* and *displaying inadequacy.* These goals identify the purposes of student misbehavior. They are usually sought in sequential order. If attention getting fails to gain recognition, the student will progress to power-seeking behavior. If that is not rewarded they move on to getting revenge and then to inadequacy. Let's examine each of these mistaken goals more closely.

Attention Getting

When students discover that they are not getting the recognition they desire, they may resort to getting attention through misbehavior. These students are trying to seek proof of acceptance through what they can get others to give them, in this case, attention. They want the teacher to pay attention to them and provide them with extra services. They disrupt, ask special favors, continually need help with assignments, refuse to work unless the teacher hovers over them, or ask irrelevant questions. Some good students can also make unusual bids for attention. They can function only as long as they have the teacher's approval. If this approval is not forthcoming, they may resort to less acceptable ways of getting attention.

Giving attention to misbehaving students does not improve their behavior, it reinforces it. Their need for attention increases. Furthermore, it causes them to be motivated by outside forces, rather than from within.

If attention-getting behavior does not provide students the recognition they seek, they will turn to the next mistaken goal—power.

Power Seeking

Power-seeking students feel that defying adults is the only way they can get what they want. Their mistaken belief is: If you don't let me do what I want, you don't approve of me. A need for power is expressed by arguing, contradicting, lying, having temper tantrums, and exhibiting hostile behavior. If these students can get the teacher to fight with them they *win*, because they succeed in getting the teacher into a power struggle. Whether or not they actually get what they want does not matter. What does matter is that they upset the teacher. Should the teacher win the contest of wills, it only causes the student to believe more firmly that power is what matters in life. If students lose these power struggles, they move on to more severe misbehavior—getting revenge.

Revenge Seeking

Students have failed to gain status through getting attention or establishing power. Their mistaken goal now becomes: I can only feel significant if I have the power to hurt others. Hurting others makes up for being hurt.

Students who seek revenge set themselves up to be punished. They are vicious, cruel, and violent. When adults punish them, revenge-seeking students have renewed cause for action. The more trouble they cause for themselves, the more justified they feel. They consider it a victory to be disliked.

Underneath their bravado, these individuals are deeply discouraged. Their behavior only elicits more hurt from others. They feel totally worthless and unlovable, and these feelings cause them to withdraw to the next mistaken goal—displaying inadequacy.

Displaying Inadequacy

At this level students feel themselves helpless and see themselves as total failures. There is no need to try anymore. They withdraw from any situation that can intensify their feeling of failure. They guard what little self-esteem they have left by removing it from social tests. Their mistaken belief is: If others believe I am inadequate they will leave me alone.

Students with this goal play stupid. They refuse to respond to motivation and passively refuse to participate in classroom activities. They do not interact with anyone. Dreikurs calls them "blobs." This mistaken goal is very difficult for students and teachers to overcome.

All of the mistaken goals are based on the belief that they provide a way to achieve significance. Most mistaken goals are pursued one at a time, but some students switch from goal to goal.

WHAT CAN TEACHERS DO?

The first thing teachers can do is identify the student's mistaken goal. The easiest way for teachers to do this is to note their own responses to the misbehavior. Their responses indicate what type of expectations the student has. If teachers feel:

- *Annoyed,* it indicates attention-getting behavior
- *Threatened,* it indicates power-seeking behavior
- *Hurt,* it indicates revenge
- *Powerless,* it indicates student displaying inadequacy

Another way to identify mistaken goals is to observe students' reactions to being corrected.

If students:	*Then their goal is:*
Stop the behavior and then repeat it	Getting attention
Refuse to stop, or increase the behavior	Power seeking
Become violent or hostile	Getting revenge
Refuse to cooperate, participate, or interact	Displaying inadequacy

After the teacher has identified the mistaken goals, the students should be confronted with an explanation of the mistaken goals together with a discussion of the faulty logic involved. By doing this in a friendly, nonthreatening way, teachers can usually get students to examine the purposes behind their behavior.

Dreikurs would have teachers ask students the following questions, in order, and observe reactions that might indicate a mistaken goal.

1. Could it be that you want me to pay attention to you?
2. Could it be that you want to prove that nobody can make you do anything?
3. Could it be that you want to hurt me or others?
4. Could it be that you want me to believe you are not capable?

These questions have three effects. They open up communication between teacher and student, they improve behavior because they remove the fun of provoking the teacher, and they take the initiative away from the student, allowing the teacher to implement actions to change behavior.

When teachers know the mistaken goals that are being aimed at they can begin to take action that will defeat the student's purposes and initiate new, constructive behavior. Here is what Dreikurs recommends teachers do in each case of mistaken goals.

Attention Getting

When teachers discover students seeking the mistaken goal of attention getting, they can either agree to go on giving attention, or they can refuse to grant attention or services by ignoring students when they are bidding for attention. Students who seek attention cannot tolerate being ignored. They would rather be punished, belittled, or humiliated, anything as long as they are getting someone to give them something. So, they create behavior that cannot be ignored by the teacher. Teachers who fall for this behavior nag, coax, scold, and otherwise reinforce the student's need for attention.

When teachers perceive that students are making undue bids for attention they should consistently and without fail ignore all such behavior. If they do so, the students will not get what they need from their behavior and will be forced to find new ways to gain recognition.

In addition to ignoring, teachers should strive to give attention to these students any time they are not demanding it. This encourages students to develop motivation from within instead of depending on attention from without.

Sometimes it is not feasible for teachers to ignore behavior that is disrupting the class. In these cases, teachers need to give attention in ways that are not rewarding to the student. The teacher may call the student's name and make eye contact without any comments. Or the teacher may describe the behavior without any trace of annoyance.

Example: "I see that you are not finishing your assignment."

One technique that has been partially effective is to privately confront the student with his goal and ask, "How many times do you think you will need my attention in the next hour?" The student will usually not know what to say. The teacher might then say, "If I give you attention 15 times, will that be enough?" This will sound like an exaggeration to the student. Then when the student misbehaves the teacher responds by saying, "Joel, number 1," "Joel, number 2," and so forth. The teacher does not comment on the behavior or scold, which would give Joel the attention he seeks, but simply lets him know that his behavior is being observed but not tolerated.

By encouraging students to seek attention through useful behavior teachers inform students that they can receive recognition through good efforts and accomplishments. This helps students feel pride in themselves. Learning to function for self-satisfaction can be one of the most valuable lessons taught in school.

Power Seeking

Most teachers react to power struggles by feeling threatened. They fight back, refusing to let students get the best of them. By fighting and winning struggles, teachers only cause students to become more rebellious and hostile and to think about getting revenge. Dreikurs believes that teachers do not have to fight with students nor give in. The best thing for them to do is not to get involved in power struggles in the first place. They should withdraw as an authority figure. The student cannot meet a goal of power if there is no one with whom to fight. Teachers may admit to the student and the class that they recognize the need for power. One way is to stop the entire class and have them wait for the disruptive behavior to cease, in which case the student is in conflict with his peers and not the teacher.

Teachers can also redirect students' ambitions to be in charge by inviting them to participate in making decisions or by giving them positions of responsibility. A teacher might take a student aside and say, "The language during phys ed is very unsportsmanlike. The others look up to you. Do you think you could help out by setting an example?" Or, in the same situation, the teacher might say, "I have a problem. It concerns the langauge I am hearing. What do you think I should do?" In this way, teachers admit that the child has power but refuse to be engaged in conflicts.

Teachers may also wish to confront the behavior openly. When a disruption begins they would say, "I cannot continue to teach when you are doing that. Can you think of a way in which you could do what you want and I could still teach?" If students cannot think of any ways, be prepared to suggest some alternatives.

By withdrawing as a power figure, teachers take fuel from a student's fire. Student's cannot be involved in a power struggle with themselves. They will not receive status or recogniton if they cannot get the best of the teacher. Teachers who withdraw thwart the purpose of power-seeking behavior.

Revenge Seeking

The goal of revenge is closely related to the goal of power. Some students feel they should be allowed to do whatever they please and should consider anyone who tries to stop them as an enemy. These students are very difficult to deal with because they do not care about consequences. Consequences only give them justification for revenge.

It is difficult for teachers to care for students who are out to hurt them. These students feel the need to hurt others because they have been hurt themselves. What they need most is understanding and acceptance. Teachers can best provide this by calling on the class to support and encourage these students. Sometimes this is best accomplished by selecting a student with high esteem to befriend the troublemaker and help him develop constructive behavior. The teacher also may be able to set up situations that allow revengeful students to exhibit talents or strengths, helping to persuade these students that they can behave in ways that bring acceptance and status.

This is a very difficult thing to ask of a class. Students who seek revenge at first reject efforts made by others. Teachers must encourage their students and persuade them that their efforts will pay off. It is awful for any student to feel unliked by everyone. It takes persistence and patience on everyone's part to change such a situation.

Displaying Inadequacy

Students who wish to be left alone usually think of themselves as thoroughly inadequate. They want their teacher to believe that they are too hopeless to deal with. Teachers often believe exactly that and promptly give up. After all, the students are not troublemakers—they are not disruptive or hostile. They are simply blobs. Students who adopt this goal usually do so for one of the following reasons:

1. They are overly ambitious. They cannot do as well as they think they should. If they cannot be the best, they will not put forth any effort at all.
2. They are overly competitive. They cannot do as well as others. They feel that they are not good enough. They withdraw from being compared.
3. They are under too much pressure. They cannot do as well as others want them to. They don't feel good enough as they are. They refuse to live up to anyone's expectations.

In each case, discouraged students feel like failures. They feel worthless and inadequate. They want to keep others from discovering exactly how useless they are.

Teachers must *never* give up on these students. They must always offer encouragement and support for even their smallest efforts. Encouragement is especially needed when the student is making mistakes. It is not the achievement but the effort that counts. Every attempt should be made by teachers and peers to make these students feel successful.

Teachers should also be very sensitive to their own reactions to these students. Any indication of defeat or frustration on the teacher's part reinforces the student's conviction of worthlessness and a desire to appear inadequate. One failure does not mean a student is a failure forever, and teachers must help encourage students to see this fact.

FOUR CASES OF MISTAKEN GOALS

Mrs. Morton's class was doing independent seat work. Every few mintues Sally raised her hand to ask for some kind of direction. She wanted to know if she should number the sentences. Should she put her name on the paper? Was this right? Mrs. Morton became very exasperated. She had had to explain things dozens of times to Sally. Finally she told Sally she would not help her during seat work anymore. She would explain the directions to the class once, and if Sally did not understand them she would have to wait and do the assignment at recess. Mrs. Morton then totally ignored all Sally's requests for help. She did however, immediately encourage Sally when she saw her working without teacher assistance.

This is an example of attention-getting behavior. The best clue was the teacher's reaction to Sally's behavior. She was annoyed. But Mrs. Morton did the best thing in this instance. She ignored Sally's bids for attention and reinforced her ability to work independently. She established logical consequences for Sally's inability to work independently.

Jerry and another student were wrestling near dangerous equipment in woodshop class. They knew this was against the rules and would result in their being removed from the class. Mr. Graves approached them and asked them to leave. Jerry refused. Mr. Graves was tempted to remove him, physically. Instead, he walked to the front of the room and told everyone to turn off their machines and put their work down. He told the students that woodshop could not continue because Jerry was behaving in a dangerous way around equipment and refused to leave the room. The class stood and waited, not without directing a few glares at Jerry. Jerry soon chose to leave the woodshop.

This is an example of power-seeking behavior. Mr. Graves's first reaction was to feel his authority was threatened. He was tempted to get into a power struggle with Jerry. However, he refused to be drawn into a fight. He freely admitted to the class that Jerry had the power to stop them from continuing. Jerry then had no one to struggle against. His power-seeking behavior was thwarted. Later, Mr. Graves offered Jerry the job of shop foreman. It would be his job to see that everyone behaved in a safe way around dangerous equipment. That put Jerry in a position of authority and met his need for power in a constructive way.

Julie was looking at a book the teacher had brought in to read to the class. Cindy came over and grabbed it away, saying she wanted to read it. Miss Allen gave the book back to Julie and told Cindy to go sit in the hall. When Miss Allen was cleaning up the room after school she found the book torn into pieces. She was shocked and hurt by Cindy's behavior. Miss Allen had punished Cindy and Cindy had taken revenge. Her revenge hurt Miss Allen, which was exactly what Cindy intended.

Miss Allen might have better handled the situation by suggesting that Julie and Cindy sit down and read the book together. Cindy might have been able to show Julie that she was an excellent reader. Julie might have shown Cindy that sharing could be fun. Cindy might have had an opportunity to feel accepted.

Mr. Redding gave the class an assignment to write a story. Everyone was writing busily, except for Kathy who was staring at her blank paper. Mr. Redding walked over to her and said, "Kathy, you can start by writing your name on your paper." Kathy did not pick up her pencil, but she kept staring at her paper. Mr. Redding felt frustrated, he did not feel like coaxing Kathy. He wanted to give up. Instead he said, "Sometimes writers need time to think before they write. I know you'll start writing when you're ready."

Kathy wanted the teacher to believe she was inadequate. If she had wanted attention she would have responded to the teacher. Instead she acted as if he were not there, hoping he would go away. Mr. Redding did not give up as Kathy wished. He offered encouragement and let her know that he had faith in her ability to do the assignment.

ENCOURAGEMENT VERSUS PRAISE

Teachers traditionally have used a variety of undesirable discipline techniques when confronted with disruptive behaviors. They have threatened, humiliated, and punished. They have waited for misbehavior and then pounced. The results have been resentment, rebellion, and hostility. Today's teachers need new approaches for effective classroom control, many of which are being explored. One of the most promising is encouragement. Dreikurs believes that encouragement is a crucial element in the prevention of problem behavior. Through encouragement teachers make learning seem worthwhile and help students develop positive self-concepts.

Encouragement consists of words or actions that convey teacher respect and belief in students' abilities. It tells students that they are accepted as they are. It recognizes efforts, not achievements. It gives students the courage to try, while accepting themselves as less than perfect. Teachers should be continually alert for opportunities to recognize effort, regardless of its results.

Encouragement facilitates feelings of being a contributing and participating member of a group. It helps students accept themselves as they are. It draws on motivation from within and allows them to become aware of their strengths.

Praise is not the same thing as encouragement. Praise is given when a task is well done. It promotes the idea that a product is worthless unless it receives praise. Students learn to receive praise from without and fail to learn to work for self-satisfaction. Praise encourages the attitude, "What am I going to get out of it?" Here are some examples showing the differences between praise and encouragement:

Praise	*Encouragement*
You're such a good girl for finishing your assignment.	I can tell that you have been working hard.
I am proud of your behavior at the assembly.	Isn't it nice that we could all enjoy the assembly!
You play the guitar so well!	I can see that you really enjoy playing the guitar.

Dreikurs outlines the following points for teachers who want to encourage students:

1. Always be positive; avoid negative statements.
2. Encourage students to strive for improvement, not perfection.
3. Encourage *effort*. Results don't matter if students are trying.
4. Emphasize strengths and minimize weaknesses.
5. Teach students to learn from mistakes. Emphasize that mistakes are not failures.
6. Stimulate motivation from within. Do not exert pressure from without.
7. Encourage independence.
8. Let students know that you have faith in their abilities.
9. Offer to help overcome obstacles.
10. Encourage students to help classmates who are having difficulties. This helps them appreciate their own strengths.
11. Send positive notes home, especially noting effort.
12. Show pride in students' work. Display it and invite others to see it.
13. Be optimistic and enthusiastic—it is catching.
14. Try to set up situations that guarantee success for all.

15. Use encouraging remarks often, such as these:
    a. "You have improved!"
    b. "Can I help you?"
    c. "What did you learn from that mistake?"
    d. "I know you can."
    e. "Keep trying!"
    f. "I know you can solve this, but if you think you need help . . ."
    g. "I understand how you feel, but I'm sure you can handle it."

There are some pitfalls, too, in using encouragement. The teacher should *not:*

1. Encourage competition or comparison with others.
2. Point out how much better the student *could* be.
3. Use "but" statements such as, "I'm pleased with your progress, but . . . "
4. Use statements such as, "It's about time."
5. Give up on those who are not responding. Always encourage consistently and constantly.
6. Praise students or their products.

LOGICAL AND NATURAL CONSEQUENCES

No matter how encouraging teachers are, they will still encounter behavior problems. Dreikurs advises setting up logical and natural consequences to help deter misbehavior and motivate appropriate behavior. Consequences are not punishment. Punishment is action taken by the teacher to get back at misbehaving students and to show them who is boss. Punishment breeds retaliation and gives students the feeling that they have the right to punish in return. Consequences are actions that follow behavior in a natural and logical way. They are not weapons used by the teacher. They teach students that all behavior results in some corresponding action: Good behavior brings rewards and unacceptable behavior brings unpleasant consequences.

Dreikurs identifies two types of consequences—*natural* and *logical*. Natural consequences are those that students experience only as a result of their behavior. They are not due to the intervention of another. For example, if a student kicks his desk and breaks his foot, he experiences a natural consequence of his behavior. Logical consequences are arranged by someone else, in this case, a teacher. If a student throws papers on the floor, that student will have to pick them up. Logical consequences imposed by the teacher are very effective except when dealing with power-seeking behavior. In that case, natural consequences control students' behavior.

Consequences must be explained, understood, and decided on by students. If they are sprung on students at the time of conflict, they will be considered punishment. When applying consequences, teachers should not act as self-appointed authorities. They should simply represent the order required by society and enforce the rules established by the students.

Consequences are only effective when applied consistently. If teachers apply them while in a bad mood, or only to certain students, students will not learn that misbehavior *always* carries unpleasant consequences. They will misbehave and gamble that they can get away with it. Students must be convinced that consequences will be applied each and every time they choose to misbehave. They will have to consider carefully whether misbehaving is worth it. Sometimes it takes time to break old behavior habits, but teachers should never get discouraged and give up on implementing consequences.

Applying consequences allows students to make their own choices about how they will behave. They learn to rely on their own inner discipline to control their actions. They learn that poor choices invariably result in unpleasant consequences. It is nobody's fault but their own. Students also learn that the teacher respects their ability to make their own decisions.

Consequences should relate as closely as possible to the misbehavior, so students can see the connection between them. For example:

1. Students who damage school property would have to replace it.
2. Failure to finish an assignment would mean finishing it after school.
3. Fighting at recess would result in no recess.
4. Disturbing others would result in isolation from the group.

Teachers should not show anger or triumph when applying consequences. They should simply say, "You chose to talk instead of doing math, so you must finish your math after school." When students choose to misbehave, they choose to suffer the consequences. Their action has nothing to do with the teachers reaction.

DREIKURS' DOS AND DON'TS

Discipline involves ongoing teacher guidance to help students develop inner controls. It should not consist of limits imposed from the outside at times of stress and conflict. Rather, it should be consistent guidance that promotes a feeling of cooperation and team effort. To achieve this feeling, Dreikurs (1982) suggests that teachers do several things, among which are the following:

1. Give clearcut directions for the expected actions of the students. Wait until you have the attention of all class members before giving directions.

2. Try to establish a relationship with each individual built on trust and mutual respect.

3. Use natural and logical consequences instead of traditional punishment. The consequence must bear a direct relationship to the behavior and must be understood by the students.

4. See behavior in its proper perspective. In this way, you will avoid making serious issues out of trivial incidents.

5. Let students assume greater responsibility for their own behavior and learning.

6. Treat students as your social equals.

7. Combine kindness and firmness. The student must always sense that you are a friend, but that you would not accept certain kinds of behavior (pp. 88–90).

8. At all times distinguish between the deed and the doer. This permits respect for the student, even when he or she does something wrong.

9. Set limits from the beginning, but work toward mutual understanding, a sense of responsibility, and consideration of others.

10. Mean what you say, but keep your demands simple, and see that they are carried out.

11. Close an incident quickly and revive good spirits. Let students know that mistakes are corrected and then forgotten.

TEACHERS SHOULD NOT:

1. Nag and scold, since this fortifies a student's mistaken concept of how to get attention.

2. Ask a student to promise anything. Most students will promise to change in order to get out of an uncomfortable situation. It is a sheer waste of time.

3. Find fault with students. It may hurt their self-esteem and discourage them.

4. Adopt double standards—one for yourself and another for the students.

5. Use threats as a method to discipline students. Although some students may become intimidated and conform for the moment, threats have no lasting value since they do not change students' basic attitudes.

REFERENCES

DREIKURS, R. *Psychology in the Classroom.* 2d ed. New York: Harper and Row, 1968.
DREIKURS, R., and P. CASSEL. *Discipline without Tears.* New York: Hawthorn, 1972.
DREIKURS, R., B. GRUNWALD, and F. PEPPER. *Maintaining Sanity in the Classroom* 2d ed. New York: Harper and Row, 1982.

·6·

THE JONES MODEL

*Body Language, Incentive
Systems, and Providing
Efficient Help*

JONES BIOGRAPHICAL SKETCH

Frederic H. Jones, a psychologist, is director of the Classroom Management Training Program, headquartered in Santa Cruz, California, where he is developing and promoting procedures for improving teacher effectiveness, especially in the areas of student motivation and management. His program provides staff development for numerous school districts. The procedures he advocates initially grew out of research and development in classroom practices, conducted while he was on the faculties of the U.C.L.A. Medical Center and the University of Rochester School of Medicine and Dentistry. His work, while not as well known as that of the other major authorities in school management and discipline, is received enthusiastically by teachers, probably because they recognize it as refinements on practices with which they are already familiar but have not seen organized into a systematic approach. Unlike the other writers, Jones has not published a book on his management system, relying instead on his "pyramid" training system, in which teachers are trained to train other teachers.

JONES'S KEY IDEAS

1. Teachers in typical classrooms lose approximately 50% of their instructional time because students are off task or otherwise disturbing the teacher or other class members.

2. Practically all of this lost time results from two kinds of student misbehavior—talking without permission (80%) and general goofing off, including making noises, daydreaming, or getting out of one's seats without asking permission (19%).

3. Most of this lost teaching time can be salvaged if teachers systematically employ three kinds of techniques that strongly assist discipline: effective body language, incentive systems, and efficient individual help.

4. Good classroom discipline results mainly from the first—effective body language, which includes posture, eye contact, facial expression, signals, gestures, and physical proximity.

5. Incentive systems, which motivate students to remain on task, to complete work, and to behave properly, also contribute strongly to good discipline.

6. When teachers are able to provide individual help to students quickly and effectively, the students are better behaved and complete more work.

MISBEHAVIOR AND TIME LOSS

During the 1970s, Frederic H. Jones and his associates conducted thousands of hours of carefully controlled observations in hundreds of elementary and secondary school classrooms in various parts of the country. Their concern lay in effective methods of classroom management, especially in how teachers attempted to keep students working on task, how they provided individual help when needed, and how they dealt with misbehavior. These observations yielded several important findings. First, they revealed that classroom discipline problems are very different from the way they are depicted in the media and perceived by the public. Even though many of the classrooms studied were located in inner-city schools and alternative schools for behavior problem students, the observers found no rampant terrorism, no bullying attacks on teachers, and almost no hostile defiance—the kinds of behavior that teachers fear and that many people believe exist in the schools, especially in urban areas. Instead, they found what Jones called "massive time wasting," which was comprised almost entirely of students talking, goofing off, and moving about the room without permission. Jones found that in well-managed classrooms, the typical student averaged one of those behaviors about every two minutes. In loud, unruly classes the disruptions often averaged 2.5 per student per minute. As teachers attempted to deal with these misbehaviors, they lost almost 50% of the time available for teaching and learning.

In his research, Jones determined that teachers generally feel frustrated in their efforts to manage classrooms. Many of those interviewed expressed bitterness that they had never received training in how to deal effectively with misbehavior. New teachers expected that they would quickly learn to maintain order in their own classrooms, but most were only partially successful, and many finally resorted to hostility and punitive measures or else threw up their hands in resignation. The results were loss of teaching and learning time, lowered levels of student learning, and high levels of teacher frustration and stress.

Jones felt that his observations confirmed what the teachers were expressing, that they had not been trained well in management skills, and that many, if not most, had not learned those skills adequately on the job. Meanwhile, Jones had been at work carefully observing and documenting the methods used by those few teachers who never seemed to have trouble with discipline. From those observations he identified specific clusters of skills that served both to forestall misbehavior and to deal with it quickly when it did occur. Three such skill clusters emerged—one having to do with *body language,* one having to do with motivation through the use of *incentive systems,* and one having to do with giving individual students attention through *providing help efficiently.* Jones now instructs teachers and administrators in the use of these skill clusters through the training program he has developed, called the Classroom Management Training Program.

BODY LANGUAGE

Discipline, says Jones, is 90% effective body language; therefore, his training program concentrates on helping teachers learn to use their physical mannerisms to set and enforce behavior limits specified in the rules established for the class. This body language involves eye contact, physical proximity, bodily carriage, facial expression, and gestures. At its most effective level, it communicates that the teacher is calmly in control, knows what is going on, and means business.

Eye Contact

Few physical acts are more effective than eye contact for conveying the impression of being in control. Skilled teachers allow their eyes to sweep the room continually, and as they do so they pause directly on the eyes of individual students. Locking eyes makes many people uncomfortable, teachers and students alike, and students often avert their eyes when teachers look directly at them. The effect is not lost, however, for the students realize that the teacher, in looking directly at them, takes continual note of their behavior, both good and bad.

Making eye contact does not seem to be a natural behavior for most beginning teachers and therefore, must be practiced before it can be used effectively. Student teachers especially seem to have a difficult time in focusing their eyes directly on the faces of individual students. They tend to look over students' heads, between them, or dart their eyes rapidly without locking onto individuals. Sometimes while teaching, they stare more or less directly ahead, failing to monitor students who are located at the back and sides of the group, or they find comfort in looking only at the faces of two or three well-behaved, actively responding students, oblivious to others not so attuned to the lesson.

These tendencies carry over into subsequent years, so it is common to encounter experienced teachers who do not use eye contact effectively. With practice, however, they can learn to focus their eyes directly on the face of each individual student with some frequency. This in itself sends a message that the teacher is aware and in control. It further serves to inhibit students on the verge of misbehavior, and it provides an opportunity to send facial expressions of approval or disapproval to students who deserve them.

Physical Proximity

In his classroom observations, Jones noted that most misbehavior occurred some distance away from the teacher. Students near the teacher rarely misbehaved. This phenomenon has long been recognized by experienced teachers, who have learned to move nearer to students who are prone to misbehave, or to seat such students near them. Jones, recognizing the powerful effects of physical proximity, incorporated it into the body language skill cluster.

Jones noted that teachers who used physical proximity did not need to say anything to the offending students to get them to behave. He, therefore, concluded that verbalizing was not needed, that in fact it sometimes tended to weaken the effect, due possibly to defensive reactions engendered in students when reprimanded verbally by the teacher. Teachers who need to deal with minor misbehavior are urged to move near the offending student, establish brief eye contact, and say nothing. The student will usually return immediately to proper behavior.

To use physical proximity effectively, the teacher must be able to step quickly alongside the appropriate student. This is difficult in traditionally arranged classrooms because students are seated in long rows of desks or at clusters of tables spread out over most of the floor space. Jones advocates seating the students at desks or tables arranged in shallow semicircles, no more than three rows deep. Walk space is interspersed within the rows. The teacher can then operate from within the arc of the semicircle, obtain easy eye contact with students, and move quickly to the side of any student. Physical proximity is thereby increased and facilitated, and the teacher can circulate more easily to provide individual help (an important consideration to be discussed later in the chapter).

Bodily Carriage

Jones describes bodily posture and carriage as aspects of body langauge that communicate authority. Students quickly become adept at reading body language, even without knowing that they are doing so. They can usually tell immediately whether the teacher is ill, tired, disinterested, or intimidated. These messages are of course conveyed through tone and strength of voice, but an equally important consideration is the way the teacher stands and moves. Good posture and confident carriage suggest strong leadership; a drooping posture and lethargic movements suggest resignation or fearfulness. Effective teachers even when tired or troubled tend to hold themselves erect and move with a measure of vigor. One should note here that on those infrequent occasions when the teacher is feeling ill, it is a good idea to inform the students and ask for their assistance and tolerance. Students usually behave with unexpected consideration at such times, although the likelihood wanes when the strategy is used insincerely or too frequently.

Facial Expression

Like carriage, facial expression reveals much to students. It can show enthusiasm, seriousness, enjoyment, and appreciation, all of which tend to encourage good student behavior: or it can reveal boredom, annoyance, and resignation, which may tend to encourage misbehavior. Perhaps more than anything else, facial expression, through winks, smiles, and contortions, can demonstrate a sense of humor, *the* trait that students seem to prize most in teachers.

The face can be put to good use in sending other types of nonverbal signals. Eye contact has been discussed as a prime example. Very slight shakes of the head can stop much misbehavior before it gets under way. Frowns show unmistakable disapproval. A firmed lip line and flashing eyes can indicated powerfully that the limits have been reached. These facial expressions are used instead of words whenever possible. They are as effective as words in showing approval, and for control and disapproval, they have the advantage over verbal rebuffs in that they seldom belittle, sting, antagonize, or encourage counterattacks from students.

Gestures

Experienced teachers employ a variety of hand signals that they use to encourage and discourage behavior and to maintain student attention. Examples include palm out *(stop)*, palm up flexing fingers *(continue)*, finger to lips *(quiet)*, finger snap *(attention)*, and thumbs up *(approval)*. These gestures communicate effectively, do not interfere with necessary instructional verbalization, and have other advantages over verbal reprimands that have already been discussed.

Body Language

How, then, might teachers use body language to advantage when dealing with student misbehavior in the classroom? Following Jones's advice, the teacher's behavior would be similar to that shown in the following episodes:

1. Sam and Jim are talking and laughing while Mr. Sanchez is explaining the process used to divide fractions. Mr. Sanchez makes eye contact with them, pauses momentarily, and then continues with his explanation. Sam and Jim probably stop talking when Mr. Sanchez makes eye contact and pauses.

    But if they continue . . .

2. Mr. Sanchez again pauses, makes eye contact, and shakes his head slightly but emphatically. He may give a fleeting palm-out hand signal. Sam and Jim probably stop talking when he sends these signals.

    But if they continue . . .

3. Mr. Sanchez moves calmly and stands beside Sam and Jim. He asks the class, "Who thinks they can go to the board and show us how to divide five-eighths by one-eighth? Tell us what to do, step by step." Sam and Jim will almost certainly stop talking now.

But if they continue . . .

4. Mr. Sanchez makes eye contact with them and calmly says, "Jim, Sam, I want you to stop talking right now."

If for any reason they defy Mr. Sanchez's direct order, Mr. Sanchez stops the lesson long enough to separate the boys, or seat them in opposite corners of the room, or as a last resort call the office to inform that they are being sent for detention. In any of these cases, a follow-up conference will be necessary with the boys, and if the defiance continues, it will need to be dealt with by the principal, vice principal, counselor, or the boys' parents.

Note that in all cases except the most severe, Mr. Sanchez used only body language. There was no verbal confrontation and only the slightest slow-downs, if any, in the lesson. Instruction continued, students were kept on task, and teaching–learning time was preserved.

INCENTIVE SYSTEMS

An incentive is something outside of the individual that prompts the individual to act. The purpose of the act is to obtain that "something," which might be a tangible object such as food, or a pleasurable condition such as going to a movie or receiving plaudits from others. Jones, in constructing his classroom management program, placed strong emphasis on incentive systems—formalized structured ways of making incentives available to students—as a means of increasing student motivation to work. All teachers know that properly motivated students tend to work more diligently at school tasks, and in so doing they learn more and cause fewer discipline problems. Jones found that a few successful teachers made good use of incentives for motivation, but that most used them ineffectively or not at all.

An incentive system, as advocated by Jones, is an organized means of making available something—in this case a pleasureable condition—that students like so much that in order to obtain it they will work diligently through the period or day. Typically, teachers have selected for incentives such things as marks, stars, having work displayed, being dismissed first, and so forth. The trouble with these incentives is that they tend to be given only to the few top achievers; the also rans, once out of contention for the prize, have nothing left with which to be motivated. In addition, for many students some of these incentives, such as receiving a star or being first in line, do not compete strongly with the joys of talking or daydreaming.

Jones seems to suggest that incentive systems, to be most effective, must meet certain criteria that few teachers take into account fully. Such criteria include genuine incentives, Grandma's rule, educational value, group concern, and ease of implementation. These criteria are described in the following paragraphs.

Genuine Incentives

What is presented as an incentive must be genuine; that is, it must be something that will cause students to work and behave, hopefully for long periods of time. This point may seem obvious, but it is often overlooked in classrooms where teachers say, "The first person to complete a perfect paper will receive two bonus points." (This works for a handful of students, but most know they have little chance to win, so they have no reason to try.) "Let's have a sense of pride in our work." (This is definitely important but the urging does not, unfortunately, strongly motivate most students.) "If you really try, you can be the best class I have ever had." (This usually sounds better to the teacher than to the students. Students might like to think of themselves as the best class, but the thought alone won't be strong enough to keep them hard at work.)

What, then, are some genuine incentives that can be used in the classroom? Tangible objects, when made reasonably available to all students, are highly motivational, far more so for most students than intangibles such as self-satisfaction or personal growth. Tangibles, however, tend to be costly for the teacher and awkward to dispense. Teachers often reject them because their use smacks of bribing the students to learn. Fortunately, students are just as eager to earn group activities that they enjoy, such as art, watching a film, or having free time to talk or pursue individual interests. Such group activities are genuine incentives; students desire them sufficiently and make extra effort to obtain them. Moreover, these activities mesh with other requisites for incentive programs, as indicated in the following discussions.

Grandma's Rule

Grandma's rule goes like this: First eat your dinner and then you can have your dessert. Applied to the classroom, this rule requires that students first do what they are supposed to do, and then for a while they can do what they want to do. In each case, the incentive is the end product of the proposition. In order to obtain it, the students must complete designated work while behaving in an approved way.

Just as children (and some adults) will ask to have their dessert first, promising to eat all their dinner afterward, students will ask to have their incentive first, pledging on their honor to work feverishly afterward. As we all know, even the best intentions are hard to fulfill once the reason for doing so is gone. Thus, teachers who wish to employ effective incentive systems must, despite student urging, delay the rewards until last and make the reward contingent on the students doing required work acceptably. In other words, "If they don't eat their beans and cabbage, they don't get their pudding."

Educational Value

To the extent that is possible, every class period throughout the day should be devoted to activities that have educational value. Work that keeps students occupied but teaches them nothing of value can rarely be justified. This principal holds for incentive systems. While few educators would be such Scrooges that they would never allow a moment of innocent frivolity, the opposite extreme of thowing daily or weekly classroom parties as incentives for work and behavior is difficult to condone from an educational standpoint. What then is the solution?

There are many educationally valuable activities that students enjoy greatly, whether they be individual or group activities. An example for individuals is free time, a specified number of minutes held at the end of certain periods or days during which students may read, work on assignments, do art work, plan with other students, work, or on individual projects. This time is not entirely free; students are not left without guidance or rules. The freedom is the choice between various options, whereby students spend useful time most enjoyably.

For the total group, educationally sound activities can be selected by vote, and all students are to engage in the same activity during the time allotted. Elementary school students often select physical education, art, music, drama, or construction activities. Sometimes they want the teacher to read to them from a favorite book. Secondary students may elect to watch a film, hold class discussions on topics of interest, watch selected demonstrations and performances by class members, or work together on producing a class magazine.

Group Concern

There is a fatal flaw in most classroom incentive systems—which is that only a few students are ever likely to earn the incentives. The students who do so are the fast working, high achievers. Slower students and the poorly behaved are those who would benefit most, but they seldom have a reasonable chance to finish first, do the most, or get the greatest number correct. They soon learn that the available incentives go to the class stars. That realization effectively removes the motivational effect that the incentives might otherwise have had. Teachers sometimes try to get around this problem by setting incentives that individual students can earn by improving on their own past performances. This can be effective in promoting both achievement and better behavior, but when every student must be kept track of closely, managing the system becomes unwieldy and time consuming.

Jones hit on an ingenious ploy for providing incentives that involve every member of the class yet remains very simple to administer. The plan hinges on causing every student to have a stake in trying to obtain an incentive for the total class. This plan, centered on group concern, provides motivation for all students to keep on tasks, behave well, and complete assigned work. Yet it requires little effort on the part of the teacher. Here is how it works.

The teacher sets aside a period of time in which the students can engage in a preferred activity. In keeping with Grandma's rule this time period must come after a significant amount of work time. It can be at the end of the school day for self-contained classes—15 or 20 minutes—or at the end of selected periods for departmentalized classes. The students are allowed to select pre- ferred educational activities such as art, music, physical fitness, reading or project work, in which they will engage during the "dessert" time. In order to earn the incentive, the students have only to work and behave as expected. By keeping on task and not causing disturbances, the class completes more work in shorter amounts of time, and the dessert time does not, therefore, take away from their normal instructional program.

The teacher manages this incentive system by using a stopwatch, prefer- ably a large one with hands that the class can see. When any student begins to misbehave the teacher simply lifts the stopwatch and clicks it on. Every second that ticks off the watch is time deducted from the period made available for the incentive. The teacher must be dispassionately firm in applying this technique. A burst of perfect behavior cannot be allowed to erase previous misbehavior, since that tells students it is all right to misbehave for a while before settling down. The teacher also cannot be talked into cancelling time lost on the promise of better behavior in the future. The students know the rules of the game from the beginning, and they know that they can choose through their behavior whether and to what extent they will earn the incentive time.

Teachers may think it unfair to penalize the entire class, through loss of time, for the sins of a few or even a single class member. In practice, this is rarely a problem because, first, the class is made to understand that this is a group not an individual effort. The group is rewarded together and punished together regardless of who might transgress. Second, this scheme brings to bear strong peer pressure against misbehavior. Ordinarily a misbehaving student obtains reinforcement from the group in the form of attention, laughter, or admiration. With the stopwatch system the opposite is true. The class is likely to discourage individual misbehavior because it takes away something that class members want.

Ease of Implementation

As mentioned, commonly used incentive systems tend to be effective for only a few class members. Those plans that bring all students into the picture tend to be difficult to implement. Jones's incentive system solves both of these problems. It gives every student an equal reason and opportunity for gaining the incentive, as well as an equal responsibility in seeing that the incentive comes to the class as a whole. It is also very easy to implement. Teachers need do only four things:

1. Establish and explain the system.
2. Allow the class to vote from time to time on which teacher-approved activities they wish to have included in the plan.
3. Obtain a stopwatch and use it conscientiously.
4. Be prepared when necessary to conduct the class in low preference activities for the amount of time that students might have lost from their preferred activity time allotment.

When It Does not Work

If Jones's incentive system loses effectiveness, it is likely to be for one of the following reasons. First, the preferred activities might have grown stale. This is cured by allowing the class to discuss the matter and decide on new preferences. Second, the class may temporarily be overly excited by unsettling occurrences such as unusual weather, a holiday, special events at school, or an accident. In such cases the teacher may suspend the incentive program for a time, with explanation and discussion. Third, individual students may occasionally lose self-control or decide to defy the teacher. In this case, the offending student should be isolated in the room or removed to the office. The teacher can establish a policy wherein the class will not be penalized for the actions of individual students that result in isolation or removal from the room.

PROVIDING EFFICIENT HELP

One of the most interesting and important findings in Jones's research has to do with the way teachers provide individual help to students who are "stuck" during seat work. Suppose that a math lesson is in progress. The teacher introduces the topic, explains the algorithm on the chalkboard, asks a couple of questions to determine whether the students are understanding, and then assigns 10 problems from the textbook to be done by students at their desks. Very soon a hand is raised to signal that a student is stuck and needs help. If only three or four hands are raised during work time the teacher has no problem. But if 20 students fill the air with waving arms, most of them will sit there for several minutes doing nothing while awaiting attention from the teacher. For each student needing help this time is pure waste and an encouragement to misbehave.

Jones asked teachers how much time they thought they spent on the average when providing help to each student who signaled. The teachers felt that they spent from one to two minutes with each student, but when Jones's researchers timed the episodes they found that teachers actually spent around four minutes with each student. This consumed much time and made it impossible for the teacher to attend to more than a few students during work time. Even if the amount of time spent was only one minute per contact, some students would have to waste several minutes while waiting.

Jones noted another phenomenon that compounded the problem. He described it as a dependency syndrome wherein some students felt so uncomfortable doing independent work that they routinely raised their hands for teacher help even when they did not need it. To have the teacher unfailingly come to their side and give personal attention proved rewarding indeed, and that reinforcement perpetrated the unnecessary dependency.

Jones thus described independent seat work as having four inherent problems—(1) insufficient time for teachers to answer all requests for help; (2) wasted student time; (3) high potential for misbehavior; and (4) the perpetuation of dependency in students. Consequently he gave this matter high priority in his classroom management training program.

Jones determined that all four problems could be solved by teachers giving help more efficiently. He suggested that this be accomplished in three steps.

Step one: Organize the classroom seating so that students are within easy reach of the teacher. The shallow concentric semicircles previously described are advocated by Jones. Otherwise the teacher uses too much time and energy dashing from one end of the room to the other.

Step two: Use graphic reminders, such as models or charts, that provide clear examples and instructions. These might show steps in algorithms, proper form for business letters, or simply written directions for the lesson. These reminders are posted and can be consulted by students before they call for teacher help.

Step three: One in which Jones puts great stock. Learning how to cut to a bare minimum the time used to give individual help. To see how this is done, consider that teachers normally give help in the form of a questioning tutorial as follows:

> "What's the problem?"
>
> "All right, what did we say was the first thing to do?" *(Waits; repeats question.)*
>
> "No, that was the second. You are forgetting the first. What was it? Think again." *(Waits until student finally makes guess.)*
>
> "No, let me help you with another example. Suppose . . ."

Often in this helping mode the teacher virtually reteaches the concept or process to each student who requests help. That is how four minutes can be unexpectedly spent in each interaction. If help is to be provided more quickly, this questioning method must be reconsidered. Jones trains teachers to give help in a very different way, and he insists that it be done in 20 seconds or less for each student. Here is what teachers do when they arrive beside the student:

> Quickly find anything the student has done correctly and mention it favorably. ("Your work is very neat" or "Good job up to here.")
>
> Give a straightforward hint or suggestion that will get the student going. ("Follow Step 2 on the chart" or "Regroup here.")
>
> Leave immediately.

Help provided in this way solves the major problems that Jones identified. Teachers have time to attend to every student who needs help. Students spend little wasted time waiting for the teacher. Misbehavior is considerably less likely to occur. The dependency syndrome is broken, especially if the teacher gives attention to students who try to complete their work without calling for assistance. Rapid circulation by the teacher also permits better monitoring of work being done by students who do not raise their hands. When errors are noted in their work the teacher can provide the same kind of help as that given to the others.

JONES'S REMINDERS FOR TEACHERS

The three skills clusters described in this chapter—body language, incentive systems, and efficient help—comprise the core of Jones's system of discipline. Reminders for teachers were presented in a report by Rardin (1978):

- Catch misbehavior early and deal with it immediately.
- Use body language instead of words. Show you mean business through your posture, eye contact, facial expression, and gestures.
- Use physical proximity in dealing with misbehaving or defiant students.
- Use group incentive systems (following Grandma's rule) to motivate work and good behavior.
- Provide individual help efficiently; aim for 10-second interactions.
- Do not use threats; establish rules and attend to misbehavior.

REFERENCES

JONES, F. The Gentle Art of Classroom Discipline." *National Elementary Principal* (June 1979) 58: 26–32.

———. "The Classroom Mangement Training Program: A Comprehensive Methoddology for Teacher Training," Duplicated training materials packet used in training programs by Frederic H. Jones, n.d.

RARDIN, R. "Classroom Management Made Easy." *Virginia Journal of Education* (September 1978) :14–17.

·7·

THE CANTER MODEL

Assertively Taking Charge

THE CANTERS' BIOGRAPHICAL SKETCHES

Lee and Marlene Canter have done extensive research about the traits of teachers known to have good control in their classrooms. Their research led to the formulation and testing of a control system they call *assertive discipline.* Their approach, which they began to disseminate in the mid-1970s, has been widely acclaimed by teachers and administrators. As of 1980, Canter and Associates had trained more than 100,000 teachers and administrators nationwide in the techniques of assertive discipline.

By profession, Lee Canter is a specialist in child guidance. He has worked in a number of child guidance agencies that attend to behavior problems in the young. He is now director of Canter and Associates, an organization that provides training in assertive discipline.

Marlene Canter collaborated with her husband in the research that led to assertive discipline. She coauthored their book *Assertive Discipline: A Take Charge Approach for Today's Educator* (1976) and she has been a teacher of the learning disabled in schools in Los Angeles, Carmel, and Irvine, California.

Assertive discipline is an approach to classroom control intended to help teachers take charge in their classrooms. It provides the means for interacting with students in calm yet forceful ways. It enables teachers to put aside yelling and threatening, offering instead a positive power that prevents their giving in or giving up. This power combines clear expectations, insistence on correct behavior, and consistent follow through, overlaid with the warmth and support that all students need.

Assertive discipline is built around principles from assertion training as they affect interactions with school students. The result is a positive approach that allows teachers to deal constructively with misbehaving students while maintaining a helpful supportive climate for best student growth.

THE CANTERS' KEY IDEAS

The following list presents the key ideas that form the core of assertive discipline. It provides a summary of the assertive model of discipline. These ideas are explained in greater detail in subsequent sections of this chapter.

1. Teachers should insist on decent, responsible behavior from their students. Students need this type of behavior, parents want it, the community at large expects it, and the educational process is crippled without it.

2. Teacher failure, for all practical purposes, is synonymous with failure to maintain adequate classroom discipline.

3. Many teachers labor under false assumptions about discipline. They believe that firm control is stifling and inhumane. It is not. Firm control maintained correctly is humane and liberating.

4. Teachers have basic educational rights in their classrooms including:

   a. The right to establish optimal learning environments.

   b. The right to determine, request, and expect appropriate behavior from students.

   c. The right to receive help from administrators and parents when it is needed.

5. Students have basic rights in the classroom, too, including:

   a. The right to have teachers who help them limit their inappropriate, self-destructive behavior.

   b. The right to have teachers who provide positive support for their appropriate behavior.

   c. The right to choose how to behave, with full understanding of the consequences that automatically follow their choices.

6. These needs, rights, and conditions are best met through assertive discipline, in which the teacher clearly communicates expectations to students and consistently follows up with appropriate actions but never violates the best interests of the students.

7. This assertive discipline consists of the following elements:

   a. Identifying expectations clearly.

   b. Willingness to say, "I like that," and "I don't like that."

   c. Persistence in stating expectations and feelings.

   d. Use of firm tone of voice.

   e. Maintenance of eye contact.

   f. Use of nonverbal gestures in support of verbal statements.

8. Assertive discipline enables teachers to do such things as:

   a. Say no, without feeling guilty.

   b. Give and receive compliments genuinely and gracefully.

   c. Express thoughts and feelings that others might find intimidating.

   d. Stand up for feelings and rights when under fire from others.

   e. Place demands comfortably on others.

   f. Influence students' behavior firmly without yelling and threatening.

   g. Work more successfully with chronic behavior problems.

9. Teachers who use assertive discipline do the following:

   a. Employ assertive response styles, as opposed to nonassertive or hostile response styles.

   b. Eliminate negative expectations about student behavior.

   c. Establish and communicate clear expectations for positive student behavior.

  d. Use hints, questions, and I-messages rather than demands for requesting student behavior.

  e. Use eye contact, gestures, and touches to supplement verbal messages.

  f. Follow through with promises (reasonable consequences, previously established) rather than with threats.

  g. Be assertive in confrontations with students, including using statements of expectations, indicating consequences that will occur, and noting why the action is necessary.

10. To become more assertive in discipline, teachers should do the following:

  a. Practice assertive response styles

  b. Set clear limits and consequences.

  c. Follow through consistently.

  d. Make specific assertive discipline plans and rehearse them mentally.

  e. Write things down; do not trust the memory.

  f. Practice the broken record technique for repeating expectations.

  g. Ask school principals and parents for support in the efforts to help students.

THE NEED FOR ASSERTIVE DISCIPLINE

Discipline is a matter of great concern in schools; it remains so year after year. Teachers hold it as their greatest concern in teaching. It is the overwhelming cause of teacher failure, burn out, and resignation. Parents and the community name school discipline far more than any other factor as the area in which they would like to see improvement. Discipline remains a source of sore concern for several reasons. Among those reasons are a general decline in our society's respect for authority, a decline in parents' insistence that their children behave acceptably in school and elsewhere, and a leniency within law enforcement and legal circles in dealing with juvenile offenders. But teachers and school administrators have to share some of the blame, too. The societal conditions just mentioned make discipline more difficult, yet much of the control problem can be placed at the feet of teachers and administrators who hold such mistaken ideas about discipline as:

1. Good teachers can handle discipline problems on their own without help.

2. Firm discipline causes psychological trauma in students.

3. Discipline problems disappear when students are given activities that meet their needs.

4. Misbehavior results from deep-seated causes, which are beyond the influence of the teacher.

These mistaken ideas about discipline cause teachers to be hesitant about controlling misbehavior. They are afraid they will do ethical or psychological harm and become reluctant to confront misbehaving students. Teachers hesitate to take action, and by the time they realize that action is necessary, the situation in the classroom is out of hand.

We must supplant these thoughts with correct ideas about discipline including:

1. We all need discipline for psychological security.
2. We need discipline as a suppressant to acts that we would not be proud of later.
3. We need discipline as a liberating influence that allows us to build and expand out best traits and abilities.
4. Discipline is necessary to maintain an effective and efficient learning environment.

THE BASIS OF ASSERTIVE DISCIPLINE

Canter and Canter (1976) say that an assertive teacher is one who clearly and firmly communicates needs and requirements to students, follows those words with appropriate actions, responds to students in ways that maximize compliance, but in no way violates the best interests of the students.

The basis of this assertive posture is *caring* about oneself to the point of not allowing others (students) to take advantage and caring about students to the point of not allowing them to behave in ways that are damaging to themselves. Such care can only be shown when the teacher takes charge in the classroom. The manner must be positive, firm, and consistent. It must be composed. It cannot be wishy-washy, hostile, loudly abusive, or threatening. These negative postures are doomed to failure. The calm, positive manner shows students that teachers do care about them, their needs, and their proper behavior. It provides the climate of support that best assists students' own self-control.

A climate of care and support rises up from what Canter and Canter (p.2) call basic teacher rights in working with students.

1. The right to establish optimal learning environments for students, consistent with the teacher's strengths and weaknesses.
2. The right to expect behavior from students that contributes to their optimal growth, while also meeting the special needs of the teacher.
3. The right to ask and receive help and backing from administrators and parents.

The climate of care also has origins in what Canter and Canter (p.8) call rights of students, when under the teacher's guidance.

1. The right to have a teacher who will limit inappropriate and self-destructive behavior.

2. The right to have a teacher who will provide positive support for appropriate behavior.

3. The right to choose one's own behavior, with full knowledge of the natural consequences that follow that behavior.

The climate of positive support and care is best provided, Canter and Canter believe, through the careful application of principles of assertion training to classroom discipline. Such application produces assertive discipline. It replaces teacher inertia and hostility with firm positive insistence. While certainly not a cure-all for problems that occur in the classroom, assertive discipline greatly helps teachers establish and maintain the sort of working climate that meets students' needs as well as their own. Canter and Canter (p.12) say that assertive discipline provides the following helps for teachers:

1. Identify situations where assertiveness will help both teacher and students; ·

2. Develop more consistent and effective communication with students;

3. Gain confidence and skills for making firmer and more consistent demands on students;

4. Reduce hostile teacher behavior, replacing it with the more effective positive, firm, composed insistence;

5. Gain confidence and skills for working more effectively with chronic behavior problems in the classroom.

FIVE STEPS TO ASSERTIVE DISCIPLINE

The material Canter and Canter present in *Assertive Discipline: A Take-Charge Approach for Today's Educator* suggests that teachers can easily incorporate the basics of assertive discipline into their own behavior. A series of five steps is implied for this implementation, which appear to be (1) recognizing and removing roadblocks to assertive discipline; (2) practicing the use of assertive response styles; (3) learning to set limits; (4) learning to follow through on limits; and (5) implementing a system of positive assertions. These five steps are explained and discussed in the paragraphs that follow.

Step 1. Recognizing and Removing Roadblocks to Assertive Discipline.   All teachers have within themselves the potential for expressing their educational needs to students. They also have the potential for obtaining student compliance for those needs. Most teachers have difficulty, however, with both the expression of needs and the acquisition of compliance that can be attributed to a group of "road-blocks" that hinder teachers in their efforts to be assertive. The first step in learning to use assertive discipline is to recognize and remove these roadblocks. Most of the roadblocks have to do with *negative expectations* about students: We expect them to act bad. We feel that conditions of health, home, personality, or environment prohibit normal behavior. This negative expectation must be recognized as false, and it must be supplanted with positive expectations.

The first thing we must realize, say Canter and Canter is that "problems or no problems, no child should be allowed to engage in behavior that is self-desructive or violates the rights of his peers or teacher (p.56)." Thus, we learn never to tolerate improper behavior in students, even when we feel they suffer from:

- *Emotional illness:* Students are too sick to behave normally, therefore all behavior must be tolerated.
- *Poor heredity:* Bad from the beginning, students are unable to act otherwise because of genetic makeup.
- *Brain damage:* Damage to the nervous system makes appropriate behavior impossible.
- *Poor socioeconomic background.* Deprivation and poverty have so dehumanized the students that they can't be expected to behave in a civilized way.

The second thing we must do is recognize a simple fact: We can influence in positive ways the behavior of all students under our direction, no matter what their problems. Recognition of this fact helps remove the roadblocks associated with negative expectations and we come to accept the following realities:

1.   *All students need limits, and teachers have the right to set them.* Teachers who fear that students will not like them if they set limits and stick to them have not paid attention to human psychology. Most of us admire and respect teachers who have high expectations, set high standards, and stick to them. We seldom respect teachers (or like them in the long run) if they take a laissez-faire approach to teaching.

2. *Teachers have a right to ask for and receive back-up help from principals, parents, and other school personnel.* All teachers hold a fear in the back of their minds that they will have confrontations with students they cannot handle. They fear the student will hostilely disobey, go out of control, or even attack physically. Teachers have the right to expect back-up assistance when and if such an event occurs to keep them from being intimidated by students and help them to be more firmly insistent on appropriate student behavior.

3. *We can't always treat all students exactly alike.* Teachers have heard that discipline is improved when standards are applied equally, when all students are treated alike. This is true up to a point. If students think a teacher is playing favorites, they may become restive. However, we all know that people respond differently to different situations. We know that some of us require stronger motivation than others. Students realize that fact, too, and when they see that one of their peers needs special help in order to reach the same standards of conduct expected of other class members, they will be understanding and accepting. They will even help, if needed. Thus, some students may have to be put on special incentive programs or behavior-modification programs before they can live up to the standards that are expected.

Step 2. Practice the Use of Assertive Response Styles   Canter and Canter (p. 16) differentiate among three styles of responses that characterize teachers' interactions with misbehaving students: *nonassertive, hostile,* and *assertive.* The first two should be eliminated, the third should be practiced.

The nonassertive response style is typical of teachers who have given in to students or who feel it is wrong to place strong demands on students' behavior. With this style teachers do not establish clear standards of acceptable and unacceptable behavior. Or if they do, they fail to back up their words with appropriate actions. Teachers using this style are passive. They feel basically powerless to control students and hope to see their good natures to gain student compliance. They will often ask students to "please try" to do their work, behave themselves, do better next time. They are not firm or insistent and end up passively accepting whatever the students decide to do.

The hostile response style is typically used by teachers who feel that they are barely hanging on to class control. They use an aversive approach, characterized by sarcasm and threats. They often shout. They rule with an iron fist and believe that to do otherwise is to invite certain chaos, and lose vital control in the classroom. Hostile responses produce several bad side effects. First, they abuse students' feelings. Second, they fail to provide for students' needs for warmth and security. Third, they violate two of the basic student rights described earlier: the right to positive limit setting on self-destructive behavior and the right to choose their own behavior, with full knowledge of the natural consequences that will follow.

The assertive response style, which teachers should practice until it becomes a natural part of their dealings with students, protects the rights of both teacher and students. With this style, teachers make their expectations clearly known to students. In a businesslike way they continually insist that students comply with those expectations. They back up their words with actions. When students choose to comply with teacher guidance, they receive positive benefits. When they choose to behave in unacceptable ways, the teacher follows through with consequences that reasonably accompany the misbehavior.

Teachers, then, should learn to eliminate nonassertive and hostile responses from their behavior, supplanting them with assertive responses. Here are examples of the three kinds of responses:

EXAMPLE: Fighting

Nonassertive	Please try your very best to stop fighting.
Hostile	You are acting like a disgusting savage again!
Assertive	We do not fight. Sit down until you cool off.

EXAMPLE: Talking Out

Nonassertive	You are talking again without raising your hand.
Hostile	I hope you learn some manners. Otherwise there's going to be trouble.
Assertive	Don't answer unless you raise your hand and I call on you.

Notice in these examples that the assertive response clearly communicates the teacher's disapproval of the behavior, followed by an indication of what the student is supposed to do. The teacher is persistent in making these responses, which will be repeated as often as necessary, in the broken-record fashion. When students behave in appropriate ways the teacher is equally quick to recognize the correct behavior and acknowledge it.

In contrast to the assertive response, the nonassertive response leaves students unconvinced that they are truly expected to behave differently. The teacher may plead with them rather than firmly directing them, may fail to communiate precisely what the students are to do or may fail to back up firm directions with actions if necessary. This lack of direction and firmness, regardless of its underlying reasons, suggests to students that the teacher is afraid of them or feels powerless to deal with their behavior. Either of these notions encourages students to misbehave.

The hostile response is counterproductive, too. It attacks the student and smacks of dislike and vengeance. It wounds students in ways that are difficult to cure. It depicts the classroom as a battleground where teacher and students are pitted as adversaries, each intent on subduing the other. Teachers who use this response style rely on you-messages, which put down the students but do not communicate clearly what is expected. They make threats that if carried out are far too severe. If the threats are made but not carried out students are reinforced in their belief that they can do as they please in the classroom.

Step 3. Learning to Set Limits.   Canter and Canter make this point very clearly: "No matter what the activity, in order to be assertive, you need to be aware of what behaviors you want and need from the students" (p. 65). They say that teachers should think in terms of specific behaviors they expect from students, such as taking turns, not shouting out, starting work on time, and listening to a student who is speaking. They suggest that teachers list the various kinds of activities they provide during the day so that within each of these activities they can decide on the specific kinds of behavior they need to see in their students. Following this step, teachers should instruct students very clearly on the behaviors they have identified. For elementary teachers, signs can be made and posted at the appropriate time in front of the room. Such signs might be made for quiet time, art period, group work, and so forth. The specific behavior expectations for each of those times are discussed and practiced. Secondary teachers will not need to make signs but they should clearly specify behaviors that are accepted for such different activities as individual work, group discussions, group projects, and teacher lecture and demonstration. It is often helpful to make short, succinct written lists of key dos and don'ts. These lists are posted in the classroom and referred to as necessary to provide constant reminders of behaviors that are desired and behavior that will not be tolerated.

Once a teacher's specific behavioral needs and expectations are established the next step is to decide how forcefully those needs will be communicated and how far the teacher is willing to go in following through on them. Canter and Canter suggest that students need to be told clearly and firmly what behaviors are desired and what behaviors will not be tolerated. It is not sufficient to say "be nice" or "work hard." The understanding should be so clear that students can tell a visitor exactly how they are supposed to be behaving at any given time.

Teachers must also decide on how they intend to respond to students when established expectations are either complied with or broken. Compliance calls for acknowledgment, using procedures in keeping with the ages and needs of the students. For most students, verbal acknowledgment is sufficient. Sometimes tangible rewards or special privileges are needed to motivate the continuance of desired behavior. In other cases, students will not want to be singled out for praise because it embarrasses them in front of the group. For them, the teacher will need to find other means, such as knowing looks, special signals, and private conferences.

While dealing with compliance is easy, dealing with violations is more difficult. It is here that assertive discipline is most effective. Teachers should not ignore inappropriate behavior. Instead, they should stop it, with firm reminders of what the students are supposed to be doing. They should clarify in their minds what they will do to follow through if and when students continue to misbehave. Knowing they will have to back up their words with actions, they should decide in advance what they will say and do. In particular they need to think through clearly how they will deal with students who are especially deviant, stubborn, and powerful.

Canter and Canter suggest *verbal limit setting*, combined with physical acts, as the vehicle for establishing expectations and follow-through procedures. Verbal limit setting has three key aspects, the first of which is called *requesting behavior*. Four general methods or approaches are suggested for use in requesting behavior from students: (1) hints, (2) I-messages, (3) questions, and (4) demands. Whenever possible, the first three should be used; demands should be used only as a last resort because they imply dire consequences if they are not met. Here is how Canter and Canter describe the four methods of requesting behavior: Hints are statements the teacher makes from time to time simply to remind students of what they are supposed to be doing, such as, "Everyone should be reading silently." I-messages tell how the behavior is affecting the teacher, such as, "It is getting so noisy I can't do my work." Questions are hints put into interrogative form, such as, "Would you please get back to your reading?" Demands direct students about what to do. Negative consequences are implied if the demand is not met; for instance, "Get back to your reading. I'd better not have to tell you again." Yet, Canter and Canter (p. 74) warn of the effects of demands. In doing so, they put forth their one and only commandment of assertive discipline: "Thou shalt not make a demand thou art not preparest to follow through upon." Ask yourself, they say, just what you will in fact do if the student defies your demand. Unless you have a response ready that is assertive and appropriate to the degree of misbehavior, think twice.

The second aspect of verbal limit setting involves the way in which the hint, I-message, question, or demand is delivered. This aspect includes tone of voice, eye contact, gestures, use of student's name, and physical touch. The tone of voice you use should be firmly neutral. It should not be harsh, abusive, or intimidating. Neither should it be mirthful, implying that you are not really serious about what you say. It should be businesslike, no-nonsense, "I-mean-what-I-say."

Eye contact is essential for the message to have full impact. Teachers should always look a student straight in the eye when setting limits and correcting. The students should see the intensity in teacher's eyes. There is one caution—teachers should *not* insist that students look them back in the eye. It is very difficult, indeed, for a young person to look directly back at an older person when being upbraided. Moreover, in some ethnic groups, younger people show respect for older people by dropping their eyes—to insist that they look you in the eye would be to insist that they make an open show of disrespect. Nevertheless, teachers should fix students with their direct gaze when correcting them forcefully.

Gestures add much impact to verbal messages. This is especially true in Anglo-American society, compared to other societal groups, where we use few gestures. Canter and Canter advocate using facial expressions and hand and arm movements to accent what is being said verbally. They warn us to stop short of waving fingers or fists in front of students' noses.

Use of students' names when delivering messages also adds impact since it personalizes the message making it more forceful and penetrating. This act especially assists messages delivered at a longer range—across the classroom or across the school grounds. The use of names gets the message precisely where it is supposed to go. It leaves no doubt in anyone's mind as to the person being corrected.

Physical touch is usually extremely effective when used in conjunction with verbal messages. Light placement of the hand on the shoulder, for example, communicates forcefulness combined with sincerity. For many students, it is the most powerful way to communicate genuine, positive concern. Again, however, we should remember a word of warning. You can't be sure in advance how each individual student will react to physical touch. Some may defiantly pull away. Occasionally, someone may thrust back physically. And it is not unknown for students to claim that a teacher pinched or pressed hurtfully. While physical touch is usually especially effective, it can sometimes produce undesirable consequences.

A third aspect of verbal limit setting is the use of the broken-record ploy when students seek to divert teachers from their intended message. The broken-record strategy involves insistent repetition of the original message. Here is an example:

TEACHER: Alex, we do not fight in this room. I will not tolerate fighting. You must not fight again.
STUDENT: It's not my fault. Pete started it. He hit me first.
TEACHER: I understand that might be. I didn't see. But you will not fight in my class.
STUDENT: Pete started it.
TEACHER: That may be. I'll watch. But you *may not fight in this class.*

You can see how the teacher was not diverted from the matter of fighting to the matter of who started it. The broken-record strategy (repetition that we do not fight in the class) maintained firm, positive insistence.

Canter and Canter present these reminders about using broken record.

- Use it only when students refuse to listen, persist in responding inappropriately, or refuse to take responsibility for their own behavior.
- Preface your repetitions with, "That's not the point . . .," or, "I understand, but . . . ."
- Use it a maximum of three times.
- After the third time follow through with an appropriate consequence, if necessary (p. 88).

Step 4. Learning to Follow Through on Limits.   By limits, Canter and Canter mean the positive demands you have made on students. By following through, they mean taking the appropriate actions when students (1) refuse to meet the demands that were set or (2) act in compliance with the demands. Either response calls for follow-through.

In the first case, the natural, undesirable consequences should be invoked. In the second case, the natural, desirable consequences should be invoked. Thus, the students choose their behavior but with advance knowledge of the good or bad consequences that will result from their choice.

Canter and Canter present four guidelines that help teachers follow through appropriately:

1. Make promises, not threats.
2. Establish in advance your criteria for consequences.
3. Select appropriate consequences in advance.
4. Practice verbal confrontations that call for follow-through.

Let us see what is suggested in each of these four guidelines.

1. *Make promises, not threats.* Assertive teachers promise; they do not threaten. A promise is a vow to take positive action when necessary. A threat is a statement that shows intent to harm or punish. Teachers have to recognize that follow-through is not always pleasant. Neither teachers nor students like the notion of staying after school or being isolated from the group. But assertive teachers recognize that limit setting and follow-through are essential to the best interests of the student.

Promises have their pleasant side as well as their unpleasant side. Follow-through should also be provided when students behave in desired ways. They should be acknowledged or rewarded for choosing to behave in ways consistent with their own best interests.

The crucial point is this: Students know what is expected of them. They can choose to behave in expected ways, or they can choose to behave in undesirable ways. If they choose the former, follow-through is pleasant for all concerned. If they choose the latter, follow-through is unpleasant for all concerned. In either case, the result does not come as a surprise out of the blue. Students have been informed of it in advance. That advance information has been given in the form of promises that the teacher has made to the class to follow through—to implement—the consequences that naturally accompany behavior chosen by the students.

2. *Select appropriate consequences in advance.* Criteria are the defining characteristics that set one thing apart from another. Your criteria for beauty, for example, are the characteristics that for you set beautiful things apart from things not beautiful. Thus, criteria for consequences are the characteristics you consider appropriate, all things being considered, for acts you will establish as your follow-through consequences. Canter and Canter suggest the following criteria as useful to teachers who wish to establish criteria.

    a.   Make sure you are comfortable with the consequences. That is, do not punish yourself along with the students as you might do if you keep them after school, or if you assign written work that will add to your reading burden.

    b.   Make sure the consequence is something the students do not like, but that it is not physically or psychologically harmful to them.

    c.   Make sure students see that the consequences you select are provided as a matter of choice for them. They earn them by what they do, good or bad.

    d.   Make sure the consequence can be applied immediately, when the students' behavior calls for it. (p 94–95)

3. *Select appropriate consequences in advance.* In accord with their criteria, teachers should select several specific consequences that can be invoked when necessary. The consequences should be of both positive and negative types. Gradations of severity should be present so that the level of consequence can match the seriousness of the misbehavior.

Examples of negative consequences teachers have found most useful are time out, loss of privilege, loss of preferred activity, detention, visit to principal, and home consequences. *Time out* is the same as isolation and refers to removal from an activity or from the classroom for a period of time. Ordinarily, isolation is applied by having the student sit and work alone in a corner of the room while the remainder of the class continues its usual routine. A more powerful form of isolation is sending the misbehaving student to another classroom for a while. This form should not be used except in severe cases. Students will be greatly embarrassed by having to go to another class with another teacher. However, this type of isolation is effective precisely because students greatly dislike being sent to another room. Of course, teachers must make arrangements in advance for such isolation.

Loss of privilege means that the students do not get to participate in something to which they have been looking forward. Examples include having to forego a special assembly, field trip, performance, film, or athletic event. This procedure could also include loss of special duties in the classroom, such as monitor, messenger, or audio-visual assistant. Loss of privilege is not effective unless the loss is significant. If it is something a student didn't care about anyway, its removal will produce little result.

Loss of preferred activity is similar to loss of privilege, except that it refers to normal class activities that students especially enjoy. These losses can be applied in the form of sitting out competitive games, doing seat work rather than art, music, or free reading (assuming they are preferred activities), and exclusion from planning and preparation for holiday parties, plays, feasts, and so forth.

Detention is the familiar staying after school. Students must report to a classroom, principal's office, or special room set up for the purpose. There they complete work they were supposed to have done during the day. Again, detention is a negative consequence only when students would rather be doing something else. Sometimes students would rather stay and help the teacher than go home. If so, detention becomes a reward rather than a punishment.

Visits to the principal are another natural consequence that most students do not like. If this consequence is to be effective the visit must be unpleasant. For this reason many principals do not like to have students sent to them. They would rather present an image of the principal as a friend to students. This posture does not help teachers, however, and teachers must be able to count on the principal to back their efforts at discipline. In order to provide this backing, principals should discuss the nature of the misbehavior with the offending student and establish positive steps that will be taken to correct it. This discussion need not be harsh but it must be firm and serious. The student must be made to understand that continued misbehavior will result in removal from school.

Home consequences like visits to the principal are a form of support the teacher must be able to count on. When the best efforts of the teacher and principal do not correct a student's self-defeating behavior, the parents must step into the picture. They must arrange for negative consequences to be applied at home in the form of loss of television privileges, isolation to the bedroom, foregoing socialization with friends, doing extra homework, or having to perform undesirable chores.

The invocation of home consequences is the most serious step normally taken in school discipline. It is a frank admission by the school that other measures, effective with the vast majority of students, have not helped this particular student behave in ways consistent with the best interests of the individual, class, and teacher. If the unacceptable behavior is not corrected through home intervention, the teacher should no longer be expected to have to work with the student. Placement with another teacher, removal from school, or placement in a school that specializes in behavior problems are possibilities for the student.

Canter and Canter point out that all these consequences should indicate one thing clearly to the student and parents: The teacher and school really care about the student. They care so much that they are prepared to use all means at their disposal to influence the student in positive directions.

Step 5. Implementing a System of Positive Assertions. Most of what has been presented so far is of a negative sort. We have considered rules and limits, and we have examined steps the teacher can take when the rules are broken. While these matters are of great concern for teachers, they reflect only one side of the discipline picture.

The other side of the picture is a positive one. It has to do with teacher follow-through when students behave in appropriate ways, when they are being good instead of being bad. Canter and Canter name several benefits that accrue to teacher and students alike when systematic attention is given to students who are behaving appropriately:

1. *Your influence with students increases.* In the negative aspect of discipline students learn to limit their behavior so they can avoid unpleasant consequences. In this positive view they learn to maximize their appropriate behavior so they can enjoy consequences that meet their needs and interests. The addition of this positive side doubles a teacher's effectiveness.

2. *The amount of problem behavior decreases.* All students want attention. If they can't get it by being good, they will try to get it by being bad. When they learn they can get attention and other things they like through being good, the demeanor of the class changes dramatically. Instead of walking the fine line that separates barely acceptable behavior from unacceptable behavior, they move toward highly acceptable behavior. There they can get what they want.

3. *The classroom environment becomes much more positive.* As mentioned, the total class demeanor changes for the better when students see that good behavior will get them attention, praise, privileges, and other things they desire. They naturally become positive in their interactions with teachers and other students. That positive stance brings rewards that far exceed those that accrue from negative behavior. (pp. 118–120)

What are some of the positive consequences that students are so pleased to receive? Canter and Canter list many of them. Included are:

1. *Personal attention from the teacher.* Special, positive, personal attention from the teacher is one of the most rewarding experiences that students can have. Most students respond enthusiastically to that attention. It is given in the form of greetings, short talks, compliments, acknowledgements, smiles, and friendly eye contact.

. 2. *Positive notes to parents.* Often, parents are informed about their children only when they have misbehaved in school. A brief note or phone call, positive and complimentary, can do wonders for both students and parents. They can provide the added bonus of rallying parents to stronger support of the teacher and the educational program.

3. *Special awards.* Students respond very well to special awards given for good work, good improvement, good behavior, help given to fellow students, courteous manners, and so forth. These awards can vary from comments stamped on papers to certificates drawn or printed for the purpose.

4. *Special privileges.* Students will try hard to earn special privileges. These privileges need not be grandiose. They can be as simple as five extra minutes of physical education, choosing a friend with whom to work for a while, or helping their teacher correct papers.

5. *Material rewards.* Many effective reinforcers come in tangible form. Again, these things need not be expensive or elaborate. Adhesive stickers are prized by primary-grade students. Older students like to receive posters, pencils, and special rubber stamps. Edibles such as raisins, nuts, and popcorn are prized.

6. *Home rewards.* In collaboration with parents, privileges can be extended to the home. Completing homework can earn extra television time. Reading an extra book can earn a favorite meal.

7. *Group rewards.* Canter and Canter discuss methods of rewarding the entire group at the same time. They include suggestions such as: (1) dropping marbles into a jar, as the entire group remains on task and works hard; and (2) writing a series of letters on the board that when completed make up a secret word, such as POPCORN PARTY, which the class then receives as a reward. (pp. 122–126)

FOUR FINAL SUGGESTIONS

Canter and Canter present many suggestions that can have strong, positive effects on students, the majority of which have been noted in preceding sections of this chapter. To conclude our overview of their model of discipline, four final suggestions will be acknowledged.

Beginning the Year

Students are usually on their best behavior during the first few days of the new school year. That is an ideal time to establish a plan of assertive discipline with the class. Canter and Canter suggest the following steps in establishing the plan:

1. Decide on behaviors you want from the students the first few days of school.

2. Decide on the negative consequences you will invoke for inappropriate behavior, as well as the positive consequences you will use to follow up good behavior.

3. On first meeting the new students, discuss and write on the board the behaviors you expect. Keep the list to five or six behaviors.

4. Ask the students to write the behaviors on a sheet of paper, take it home, have their parents read and sign it, and return it the next day.

5. Stress that no student will be allowed to break the rules. Tell the students exactly what will happen each time a rule is broken (first, second, third offense, and so on).

6. Tell students what you will do as you see them complying with the rules (such as marbles in the jar for credit toward later activities).

7. Stress that these rules help the class toward their responsibility of learning and behaving acceptably.

8. Ask students to repeat orally what is expected, what will happen for violations, and what will happen for compliance.

9. Prepare a short letter to send home to each parent, indicating your plans for behavior, your intention to keep parents fully informed of their child's progress, your need for their support, and your pleasure in collaborating with them toward the benefit of their child.

10. Implement the assertive discipline immediately (pp. 136–139).

Making Assertive Plans

Canter and Canter have found that while most teachers make lesson plans as a routine matter, virtually none make discipline plans (pp. 146–148). They believe that making discipline plans is important and helpful. They urge teachers to make discipline plans according to the following steps:

1. Identify any existing or potential discipline problems.

2. Specify the behaviors you want the students to eliminate or engage in.

3. Decide on negative and positive consequences appropriate to the student and situation.
4. Decide how to implement the negative and positive consequences.

Mental Rehearsal

Mental rehearsal is the process of visualizing specific situations in which you will need to respond assertively. This clear visualization and premeditated assertive responding help make the process become a natural part of your behavior. This rehearsal is especially effective when done in conjunction with the assertive-discipline plans discussed in the previous section. It allows you to practice verbal confrontations in advance, thus ensuring that you will respond in firm, insistent ways rather than in a hostile, defensive, or wish-washy manner.

Practicing Interventions

While mental rehearsal is effective, and while it is usually the only available way to practice confrontations in advance, practice with a person is more effective yet. The following is Canter and Canter's scheme for practicing positive interventions (pp. 121–122). The same scheme is used for practicing negative interventions, recognizing that a more firm, insistent tone would be used. With a partner do this:

STEP 1   Say, "I really appreciate your help in class," while looking over your partner's shoulder.
STEP 2   Say, "I really appreciate your help in class," while looking your partner straight in the eye.
STEP 3   Using your partner's first name, say, "Frank, I really appreciate your help in class," while looking him in the eye.
STEP 4   Say the same thing using eye contact and first name. In addition, touch your partner on the shoulder.
STEP 5   Repeat STEP 1, exactly.
STEP 6   Repeat STEP 4, exactly.

CONCLUSION

This concludes the overview of the Canter and Canter model of assertive discipline. You can see that it integrates within its scope ideas from several other models, such as behavior as choice, logical consequences rather than threats or punishments, positive reinforcements for desired behavior, and addressing the situation rather than the student's character. Its unique contribution is the view that teachers must care enough about students to limit their self-defeating behavior, that they must insistently and firmly guide students and apply natural consequences of student behavior, and that they have the right to count on full support from administrators and parents if their best efforts with students come to naught.

REFERENCES

CANTER, L. "Be An Assertive Teacher." *Instructor* 88 (November 1978) :60.
_____. "Taking Charge of Student Behavior." *National Elementary Principal* 58 (June 1979) :33–41.
CANTER, L., and M. CANTER. *Assertive Discipline: A Take-Charge Approach for Today's Educator.* Seal Beach, Calif.: Canter and Associates, 1976.

SUPPLEMENTS TO
THE MODELS

·8·

SERIOUSNESS, RULES, AND GREAT EXPECTATIONS

Suppose it were possible to go into a large school district and obtain from the personnel director two lists of teachers: the first would name a few teachers considered to be strongest in class control and the second would name a few teachers considered to be weakest in class control. Suppose you then studied the teaching traits of people on those two lists. You would probably find interesting differences between them in many areas, almost certainly including the following:

1. Seriousness about teaching and learning.
2. Class rules for personal conduct and work that are clear, reasonable, and consistently enforced.
3. Great expectations, which mean that the teacher fully expects students to behave well and learn rapidly, and continued reiteration of those expectations to the students.

These three factors in class control are fundamentally important and merit further examination.

SERIOUSNESS

Have you ever read the dictionary definitions of the word serious? If so, you might have the wrong idea about what seriousness means in teaching. In defining *serious,* dictionaries use such gloomy terms as grave, solumn, demanding, weighty, dangerous, and apprehensive. You have to move past those words to get at the meaning intended here. Further looking will lead you to words such as earnest, thoughtful, and important. However, finally when you read explanations of synonyms for "serious" you find the way the term applies to good teachers. *Webster's New Collegiate Dictionary* puts it this way: "Serious implies a concern for what really matters."

Seriousness in teaching means exactly that: *concern for what really matters in schooling.* As discussed earlier, different people hold different ideas about what really matters in schooling. Although their opinions seem to be dissimilar, many of them are remarkably alike. Almost unanimous agreement exists regarding (1) maximum learning in academic areas, (2) courtesy and respect for others, and (3) pursuit and development of talents and abilities. Teachers are serious about teaching and learning when they show continued concern over student progress in these three aspects of schooling.

But how do we distinguish between serious and nonserious teachers? Certainly not by asking them. Of all teachers, 99.9% will avow complete seriousness about their work with learners.

Therefore, to make the distinction, we must examine what teachers do in their work on a day-to-day basis. Such an examination reveals that teachers characterized by seriousness continually and consistently do the 10 things listed below. They show these traits in the ways they talk, work, and interact with others.

TEN TRAITS OF SERIOUS TEACHERS

Teachers who are serious about their performance:

1. Value education;
2. Value learning;
3. Value the golden rule;
4. Prepare adequately for instruction;
5. Give their best effort in teaching;
6. Keep students on task;
7. Follow up;
8. Take the extra step;
9. Presevere;
10. Communicate with parents.

After glancing over this list one might conclude that this section has moved from a treatise of discipline to a treatise on good teaching. This notion only shows how closely the two are intertwined. Teachers who are truly serious about schooling as shown by these 10 traits have much better class control on the average than do teachers who lack them. A brief examination of these traits will reveal the powerful role that each plays in class control.

Value Education

To value something means to believe firmly that it is true and good. One's values are made known to others by (1) talking positively about them, (2) behaving in accord with them, and (3) helping others move toward them.

Serious teachers value education. They still believe firmly that education is the best path to the individual good life and the only means of perpetuating a democratic society. They make their views known, when necessary, to parents and colleagues. They make them known continually to the students they teach. They do not preach or cajole, but rather explain and avow. They give real-life examples of what they mean, in terms that students can understand. They help students explore realistic life goals and show how education can lead to those goals.

Value Learning

Serious teachers value learning. They think it is good and worthwhile, whether as a practical means to a goal, as a way of forming a life habit for inquisitiveness and information gathering, or as an enjoyable end in itself. They show this value in various ways. One way is by making sure that genuine learning pervades all classroom activities. Seldom do serious teachers condone busy-work just to keep students occupied. Something new is to be learned regularly. A second way is by making full use of resource people, reference materials, supplemental instructional materials, and class projects that require basic learning for successful completion. A third way is to help the class present public displays of creative and productive work. Parents, teachers, and other students view the displays and presentations. A fourth way is to produce a class publication that includes samples of students' work, annotated references of subjects and topics being studied in class, and a regular listing of new and interesting information that students have acquired. A fifth way is for teachers to show that they themselves are avid learners. They can discuss their learning activities with the class, show examples, and do demonstrations. This teacher-as-learner example can be one of the most powerful influences of all. This method only reflects the old adages—seeing is believing; actions speak louder than words; we all learn more through imitation than through any other avenue.

Value the Golden Rule

"Do unto others as you would have them do unto you." Treat others as you want to be treated. Think of how you like to be spoken to and speak to others in that way. Think of how you like to be recognized and thus recognize others in the same manner. One could go on and on with this kind of advice. Serious teachers have found it to be a most desirable guide to behavior—easy to understand, easy to apply, effective, and contagious. It teaches positive habits that have lifelong value. It helps as much as anything else in reducing conflict in the classroom. As conflicts shrink, class control improves.

You may think it odd that serious teachers put such emphasis on the golden rule. You may be remembering teachers who embodied the first definition of *serious*—stern, demanding, harsh, inflexible, frightening. If so, think about the second definition of *serious*—caring, determined, concerned, dedicated. This helps remind us that one can be serious about anything, serious about enjoyment, serious about good feelings, serious about the pleasures of treating others well and having them treat us well in return.

In many respects, teaching students to live by the golden rule is one of the most valuable things we can do. We all lament the growing rates of crime and vandalism. We are distressed by a pervasive unwillingness to get involved with other people's problems. We wonder what happened to old-fashioned courtesy. We see school students exhibiting disgusting behavior, some of it criminal. We wring our hands in despair or submissively resign ourselves to a "what-can-I-do" attitude.

Serious teachers know they can do a great deal. True, some groups of students seem beyond hope. While plentiful, such students are still far from being the rule. Most students want to be treated well. When they are, they become better able to treat others well. Most students want to know about manners and etiquette, even though older ones may be publicly derisive of such social niceties.

Serious teachers do two things. First, they always model in their own classroom demeanor the behaviors they want their students to acquire. They are always polite and helpful. Second, they talk with students about golden-rule behavior, insist that they follow its percepts, arrange practice sessions as necessary, and reinforce students when they exhibit desired behavior. If teachers are wise they do a third thing as well. They inform the students' parents about what they are attempting to achieve and ask for support from home.

Prepare Adequately

All teachers know that students can acquire a good deal of school learning more or less on their own, without much instruction. This phenomenon is known variously as spontaneous learning, learning on their own, and learning despite the teacher. But teachers also know that students learn faster, easier, more correctly, and in greater quantities when given good instruction that guides, explains, urges, reinforces, and holds students accountable. Coincidentally, that kind of instruction cuts down markedly on the amount of disruptive behavior in the classroom.

Therefore, serious teachers must routinely prepare thoroughly for each day's teaching even though they could get by without such preparation. Better teachers are able to teach off-the-cuff when necessary. They can ad lib, improvise, and teach from the basis of personality rather than organization. However, they know that when they do so they risk shortchanging their students.

Serious teachers know the facts of teaching—every single thing cannot be planned in advance, even the best devised plans sometimes fall short of the mark, and unexpected happenings call for spur-of-the-moment revisions. But they also know that day in and day out better planning leads to better learning and better classroom control.

Give the Best Effort

Serious teachers make a more determined effort to teach well than do average teachers. They plan, communicate, motivate, encourage, insist, and follow through. They do these things thoroughly and consistently, even when they feel like saying, "What's the use?"

No one teaches hour after hour at their full capacity. Everyone, including the very best in any profession, has ups and downs. Serious teachers recognize that fact. When they are much below par they often admit it to the students and ask for their special help. They also plan against the lows, going farther than usual to motivate students and enliven instruction. The good days take care of themselves.

Serious teachers seldom are completely satisfied with their performance. Despite diligent work they often feel they could have done better. When outside observers compare teachers' efforts, it becomes clear that serious teachers come close to giving their best effort consistently. Observers can also see that students are aware of the efforts teachers make. Students tend to pick up on those efforts, responding positively in classroom work and behavior.

Keep Students On Task

In the late 1970s, the California Commission on Teacher Preparation and Licensing began a study that continued for several years. The commission wished to identify teaching traits and behaviors that contributed to success in teaching. The study, called the Beginning Teacher Evaluation Study (BTES), identified several teacher behaviors that correlated with student learning. Most of the behaviors studied showed very low correlations with student learning. One, however, showed significant (though still relatively small) effect. That was behavior that kept students on task in learning. It was found that the more time students remained actively engaged in learning the material at hand, the more they learned. This finding corresponds with common sense. It is worth noting, however, because many commonsense expectations fail to prove out under close scrutiny.

Serious teachers make a determined effort to keep their students engaged actively with the tasks at hand. They use a variety of means to do so. They select worthwhile, interesting learning activities. They make sure that the ideas are within students' reach and that the work is challenging but can be accomplished fairly easily. They pace the work to match students' attention spans, vary it to prevent monotony, and provide assistance to overcome frustration. They enliven the activities with humor and surprise and provide interesting applications of material being learned. They try to keep students active physically, mentally, and emotionally. All these efforts help students stay on task. The students in turn learn more and of course have less time and inclination to misbehave.

Follow-Up

All of us have had teachers who began like a storm but ended in the doldrums. They promised so much but delivered so little. Maybe they made dire threats but did not carry them out even when they should have, or they made assignments but never checked to see if and how well they were completed. Such teachers failed to follow up on what they started.

Serious teachers finish what they start. At times of course they offer suggestions or begin actitivies that do not pan out. Naturally they do not stick doggedly to a bad idea. They discuss its limitations with students, then change plans. Everyone knows what is going on. Except when ideas go sour, however, you can find those teachers as involved at the end as they were at the beginning.

To be more specific, serious teachers give students tasks that are worthwhile—valuable assignments worthy of being completed. They check student work at two points during progress. They check for errors or obstacles which they correct or remove. At completion, they check again to be sure the work is correct and understood.

Serious teachers, in consultation with students, establish rules that govern behavior in the classroom. They monitor compliance with the rules. Students who break rules suffer reasonable consequences that have been discussed in advance. For the students' sake, the rules must be enforced.

Serious teachers do what they say they will do, when they say they will do it. You can count on them. If they promise to have materials ready on Tuesday, that is what they will do. If they promise a reward for good behavior, they will certainly come through with the reward. If they threaten to call your mother when you misbehave, you know they will surely do so. These are examples of following up in teaching. Serious teachers give students important work and they expect proper behavior. They give all possible help along the way. And they will be there at the finish, to approve, acknowleged, redirect, or otherwise see each thing through to a proper end.

Take the Extra Step

Two traits clearly set a serious teacher apart from others. Those are taking the extra step, discussed here, and its close partner, perseverance, discussed in the next section. Both show willingness and determination to help students learn and behave acceptably.

Most of us can recall teachers who took that extra step for us, who went above and beyond the call of duty because they cared about our learning. We remember those teachers as excellent in their work. Maybe they did not tell the best jokes; maybe they were not the prettiest to look at; maybe we did not have a barrel of fun in their classrooms. However, we learned, grew, and progressed because they were always willing to do more than we asked, more than we expected.

What are examples of taking the extra step? Get a group of people together and they can think of many.

- Making a goodwill visit to a student's home.
- Staying after school to help a project.
- Arriving early to give special help or make-up work.
- Sending post cards to students while away on vacation.
- Meeting with parents to iron out difficulties.
- Arranging for field trips, special guests, exhibitions, performances, and celebrations.
- Making time to talk privately with each student once in a while.
- Finding ways to draw attention to fine work done by the class.

One could go on and on, but the point is obvious: Serious teachers are continually looking for ways to help their students. They do those things even when inconvenient. That is taking the extra step.

Perseverence

The Hoosier Schoolmaster (Eggleston, 1871) is a classic book in American education. Set in the 1850s, it describes the life of a young male teacher in a one-room school an Indiana. His students were of all ages, some much larger, stronger, and tougher than himself. The rough older boys prided themselves in having run off the previous three schoolmasters. They intended to do the same thing again. But the Hoosier schoolmaster wouldn't be defeated, even though the bullies did their worst. He said to himself, "I'll be a bulldog. I'll set my teeth into this job. I'll hang on. I'll never let go. I'll never give up."

Most teachers don't get beaten up these days (some still do on occasion), but they all encounter recalcitrant students who may be stubborn, resistant, slow, or doing any and everything to get attention. Whatever the case, they are slow to learn and fast to disrupt. That distressing combination often makes teachers throw up their hands in resignation. But serious teachers do not resign. Like the Hoosier schoolmaster, they are bulldogs. They set their jaws and never give up. If Sally has to have long division explained 20 times, that is what she gets. If George thinks his atrocious playground behavior will outlast the teacher's resolve to correct it, he has another thought coming.

Serious teachers just do not give up. They stay in there pitching, even when average teachers say, "Enough, already!" Their magic is that they often make the slow faster, the stubborn more willing, and the ruffian more gentle. Sometimes they do not succeed. Even then, they, their students, and the students' parents all know they have given their best.

Communicate with Parents

Chapter 11 is entitled "Parents as Teachers' Best Friends." Experienced teachers need friends and pass along these nuggets, worth more than their weight in pure gold:

- For routines to go smoothly at school, be on best terms with the school secretary.
- For your classroom to stay in tip-top shape, be on best terms with the custodian.
- For help with your students' learning, be on best terms with their parents.

Parents sincerely want their children to learn and behave in school. The trouble is that they do not know how to help. They do not know what is expected; they do not know how school is conducted; they do not know how to tutor at home; they do not know how to arrange good homework settings.

It is not difficult to inform parents about all of these things. Once you indicate clearly what you hope to do for the students and how parents can help, you will find a cadre of staunch supporters. Serious teachers make the effort to communicate with parents. They know that the small amount of work involved pays huge dividends. They invariably have systems for communicating. Often you see them use telephone calls, notes, newsletters, and personal conferences. They send many messages through the students that describe (1) *what* they intend to accomplish with each student, (2) *how* parents can help at home, and (3) *how* and *when* they can be contacted in return. They make sure to follow up on the items communicated to parents.

When the parents see evidence of this interest in their child, they will do much to help and support the teacher. This push from home increases student learning and it cuts down markedly on student misbehavior. One caution: Good communication does not imply being on closest terms with parents. To be most effective, teachers should always be professional. They should be friendly and kind, but they should be businesslike. Otherwise some parents will see them as wishy-washy and will eagerly tell them how to teach the class.

CLASS RULES

Every class needs a set of rules that governs two things—work habits and personal behavior. To be most effective those rules must be jointly formulated, reasonable, positive, succinct, observable, public, enforceable, and enforced. Penalties for breaking the rules should be understood in advance. When the rules are broken, those penalties must be applied immediately, consistently, and impartially, without malice. Obsolete or unnecessary rules should be dropped. All rules should be seen as law. They are to be obeyed. If unreasonable, they can be changed, but so long as they are in effect they apply to everyone, students and teacher alike. Let us examine elements of good class rules.

Jointly Formulated

Students should take part with the teacher in establishing class rules. When people help make rules they are more likely to see them as reasonable and they are more likely to follow them. This is true for adults and for most school students. The teacher has responsibility for initiating rules discussions, for keeping rules short and positive, and for ensuring that penalities for breaking them are reasonable. Students should make suggestions about desired behaviors, enforcement, and penalties. If they are very young, in kindergarten or first grade, they cannot give significant input. Still, they should be consulted. Each rule should be explained carefully so that students understand clearly what it means, why it is needed, and what will happen if it is broken. Young children should receive guided practice in doing what the rules require. They should see examples of behavior that breaks the rules, but they should not practice rule-breaking behavior.

Reasonable

Curiously, when groups of people make rules for themselves they often go overboard and make too many. They makes rules that do not affect significant behavior and rules relating to character instead of behavior. It is the teacher's responsibility to make sure the rules are reasonable—that they focus on important behavior, are understandable, can be remembered, and can be practiced.

Positive

Authorities urge teachers to formulate rules in positive, rather than negative terms (i.e., saying what students should do, rather than what they should not do.) Remember Ginott's dictum, correcting is directing? He means that the best way to correct misbehavior is to show students how to do it right. Good rules do the same thing. They tell students how to behave correctly. Here are some examples:

1. Raise hands and take turns. (Instead of "No talking without permission.")
2. Be polite to others (Instead of "Don't interrupt." "Don't hit." "Don't take cuts in line.")
3. Plan ahead to get all work done on time. (Instead of "Don't turn work in late.")

Attention should be drawn to negative behaviors, too, so students know what to avoid. This should be done in discussions about the rules, and before concluding the discussion attention should be redirected to the positive.

Succinct

Ginott advised teachers to use laconic language when dealing with student misbehavior. Laconic language is very brief and to the point. It focuses attention on the matter at hand and lets the student know what to do, without haranguing, preaching, or moralizing.

Class rules should be similarly succinct—brief and to the point. That makes them more effective and easier to remember. Here are some examples:

1. Raise hands out before speaking. (Instead of "We always raise our hands and wait to be called on before speaking because we don't want to be rude to others by interrupting them.")
2. Take turns. (Instead of "We will take turns in everything we do, so that everyone will get an equal chance.")

Longer explanations can be made during rules discussions so that students understand the reasons behind the rules, but they will be better able to remember the rules in their succinct form.

Observable

Rules should be addressed to behaviors that can be observed. It is not useful to make rules about being good, polite, considerate, or respectful unless students know plainly what one does when showing those qualities. It is better to name specific acts, times, and conditions when possible, which was done in previous examples dealing with raising hands and getting work in on time. Other examples might be:

- Sit down and begin work promptly.
- Always say please and thank you.
- Stay in our seats.

The obvious difficulty with stating specific behaviors in rules is that you end up with too many rules. Each behavior you aim for could be stated as its own rule. You might thus have 50 or 100 rules, which of course would not do. Students do well to remember as many as 3 rules in kindergarten, up to 6 or 7 in upper grades. Therefore, a compromise, to compose only enough rules to cover areas of main concern, must be made. These rules will have to be rather general. Within each of the rules will be a few specific behaviors that students can discuss, practice, and remember. Here are examples:

1. A rule for work in the classroom.

   Written   Always do your best work.
   Discussed   Start on time.
                  Finish on time.
                  Be neat.
                  Do your work so that your parents would be happy to see it.

2. A rule for classroom visitors.

   Written   Treat visitors as special.
   Discussed   Greet them.
                  Offer them a chair.
                  Show them some of your work.
                  Be especially kind and helpful to substitute teachers.

3. A rule for classroom behavior.

   Written   Be kind to others.
   Discussed   Be friendly.
                  Speak politely—say please, excuse me, thank you.
                  Help someone every day.
                  Take turns.

4. A rule about behavior outside the classroom.

   Written   Obey the school rules.
   Discussed   Walk, do not run, in corridors.
                  Use clean, polite language.
                  Walk bicycles instead of riding them on school grounds.
                  Be a good example for others.

These example show how to make a few written rules that cover important areas of behavior while still giving attention to several discrete kinds of behavior that fit within the rules.

Made Public

The main rules, about three to six in number, should be made public. They should be written in large letters and displayed in a conspicuous place where they can be seen by students, teachers, and visitors. Attention can be drawn to them regularly as a form of review. When violations occur, the rule can be pointed to by the teacher. Discussions, if needed, can refresh memories on specific behaviors for which the rule calls. Many teachers like to post slogans about the room that draw attention to the rules and specific behaviors. examples of such slogans are:

- The only way to have friends is to be one.
- Manners are happy ways of doing things.
- Be kind, for everyone is fighting a hard battle.
- Courtesy is making others feel good.
- Your tongue weighs practically nothing. Are you strong enough to hold it?
- We get what we earn.
- Try to listen more than you talk.

These slogans can be added one at a time on display in the room. They offer focal points for discussions with the students, and they are a good vehicle for review of class expectations. One caution that must be remembered, however, is that if the slogans and rules remain posted in the same place all year and attention is not drawn back to them regularly, the students stop seeing them. Their mere presence is not enough.

Enforceable

Rules that cannot be enforced are worse than useless. They are counterproductive because they tell students that rules do not mean a thing. For that reason, teachers must be sure that rules, jointly formulated and publicly displayed, can be adhered to by all involved.

Some rules that sound fine simply cannot be enforced. Reasons for that condition include limited teacher power, limited ability to observe, customs of the community, and individual traits of the students. The following cases show examples of rules that cannot be enforced.

1. *Finish all work on time.* If you have students who are handicapped, immature,

or very slow workers, this rule is unreasonable. It might be changed to "Do our best to finish work on time."

2. *No swearing.* If your students come from neighborhoods where swear words fly like flakes in a snowstorm, you will not be able to enforce this rule. It would be better to compose one that says "We will improve our language every week." You can then discuss specific language usage and keep a graph of class opinion about improvements.

3. *Eat three balanced meals a day.* Forget this one. It is a good idea, but as a rule it is a dead-end street.

Enforced

Once rules have been established, they must be enforced. However, before they can be enforced, they must meet the ciriteria discussed in the previous paragraphs of this chapter. In particular, rules are more enforceable when they are reasonable and when they have been composed cooperatively by teacher and students. Moreover, there should be few surprises in rule enforcement. Students should know the penalties in advance. When they break a rule, the appropriate penalty is assessed, dispassionately and matter-of-factly.

This dispassionate and matter-of-fact penalty assessment is embodied in a concept called *logical consequences.* Such logical consequences are reasonable penalties. Students know about them in advance. If their behavior violates class rules, the penalties come as a logical consequence of the behavior they have chosen.

Choice of behavior and logical consequences are cornerstones of Glasser's view of discipline. He feels that we all choose to behave the way we do. Good behavior is simply good choices. Bad behavior is bad choices. When students choose bad behavior for themselves they are simultaneously choosing the consequences (penalties or punishments) that inevitably accompany that bad behavior.

This approach allows teachers to enforce rules with a minimum of anger, distress, or ill feelings. Students probably will not like the consequences, but they have in effect chosen them. The teacher can even show sympathy for their unfortunate choice (but not back away from enforcement. That would render the entire system ineffective). The teacher can also follow up as Glasser suggests by helping the student make a new commitment and a new plan of action for making better choices of behavior.

Threats and warnings deserve brief consideration at this point. Most teachers use them far too much, while students continue to push to see how far the rules will bend. This, in turn, causes teachers anxiety, and when teachers finally decide to impose consequences, hostility and ill feelings are likely to result for everyone.

It is better never to make threats. It is enough for students to know the rules and the penalties that automatically arise when rules are broken which makes threats unnecessary. When angered, teachers are prone to say things that are difficult or impossible to carry out. The problem then becomes compounded.

An occasional warning can be used in place of threats. The warning should be given only once. If students do not know that, teachers should make it plain. The warning can consist of mentioning the rule that is being violated. It can be given in the manner suggested by Ginott with the teacher using an I-message—"It is so noisy, I can't do my work." Also, the warning can be directed more pointedly: "The next time I have to mention talking, I must enforce the penalty that you seem to be choosing." Then the teacher must follow through if necessary. It is acceptable to give warnings once, matter-of-factly. Warnings should never be given a second time, because that only keeps students guessing. Instead of second warnings, logical consequences should be invoked.

Penalties

We hear so often that the punishment should fit the crime (and so it should), but we must remember that breaking class rules is not a crime in any legal sense of the word. Still, punishment can be administered for breaking class rules if it is reasonable and administered dispassionately. Basically, this implies that one can make students stay after school, do extra work, or relinquish privileges. One can even administer corporal punishment without being angry at the time and having a witness. *Never, never* strike a student (or pinch, pull hair, or shove) while you are angry. Few teachers use corporal punishment. It is considered inhumane and degrading and produces unwanted side effects. Parents seem eager to sue if corporal punishment has been used by a teacher. Therefore, even when teachers are legally correct in their actions, they still have reason to fear living with the headaches of legal suits, dealing with lawyers, making court appearances, and experiencing emotional distress.

What then are suitable kinds of penalties for those who break rules? The underlying requisites of interventions and penalties are:

1.   Stopping the misbehavior;
2.   Showing the student how to behave correctly;
3.   Making right what was done wrong, if possible;
4.   Acting in a manner that does not degrade the student;
5.   Allowing good personal relations to continue;
6.   Serving to improve behavior.

The models of classroom discipline presented in earlier chapters made many suggestions for good interventions and penalties. Those suggestions fit nicely into a scheme of preventive control, supportive control, and corrective control.

Preventive control consists of measures taken to reduce the incidence of misbehavior before it occurs and could include such steps as:

1. Providing interesting activities;
2. Arranging schedules that allow frequent changes of pace;
3. Making class rules and discussing them;
4. Establishing ongoing behavior modification programs;
5. Notifying parents when having contests and finding other means for establishing student desire for good behavior.

Supportive control refers to steps taken to nip misbehavior in the bud, to catch it at its earliest stage and redirect it. Examples of such steps would include:

1. Implementing ongoing behavior modification.
2. Watching students, moving among them, and helping them with difficulties they encounter.
3. Changing pace or interjecting humor when frustration or boredom begins to build.
4. Holding regular class discussions about both positive and negative feelings to iron out problems before they become serious.

Corrective control refers to the steps taken after misbehavior has occurred. Nonpunitive measures often include:

1. Taking time out—sitting apart from the class (but within view) for a time.
2. Making right what was done wrong or making it up through good deeds.
3. Asking the misbehaving student in a friendly tone of voice what he or she is doing. Have him or her make a value judgment about it.
4. Conferencing privately with the offending student, addressing the situation and the behavior rather than the student's character.
5. Calling parents if the misbehavior continues.
6. Having an administrator remove the student if nothing else works.

GREAT EXPECTATIONS

Perhaps you remember the musical play, *My Fair Lady,* in which an English gentleman succeeds, after various trials and tribulations, in transforming a cockney girl into a lady of fine speech and manners. That theme came from an ancient Greek drama entitled *Pygmalion* about the king of Cyprus who fell in love with an ivory statue that he had made. When Pygmalion was at his prayer, Aphrodite gave life to the statue.

In 1968, Robert Rosenthal and Lenore Jacobson published a book entitled *Pygmalion in the Classroom* that reported studies purported to show that students tend to live up to what is expected of them. If they are led to believe firmly that they will do well, students tend to do so. If they really believe they will do poorly, then they follow suit. Rosenthal and Jacobson introduced the term *self-fulfilling prophecy*, which they used as a label for the phenomenon of people's behavior reflecting what was genuinely expected of them. The term is now used widely.

The conclusions reported in *Pygmalion in the Classroom* have been roundly criticized, mainly because of the methods of research and data interpretation that were used. Nevertheless, most authorities agree that student behavior is influenced by expectations that teachers hold. Teachers who are good at classroom control corroborate that view. They tell you that you get pretty much from kids what you expect to get. That is over the long haul, of course, because problems arise daily that have to be solved. Students need to be talked with regularly. But through those talks, the set standards and the procedures used for correcting misbehavior, teachers can make known the essentials (1) they expect humane behavior from students; (2) they themselves will behave in humane ways; (3) their students can be the best; and (4) being the best one can be a goal worth striving for. Truly believing in students, truly expecting the best from them are the great expectations that influence behavior so powerfully.

SUMMARY

So many different ideas have been presented in this chapter that it seems desirable to summarize them. These ideas have to do with the roles that teacher seriousness, class rules, and great expectations play in student behavior and discipline.

Serious teachers were defined as those who truly value education, learning, and the golden rule. They prepare adequately for teaching, give their best effort, keep students on task, follow up with students, take the extra step, never give up, and communicate well with parents. Each of these traits influences how students behave and learn.

Rules tell students what is permitted in the classroom and what is not. They should be formulated by teacher and students together. They should be reasonable, positive, succinct, observable, public, enforceable, enforced, and call for appropriate penalties when broken. Rules remove much guesswork and game playing. Punishments should be constructive, and they should be applied consistently and without malice as the natural consequence of misbehavior.

Great expectations mean truly expecting the best of students and continually letting them know that. Students are rarely angelic. They misbehave under the best of circumstances. Still, they tend to behave in ways genuinely expected by the teacher. Expect the best, and students will lean in that direction.

REFERENCES

EGGLESTON, E. *The Hoosier Schoolmaster.* New York: Grosset and Dunlap, 1899.
ROSENTHAL, R., and L. JACOBSON. *Pygmalion in the Classroom.* New York: Harper and Row, 1968.

·9·

MODELS, MODELING, AND IMITATION LEARNING

MODELING

Modeling is a process of teaching through example that produces learning through imitation. It is not yet widely recognized or systematically used, though in the past decade it has received detailed attention. The evidence coming from that attention has established that for most social, behavioral, cognitive, and affective learning, modeling is the most effective of all methods of teaching.

Perhaps the greatest strength of modeling, from a teacher's viewpoint, is that it describes a learning process, and in the very same terms it suggests teaching procedures. That unity of terms and processes allows for teaching and learning to be considered as joint aspects of the same effort, instead of depicting teaching as a set of acts that causes students to go through a separate set of acts. This parallel of teaching to learning makes modeling uniquely useful to teachers.

Along with its practicality in teaching, modeling brings a host of added benefits. It is efficient, it provides remarkable guidance while reducing learner labor and error, and it greatly speeds the learning of complex behaviors. Most of all, modeling is the best way to teach students how to behave acceptably in the classroom.

In this chapter we shall see how teachers use modeling to help students learn both subject matter and good behavior. First, however, let us see what is required in teaching through modeling. Effective modeling requires three essential conditions.

1. A Clear, Concise, Accurate, Attractive Example (Model) for Learners to Observe. This model can depict concepts, relationships, processes, or behaviors. The model can be a live or recorded person, a verbal description, a graphic or pictoral representation, or a tangible three-dimensional object. Models can be used alone or in combination.

2. Careful Attention by Observers to the Modeled Event. The crucial elements, features, aspects, relationships, and so forth must be noted in the modeled event. Attention can be directed by telling learners in advance what to observe. It can be redirected during the event as necessary. It will be increased by attractive models showing useful, interesting behavior or information.

3. Retention (Remembering) by Observers of What is Shown by the Model. Retention allows students to reenact at a later time what they observed during modeling. Coding, directed attention, emotional involvement, practice, and reinforcement are among established means of improving retention.

Learning through modeling is further enhanced by the following, which are helpful though not essential to the process.

4. Practice in Reenacting the Observed Concept, Process, or Behavior.   The learners practice the new learning in order to refine and strengthen it.

5. Corrective Feedback and Reinforcement.   Corrective feedback during practice helps learners reenact the modeled behavior more accurately. Reinforcement also increases accuracy. In addition, it can increase the likelihood that the learner will use the new learning in appropriate situations.

WHAT RESEARCH SAYS ABOUT MODELING

Well over 200 studies dealing with modeling have been conducted since 1960 that provide a solid research base to support its elements, procedures, and effectiveness. Albert Bandura of Stanford University deserves major credit for developing modeling as a teaching process. He recognized and documented the powerful influence that modeling exerts on behavior. The more he looked into it the more he saw that modeling's component parts could be analyzed and refined in the laboratory. That meant experimentation, which in turn stirred up much research activity.

Special education was the first branch of public education to recognize the power of Bandura's work. People who work with the mentally retarded or educationally handicapped are ever watchful for procedures that speed and strengthen learning. They had earlier received a great boon with principles of reinforcement and behavior modification. Now, modeling was unveiled, and when used in conjunction with behavior modification, it produced results that surpassed those of any previous technique.

Modeling's effectiveness is not limited to special education. Its powers are even more notable in the regular classroom. We have a growing body of evidence that suggests it is our most effective method for teaching many of the objectives within the three great domains of learning: *psychomotor* (physical behavior), *cognitive* (knowledge and its use), and *affective* (emotions, attitudes, and values).

The many research studies carried out in modeling provide a body of generalizations that can be considered principles of modeling, some of which are presented in the following list.

Effectiveness of Modeling

   1.   Modeling effectively teaches behavior, concepts, cognitive skills and processes, language, creativity, values, attitudes and interests.

2. Modeling teaches effectively not only through individual example but also through group example, simulations, psychodrama, behavior rehearsal, and role play.

3. Learnings acquired through modeling are generalizable. They are not limited just to replication within identical settings, but spread to numerous other situations and contexts.

Traits of Models

4. Traits of the model provide the main motivators for observational learning. They attract and hold attention, and they can increase observers' desire to emulate the observed behavior or process.

5. Model traits known to be effective in enhancing observational learning include attractiveness, familiarity, meaningfulness, clarity, prestige, social status, creativity, skill, brightness, known success, warmth, nurturance, and an obvious desire to help.

Teacher as Model

6. Teachers are prime models for classroom instruction. They, more than any other models, possess the variety of traits known to enhance observational learning.

Filmed Models

7. While live models tend to be more effective, models presented by means of film and television can be powerful.

Peers as Models

8. Evidence points to peer modeling for both children and adults as one of the most powerful influences in the acquisition of social behavior, interests, values, morals, sex roles, language, and cognitive skills.

Verbal Models

9. Verbal models alone, or in combination with other models, are highly effective. They assist learning by clarifying, organizing, focusing attention, providing cues for retention and reenactment, and increasing the likelihood of generalization.

Graphic and Three-Dimensional Models

10. Both graphic and three-dimensional models effectively transmit behavioral, cognitive, attitudinal, and emotional learnings.

The Self as Model

11. It has been shown that clearly visualizing oneself behaving in a desirable fashion can lead to improved performance.

Motivation as Model

12. Motivation is useful in attracting, focusing, and maintaining observer attention. This motivation is affected by personal traits of the models, teacher guidance, peer pressure, and reinforcement from the teacher.

Verbalization in Modeling

13. Verbalization refers to labeling of observations and to "talking through" acts and processes. It improves the speed of learning and the ability to recall and reenact the modeled events.

Feedback in Modeling

14. Corrective feedback, given when learners are reenacting the modeled event, improves accuracy, especially for complex behaviors, processes, and concepts.

Retention in Modeling

15. Retention—what one remembers after observing a modeled event—is improved through intent to remember, usefulness of the learning, verbalization, concise labeling, continued practice and continued application.

Reinforcement in Modeling

16. Reinforcement used in conjunction with modeling usually speeds and strengthens learning.
17. Vicarious reinforcement—seeing the model being rewarded—increases imitative behavior.

Danger in Modeling

18. Modeling can effectively produce *undesirable* behaviors, just as it does desirable behaviors. Caution is required.

MODELING APPLIED TO DISCIPLINE

Modeling is a process that occurs continually in life and accounts for the natural development of social behavior, customs, attitudes, values, and interests. Under laboratory conditions it has been used to build, strengthen, and weaken many different kinds of behaviors including moral orientations, aggression, and general styles of individual and group behavior. Evidence shows that the process can be applied easily and effectively to modify all types of behavior that receive attention in classroom discipline.

Of particular interest in discipline are the behaviors associated with personal relations, self-concept, and classroom demeanor. Personal relations include such things as courtesy, manners, mutual support, and consideration for others. Self-concept has to do with an individual feeling of acceptability, competence, and belongingness. Classroom demeanor includes the numerous student acts that have bearing on classroom stability, calm, purposefulness, and order. It includes such things as moving about the room, asking permission, talking out, treatment of visitors, and support of substitute teachers.

The remainder of this chapter addresses the role that modeling can play in classroom disicpline. To help you understand what that role can be, how it functions, and how it is applied, discussions are presented within the following topics: modeling and principles of learning, effective models, steps in teaching through modeling, specific plans for teaching good behavior, specific plans for teaching manners and attitudes, and a review of modeling.

MODELING AND PRINCIPLES OF LEARNING

If you reflect for a moment on the established principles of learning, you will see that modeling flows naturally into them. Over the decades, researchers and practitioners have formulated generalizations about learning that hold true for most learners, under most conditions, most of the time. Having passed the tests of time and practice, these statements have earned the distinction of being called principles. Among principles of learning, the following are preeminent. Students learn better when:

1. They are informed in advance as precisely as possible what they are expected to do and to learn.
2. They have a motivation level sufficient to enable them to pay close attention and proceed diligently through the learning activities.
3. They are able to practice the new learnings immediately and often in appropriately meaningful situations.
4. They receive suitable feedback as to the accuracy of their efforts and mistakes they are making, plus reinforcement for suitable efforts and improvements.
5. They are able to apply their learnings to the solution of realistic problems within realistic situations.

It follows that teachers teach better when they provide the conditions under which students learn better. This is not to imply that teaching is a simple task. It is not. But when skillful teachers adept at setting good learning environments and establishing good personal relations put modeling to use, they naturally provide the conditions named in the five principles listed. Here is how modeling meets these conditions:

1. *Knowledge of expectations* is provided very clearly through the modeled
    event. Students are to replicate the model. Since they see or hear it, often
    in conjunction with verbal descriptions, they know precisely what is
    expected. Before the 1960s, students usually knew only vaguely what
    they were supposed to learn. Behavioral objectives then considerably
    sharpened their view (and that of their teachers). Modeling now provides
    another step forward for student knowledge of expectations.

2. *Motivation* in modeling comes from various sources. It can be established
    quickly at a high level by using live models that are attractive, prestigious,
    expert, and enthusiastic. Graphic and tangible models motivate highly
    when they are novel, colorful, and clear. Motivation is maintained
    through advance organization, vicarious and direct reinforcement, stu-
    dent enjoyment, and obvious worth of what is being learned.

3. *Practice* has clear direction in modeling. The students attempt to reenact
    the modeled behavior precisely. Practice is provided in various forms—
    covertly when students attempt to see themselves in their minds' eye
    performing correctly and overtly when they physically reenact the
    behavior. Ideal practice conditions allow all students to reenact the behav-
    ior so errors can be noted and corrected.

4. *Corrective feedback and reinforcement* enhance the effectiveness of model-
    ing. These concepts are easier to apply with modeling than with many
    other methods because both students and teachers know that the repli-
    cated behavior should match the modeled behavior. When errors are
    made, the teacher can specify exactly what needs to be done differently.
    This specification can be made humanely and constructively simply by
    remodeling and guiding student reenactment. Similarly, reinforcement
    specifies exactly what the student is doing right. This makes reinforce-
    ment more effective than when it is given in statements that are positive
    but vague.

5. *Application* of new learnings does not occur naturally and better with
    modeling than it does with other methods of teaching. However, learn-
    ings acquired through modeling have excellent application potential.
    They are quite precise, allowing students to use them purposefully and
    competently.

These five points make up the heart of the modeling method of teaching.
You will find them stressed and restressed in the prototype lessons that appear
later in the chapter.

EFFECTIVE MODELS

Effective modeling can be done behaviorally (live or filmed demonstrations), verbally (oral or written descriptions), and graphically (photographs, cartoons, drawings). Evidence suggests that a combination of two or more models used together is more effective than one alone. That is, while models are demonstrating a behavior, for example, they may also describe orally what they are doing and why.

For teaching acceptable classroom behavior, live models are most effective. Teachers are very effective in this role as are other adults. Peer models, used correctly, are very effective also.

Models are effective to the degree in which they capture attention, hold attention, and tend to be imitated. Traits of live models that contribute to their effectiveness include:

1. Level of competence shown by the model;
2. Purported expertness of the model;
3. Celebrity status of the model;
4. Social power of the model;
5. Model ability to reward imitators;
6. Age of the model;
7. Sex of the model;
8. Ethnic status of the model;
9. Physical attractiveness of the model;
10. Personality attractiveness of the model.

When systematic reinforcement is applied to observers during modeling, the effects of model traits become less powerful. For example, an unattractive model can be more effective than an attractive model if observers are rewarded when they imitate the model's behavior.

Effective traits of verbal and graphic models have not been explored systematically but desirable qualities of such models would probably include (1) clarity, (2) succinctness, (3) apparent correctness, and (4) attractive format, style, and language.

STEPS IN TEACHING THROUGH MODELING

Bandura's experimental work in modeling did not deal with teaching. It dealt with spontaneous imitation learning, especially in areas of fears, phobias, and interpersonal relations. The experimental work done by others following

Bandura's footsteps has delved into many other aspects of imitation learning, including traits of models, generalization of learning acquired through imitation, theorectical components of imitation learning, and effects of reinforcement on imitation learning.

Thus, modeling as a teaching process has grown out of attempts to apply its principles to the classroom. This happened first in special education and is only now occurring in regular classroom instruction. One realizes, of course, that the process of modeling has always been crucial in learning and teaching, and that it is essential to the socialization of numerous species of animals besides man. But it is only now that its principles are being refined and applied in a systematic, organized, and technical way.

In the mid 1970s the special-education department of the Cajon Valley, California schools devised and implemented a five-step sequence for teaching handicapped students through modeling. I collaborated with them in applying and refining the process in regular classrooms. The sequence proved easy to learn, easy to apply, and very effective in promoting various kinds of learning. Following are the five steps of the process. Later you will see them applied to actual teaching plans.

STEP 1. *Provide a good model for the students.* (The model should incorporate as many desirable traits as possible.)

STEP 2. *(Call for group verbal reenactment in unison of what was modeled.* (Repeat two or three times. Be sure all students participate.)

STEP 3. *Ask for volunteers to reenact the modeled event individually.* (Usually two volunteers suffice. This step serves three purposes. First, it allows the teacher to assess correctness of the replication. Second, it serves to remodel the behavior for other class members. Third, it provides opportunity for the teacher to reinforce the correct behavior. The reinforcement occurs vicariously for the other members of the class.)

STEP 4. *Draft two nonvolunteers to replicate the modeled behavior.* (This step serves the same three purposes as STEP 3.)

STEP 5. *Have students apply the new learnings immediately in a realistic situation.* (This application provides additional practice and it further establishes the value of the learning. These conditions aid retention and transfer of learning.)

In applying the steps you realize that the model is not presented cold, out of the blue. As with any other lesson, the stage must be set for student involvement. Some people use an air of exuberance, mystery, or surprise. Others preview what is to come, what should be learned, and what is to be achieved by the learning. The beginning leads into the model, which in turn guides the remainder of the lesson.

The five-step sequence is designed to cut student errors to a minimum. Still, students will make some errors. When they do, the teacher does not point to the guilty individuals. Instead the behavior is remodeled, as it first was. Then students are called on again for reenactment. This recycling procedure provides two benefits. One is that it avoids student embarrassment or hurt. Another is that group attention is diverted from the error and directed back immediately to an appropriate response.

During the entire process, teachers remember to provide feedback and reinforcement. The two are most effective when combined. They should specify in positive terms what the student is doing right. Negative comments are not used. Comments that are positive but vague are kept to a minimum. Instead of saying, "Good," "That's fine," "Nice work," the teacher might say, "Good. You are remembering to raise your hand before talking." Most of us do not use enough reinforcement and encouragement with our students. It takes practice to remember to reinforce students by telling them what they are doing right.

SPECIFIC PLANS FOR
TEACHING THROUGH MODELING

This section presents six specific plans for teaching desired behavior. The first three deal with aspects of classroom demeanor and the second three with manners and attitudes. Each plan is divided into two parts, background and application. The background tells about the plan and preparations that should be made for its use. The application details its actual use with a group of students.

Plan 1. How to Read in a Group

Background. This two-part lesson teaches students five important behaviors for reading in groups. Those behaviors are:

1. How to sit;
2. How to hold the books;
3. How to follow along with the reader;
4. How to read loudly;
5. How to read with expression.

The teacher first models for a group of five students. They are told that they will teach the rest of the class. The five students then model the behaviors in the form of a demonstration for the class. The lesson effectively improves group reading behavior for students from first through sixth grade. With modifications it can be used to teach desired behaviors in group activities at all grade levels.

Objective. Upon completion of this lesson students in reading groups will be able to sit correctly, hold their books properly, follow the reader accurately, and read aloud with suitable volume and proper expression.

Application

PART 1

Initiate
Bring five students to the reading circle. Give them reading books opened to the same page. Tell them there are good ways and poor ways to read in the reading group. We are going to learn the good ways—how to sit, hold the book, keep up with the reader, read loudly, and read with expression.

Teacher models/Group reenactment
Model each behavior for the students: sitting, holding the book, keeping up with the reader, reading loudly, and reading for expression. After modeling each behavior call on the group to reenact it together.

Volunteer reenactment
Call on volunteers to reenact each behavior.

Draftee reenactment
Call on nonvolunteers to reenact each behavior.

PART 2

Have this group of five students model how to read in a group for the remainder of the class. They can do it as a skit, with a different student modeling each behavior. The teacher directs the modeling sequence to obtain group, volunteer, and draftee reenactment.

Immediate application
Follow with group reading lessons. Tell the students you will be looking for those who remember all five parts about reading in the group.

Continued application
Ask students to recall the five important behaviors at the beginning of subsequent group reading sessions.

Plan 2. How to Behave in the Math Center
(Lab, Shop, Kitchen, etc.)

Background. This lesson teaches students how to conduct themselves when using the math learning center. It applies equally to any other part of the curriculum where specific duties, behaviors, and manners are desired.

Older students from another class model the behaviors. Arrangements are made with them and their teacher in advance, and they practice before or after school the behaviors they are going to model. The lesson is effective for learners at any grade level.

Objective. As a result of the lesson the students will demonstrate these modeled behaviors when using the math center: (a) how to go to the center; (b) how to select an activity and begin work; and (c) how to ask for help when needed.

Application

Initiate
"Class, we have a special surprise today. I have invited some students from Mrs. Simmons' class to show us how they work in the math center. They will use our center, and they will show you how they do these things I have written on the board."
1. How to go to the center.
2. How to select an activity.
3. How to ask for help.

Students model
"Let's watch how they do these three things." The models, who are seated, get up, go to the center, select an activity, and being to work. After a moment, one raises a hand. The aide or teacher responds.

Volunteer verbal reenactment
Call on volunteer students to:
1. Recall the three things being modeled.
2. Describe how students went to the center, selected an activity, and asked for help.

Draftee reenactment
Call on nonvolunteers to do the same.

Immediate application
Thank the models and allow them to return to their class. "Now let's see if we can do as well as the older students did. I will call on four people to show us what they have learned." Call four names. Those people go to the center and begin to work. Repeat with others, if desired. (Give feedback and reinforcement with specific mention of what was done correctly.)

Continued application
Periodically review desired behaviors. When students violate them, correct individually and/or follow with group discussions.

Plan 3. Ignoring Inappropriate Behavior

Background. This lesson teaches students how to ignore inappropriate behavior they see in the classroom. Their ignoring of such behavior removes the reinforcement that misbehaving students get from peer attention. The lesson is conducted by means of group discussion and role playing. Peers model the ignoring behavior. They also model the reinforcing responses made to students who ignore the inappropriate behaviors.

The lesson can be used effectively in Grades 1 through 6. In fifth and sixth grades, however, the point must be stressed that this is a serious activity, even though it may be fun. Otherwise students may decide to mimic the inappropriate behaviors rather than ignore them. Be sure to discuss the effects of inappropriate behaviors, how they disrupt lessons, and how they can hurt others' feelings.

Objective. As a result of this lesson, students will be able to:

1. Name at least three acts that are inappropriate in the classroom.
2. Tell and demonstrate the meaning of *ignore*.
3. Improve in their tendency to ignore inappropriate behavior when it occurs.

Application

Initiate
"Class, sometimes we see students in our group do things we know are not right, things that show bad manners. Have you ever noticed people doing those things? What are some of them?" (List on board as students mention them. Elicit mention of name calling, loud laughing, making noises, talking out, etc.)

"Sometimes when we hear or see someone do these things, we think it would be funny to do them, too. Soon, everyone is doing them. The result is that we can't get our work done. We annoy other people, and sometimes hurt their feelings. Because these acts disturb our work and hurt peoples' feelings, they are inappropriate. Inappropriate means they are not the right thing to do in the class. When you see inappropriate behavior, what you should do is ignore it. Ignore means you don't pay any attention to it.

"Today we are going to practice ignoring inappropriate behavior. Let's take some of the behaviors listed on the board. We will role play how to ignore them. Role play means to pretend we are really doing the things. I would like four of you to help me, please."

Peers model

"Fine. Sit in these four chairs. Tom, choose one of the behaviors listed on the board. When we begin, you can do the inappropriate behavior. Sarah and John will be students.

"They will ignore Tom—pay no attention at all to him. Lupe, you be the teacher. When you see Sarah and John ignoring Tom's behavior, thank them for ignoring it. You can let them help you collect the papers since they did what they knew was right. The rest of you are the audience. Be very quiet. You will get a chance to role play, too, if you are quiet and pay attention. All right, Tom, begin."

Group reenactment

Repeat with other students role playing ignoring inappropriate behavior.

Application

"I will be looking to see who can ignore behaviors in the class. I will find a way to thank you when you do." (Be sure that students who play the teacher's role do not say hurtful things about the offender.)

Plan 4. I Am Likeable and Capable (IALAC)

Background.   This lesson helps students become aware of the damaging effects of criticism, sarcasm, and ridicule, and it teaches students how to speak to others in ways that bolster their self-esteem. It is adaptable to all grade levels.

Three kinds of models are used: graphic, teacher, and peer. The teacher describes the graphic model and demonstrates good and poor ways of speaking to others. A peer model demonstrates some damaging kinds of remarks. The teacher then models positive remarks that help repair damage done to self-esteem. The graphic model can be made to look like Figure 9.1.

FIGURE 9.1.   *A graphic model of the technique.*

Each letter is then used to describe what it stands for. For example, "*I*—me, myself, separate person, different from everyone else; I look different, I act different, my feelings are different, etc." Continue with *likeable* and *capable*.

Objective.   As a result of this lesson, students will increase the number of positive comments they make to each other.

Application

Initiate
Show model of letters IALAC on chart. Tell students each letter will help them feel better about themselves, more likeable and capable, and teach them how to make others feel better, too. Discuss meanings of likeable and capable. Discuss the importance of feeling good about ourselves. Give each student an IALAC tag, a 3″ × 5″ card with IALAC written on it.

Teacher models, group reenacts
Say, "I am likeable and capable. Maureen, are you likeable and capable? Let's hear you say after me—I am likeable and capable." Continue. Have all students say it together.

Peer negative model
Awareness: Peer leader models behaviors that cause people not to feel likeable and capable. When student model makes remarks that criticize others the students tear a small piece off their IALAC tags.

Teacher positive model
Model behaviors that repair damaged IALAC—such as, offering help, showing consideration, going out of the way to be kind, helping one see the positive side. This is done in role-playing pairs—first teacher and student, then

Paired reenactment
Student–student pairs practice saying IALAC corrective remarks.

Volunteer reenactment
Teacher describes a situation in which a student's work has been criticized harshly by the teacher. Ask for volunteers to reenact positive responses.

Draftee reenactment
Call on two nonvolunteers to make some positive comments, either to the same or to a new hypothetical situation.

Immediate application
Each student makes a new IALAC tag and wears it the remainder of the period. Teacher and students consciously make positive remarks to each other.

Continued application
Periodically review IALAC, concern, compassion, etc., in group discussions. Call for continued and renewed efforts from students to make positive, supportive comments to each other.

Note

Remember to reinforce all desired student responses. Use verbal praise that specifies what was done right. Be sure that the negative-model aspect of the lesson is kept in perspective. The tearing of the IALAC tags could become reinforcing to undesired behaviors.

Plan 5. Active Listening to Others

Background.   This lesson, appropriate for third grade through high school, provides the rationale for the active-listening theory. It is useful for improving communication and enhancing self-concept. Students are taught to use several door-opener statements, such as, "I see," "Go on," "I'm listening," "Tell me more," and "Uh huh." They also receive practice in decoding the hidden, emotional messages in conversation and in supplying the feedback called for by those messages.

Two graphic chart models are needed, one that shows door-opener statements and another that shows decoded messages. They are shown in Figure 9.2. Puppets may be used to assist in the role-playing situations. It is helpful to have on hand several index cards on which various problems around which role-playing situations can be built are written.

"I hate Mr. ..."
(I wish he liked me.)

"This work is stupid!"
(I don't understand it.)

"I don't want to play."
(They don't want me.)

"Uh huh."
"Tell me more about that."
"I see."
"You feel that..."
"I think I understand..."

FIGURE 9.2.   *Graphic chart models of door-opening statements and decoded messages.*

Objective. After completing this lesson, the student will be able to (1) explain why active listening techniques are valid and useful and (2) use both door openers and active-listening feedback statements in their conversations, when appropriate.

Application

Initiate
Discuss with students the importance of effective communication. Demonstrate what can happen when people cannot communicate. Try using a teacher–puppet skit of a deaf person who always misunderstands, or better yet, a skit of Abbott and Costello's "Who's on First" routine. Have students identify what the communication problem entails.

Introduce model
Show "Listening Tips" chart. Have students read door-opener statements with teacher. Explain that with these phrases, you will show how they can help people talk about their problems.

Teacher models
Using the puppet or a volunteer as the "problem owner," the teacher models a short conversation, using the door openers.

Group reenactment
Teacher has the puppet or volunteer talk to the entire group as they respond with the door openers from the chart.

Volunteer reenactment
Ask for two student volunteers to talk, using door-opener statements.

Draftee reenactment
Call on two nonvolunteers to talk, using door openers.

Introduce model
Using the "What Feelings Do We Hear" chart, discuss with the students how different feelings can be heard in voices and expression.

Teacher models
Teacher demonstrates some problem situations where feedback statements from the chart would be appropriate.

Group reenactment
Repeating the same situations modeled by the teacher, have the entire group use feedback statements from the chart in reply to the problems.

Volunteer reenactment
Call on two volunteers to discuss problems, using both door-opener statements and feedback responses. Have the rest of the class count how many times each type of statement is used, and if any other comments (advice, judgement, etc.) are used.

Draftee reenactment
Call on two nonvolunteers to discuss problems following the same procedure used with volunteer reenactment.

Immediate application
At the close of the lesson ask students to summarize and evaluate how active-listening techniques would be helpful to them in talking with their friends and classmates. Be sure to reinforce any active-listening techniques used by students during the day.

Continued application
Periodically review the "Listening Tips" chart and elicit from children actual experiences when these tips helped or could have helped them. Continue reinforcement of active listening done by students during the day.

Plan 6. How to Behave with a Substitute Teacher

Models and activities used in this lesson teach students the vulnerability of substitute teachers, the feelings they have in attempting to perform their jobs, how students can help substitute teachers, and the information about the classroom that the substitute would need in order to work effectively.

Two charts are needed for models. They can be copied from Figure 9.3. Colored pens can be used for emphasis.

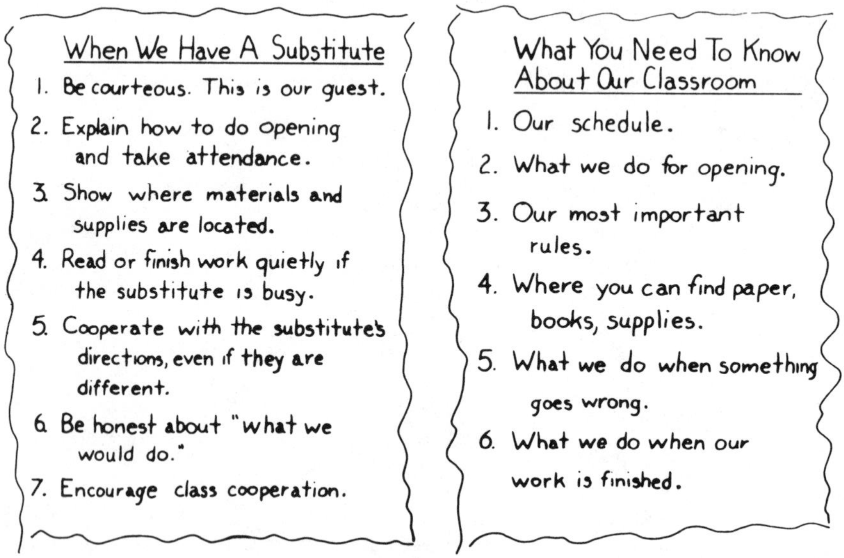

When We Have A Substitute
1. Be courteous. This is our guest.
2. Explain how to do opening and take attendance.
3. Show where materials and supplies are located.
4. Read or finish work quietly if the substitute is busy.
5. Cooperate with the substitute's directions, even if they are different.
6. Be honest about "what we would do."
7. Encourage class cooperation.

What You Need To Know About Our Classroom
1. Our schedule.
2. What we do for opening.
3. Our most important rules.
4. Where you can find paper, books, supplies.
5. What we do when something goes wrong.
6. What we do when our work is finished.

FIGURE 9.3.   *Charts for graphic models.*

Objective.   After completing this lesson the students will be able to:

1. Identify and recognize the feelings of insecurity and newness that substitute teachers have.
2. Identify and perform behaviors helpful to a substitute in the classroom.
3. Identify and prepare an orientation plan for substitutes.

Application

Initiate
Discuss with students what types of feelings they have when they are in new situations, or when they must perform a job under harsh criticism. (insecurity, helplessness, frustration, anger, etc.) Select a peer leader. Send him from the room while an object is hidden somewhere in the classroom. Tell the students that their role in the situation will have three parts:
1. When the student first reenters the room is silent; no encouragement or discouragement is offered in the search for the hidden object.
2. At a signal from the teacher, students will criticize and offer misleading hints.
3. At a second signal from the teacher, students will encourage and offer hints to the student. Have the student relate feelings that were experienced during each condition. Write comments on the board. Ask students to recall statements and behaviors that were most helpful to the student under stress. Write these on the board.

Peer models
Call on prestigious students to model helpful statements that are written on the board.

Volunteer reenactment
Call on two volunteers to reenact helpful comments and behaviors.

Draftee reenactment
Call on two nonvolunteers to reenact helpful comments and behaviors.

Application
Ask students to reiterate how this experience can help the substitute teacher in the performance of the job. Have them suggest how they might apply the helpful behaviors and statements.

Introduce second model
Tell the students you are going to set up role-playing situations in which they will use these helpful behaviors. Show the chart that contains hints on helpful ideas. Review notes on the board.

Teacher models
Select a student to play the role of substitute teacher. Teacher models providing helpful behavior to the substitute. Use suggestions from teacher-made chart or from student comments written on the board. For example the student explains the opening activities procedure to the substitute.

Paired reenactment
Divide the class into pairs. One person is the substitute and the other is a student. *Example:* Substitute has just entered the room and is looking over teacher's notes. Student approaches respectfully and explains normal class routine.

Volunteer and draftee reenactment
Call on two volunteers, then two nonvolunteers (in pairs) to reenact their role performance.

Immediate application
Conduct a group discussion on (1) what an individual can do when an entire group is misbehaving with a substitute; and (2) what an individual can do when a substitute does not know where important items are located.

Continued application
Assign groups, individual students, or the entire class to work on putting together an "Orientation Plan Book for Substitutes," using the class chart as a guide. Assign individuals to act as substitute guides for days when the teacher is not present.

REVIEW OF DISCIPLINE THROUGH MODELING

What is Modeling?

Modeling is a process of teaching through example and learning through imitation. The process accounts for the learning of most social behavior. It is instrumental in the acquisition of knowledge, values, interests, attitudes, and accepted modes of behavior.

How Does Modeling Work?

Research into modeling indicates that the process involves the following components and functions:

1. *Demonstration:* An act is demonstrated, depicted, or explained.
2. *Attention:* Observers focus their attentional processes on the demonstration, depiction, or explanation.
3. *Memory:* Observers code and store the observed information, so they can recall and reproduce it when appropriate.

It has been further established that the process is usually enhanced when the following conditions are added:

4. *Practice:* Observers reenact what they have observed.
5. *Feedback:* Reinforcement, suppressors, and corrective feedback can be used to shape students' reenactments.

Who or What Can Serve as Models?

Effective models include teacher, peers, other adults, films, photographs, cartoons, diagrams, three-dimensional objects, puppets, and oral and written descriptions. Verbalization about the model or process usually increases its effectiveness.

What Do Teachers Do in Modeling?

The teacher's role in modeling is as follows:

1. Selects behavior to be learned.
2. Selects most appropriate models.
3. Sees that the behavior is modeled clearly, accurately, and succinctly.
4. Assists in helping observers focus attention on what is being modeled.
5. Assists observers in remembering what they saw.
6. Provides for suitable practice in reenacting the observed behavior.
7. Provides corrective feedback during student reenactment.
8. Provides reinforcement following desired behaviors.

These role functions can be carried out efficiently using the five-step process of modeling, group reenactment, volunteer reenactment, draftee reenactment, and application.

What Do Students Do during Modeling?

The students' role in modeling is as follows:

1. Focus attention.
2. Remember what is observed.
3. Reenact the observed behavior when appropriate.

REFERENCES

BANDURA, A. "Modeling and Vicarious Processes." Ch. 3 in *Principles of Behavior Modification,* edited by A. Bandura. New York: Holt, Rinehart and Winston, 1969.
_____. *Social Learning Theory.* New York: General Learning, 1971.
_____. "Analysis of Modeling Processes." *School Psychology Digest*4(1) 1975:4–10.
BELCHER, T. "Modeling Original Divergent Responses: An Initial Investigation." *Journal of Educational Psychology*67 (1975):351–8.
BOTVIN, G., and F. MURRAY. "The Efficacy of Peer Modeling and Social Conflict in the Acquisition of Conservation." *Child Development*46 (1975):796–79.
COHEN, S. "Models Inside and Outside the Classroom: A Force For Desirable Learning." *Contemporary Education*51 (Summer 1980):186–188.

LEPPER, M. et al. "Generalization and Persistence of Effects of Exposure to Self-Reinforcement Models." *Child Development*46 (1975) :618–30.

MELAMED, B., and L. SIEGEL. "Reduction of Anxiety in Children Facing Hospitalization and Surgery by Use of Filmed Modeling." *Journal of Consulting and Clinical Psychology*43 (1975) :511–520.

OMIZO, M. et al. "Modeling: An Effective Teaching Strategy." *Academic Therapy*18 (January 1983) :365–368.

SAYOTSKY, G. et al. "Learning to Cooperate: Effects of Modeling and Direct Instruction." *Child Development*52 (September, 1981) :1037–1042.

SCHUNK, D. "Modeling and Attributional Effects on Children's Achievement: A Self-Efficacy Analysis." *Journal of Educational Psychology*73 (February 1981) :93–105.

·10·

THE SWEET SMELL
OF SUCCESS

SUCCESS AND FAILURE

Over 100 years ago Emerson wrote that "success in your work . . . is hat and coat, is food and wine, is fire and horse and health and holiday." Success is also very motivating, sufficiently so to produce the homily "nothing succeeds like success." But what does success mean? The answer seems simple enough, yet the word is trite and its meaning therefore requires examination. To get a grasp on the meaning of success we can consider concepts like intent, accomplishment, self-judgment, feedback, recognition, and failure.

Intent refers to what we hope to accomplish and how quickly we hope to attain our goal. In teaching and learning, intents are called objectives. We try to state them in behavioral terms, that is, in terms of actions that can be observed. In this way we know what we are trying to achieve and we have an observable, objective standard that tells us whether we have accomplished what we had intended. Sometimes we state objectives in terms of experiences. We refer to experience objectives when we believe that an experience is eminently worthwhile, but we cannot say what the observable outcome should be. An example of an experience objective is holding and petting a rabbit. We cannot specify the outcomes. Yet most teachers agree that holding and petting a rabbit is a most worthwhile experience for young children.

Accomplishment refers to whether and to what extent we have reached stated objectives, and it is necessary for recognizing success. If we do not reach our goals we cannot consider ourselves successful. At best we can compliment ourselves on making a good effort.

Self-judgment is a check on ourselves. We look to see whether we have made a strong effort, performed at our best, or slid by with the least effort. Often, we only know within ourselves the truth and that, in the long run, determines whether we see ourselves as successful or unsuccessful.

Feedback from others is also important in a personal view of success. What others say about our efforts and how they say it tell us whether they consider us successful.

Recognition, the final element in determining success, is essential, too. When we know we have made our best effort and have come close to reaching our goals, even if we have received helpful feedback, the feeling of success might never occur unless our efforts are recognized by others. Recognition means that people who are important to us know our efforts and seem to appreciate them. The importance of recognition illustrates the key role that others play in the perceptions we have of ourselves.

Failure means that we did not accomplish our intents, that we know we performed half-heartedly, or that we received no recogniton at all, leaving us with the feeling that what we did was unimportant.

Is failure good for us? We often hear that it is. People say, "We learn by our mistakes"; "Experience is the best teacher"; or "The reach must exceed the grasp." There is no doubt that we *can* learn from our failures and that we ought to do so, when possible. Of course we learn from trial and error, and we learn from the school of hard knocks. But that does not mean that failure is the best-paved path to learning. Evidence points to the contrary. Failure is bad for students. It hurts self-image, decreases motivation, and leaves a residual feeling of incapability. Therefore, we should not include failure as an important part of teaching. It does little to help students and can do much to harm them. When failure does occur, as it surely will even when we are making our best efforts, it should occur in a fail-safe environment. There students know it is acceptable to make mistakes, that they can fail when giving their best. They know, however, that failure is unacceptable if it results from lack of effort.

Here it is important for us to distinguish between two senses of the word "failure." The first sense relates to those conditions just mentioned—trying hard but not quite reaching the objectives, making errors, missing the mark a bit. Those kinds of failures are really just errors. They are benign. They are not hurtful unless made so by teacher or peers. The second sense of the word failure has to do with a pervasive feeling of incompetence, inferiority, and incapability that can develop in any person. That sense of failure comes from many sources: consistent, repeated errors; derisive, sarcastic feedback; continued lack of acceptance from others important to us. Those things produce a lasting sense of failure that affects individuals in all aspects of school. That sort of failure cannot be considered good. Its effects are too damaging and too lasting to be considered valuable in any way.

WHAT EXPERTS HAVE SAID

Many experts in counseling, therapy, and teaching have explored the effects of success and failure. They are unanimous in extolling the virtues of success and in deploring the detriments of failure. The following paragraphs give attention to the ideas of a few of those writers.

Self-Concept

Many people have investigated self-concept, that is, the opinions that each of us holds about ourself. Their investigations have made it increasingly evident that what we believe about ourselves directly affects the ways we learn, relate to others, and function in life.

Self-concept is built on experience. A strong self-concept grows out of successful functioning in different aspects of life. A poor self-concept grows out of lack of success, out of failure—failure to achieve, failure to gain acceptance, and failure to find warm relationships with other people.

If we sum the findings and opinions about self-concept, we must conclude that for strong self-concept, nothing is so important as success. Nothing is so damaging to self-concept as failure.

Freud

Sigmund Freud explored the growth of human personality. He found that in the earlier stages of life success with major life tasks resulted in adequate personality development, while failure with those life tasks resulted in fixations and defense mechanisms that hindered normal functioning.

Freud gave special attention to the "libido" as the driving life force. The libido was sexual in nature, though diverse. Its locus was not confined to the genitals, but was spread through many parts of the body. Freud believed that human personality depended in large part on what happened to the libido-energized individual during two stages of early life, the oral stage and the anal stage.

In the oral stage of early infancy the libido exerted its influence mainly in the mouth and was responsible for the pleasures associated with sucking. When babies were allowed sufficient sucking combined with simultaneous gentleness and kindness, their personalities pushed ahead in healthy ways. If they did not receive sufficient sucking, if they did not feel warm and loved and cared for, they developed oral fixations, that remained with them thereafter.

In the anal stage of early childhood the libido influenced the process of toilet training. When the child was treated gently, with care and appreciation, and not made to feel dirty, naughty, or unloved, healthy personality development continued. If scolded and viewed with distaste or contempt, the child developed anal fixations that remained throughout life and caused the individual to function in less than optimal ways.

Freud also described other stages, other fixations, and many defense mechanisms that grew out of people's inability to cope successfully with primary life functions.

Erikson

Erik Erikson, described "eight stages of man" that spread across the normal life span. Each stage was centered around one primary goal. Successful resolution of that goal brought adequate personality development. Unsuccessful resolution brought a damaged personality, resulting in the individuals being unable to function to the fullest.

Three of Erickson's stages overlap the typical school years. Each of these three stages begins with the letter "I." Teachers can think of them as Erickson's three I's: initiative, industry, and identity.

Initiative is the major goal of the stage that occurs between the ages of 3 and 6. It is the time when children's powers are growing rapidly. They have a great desire to explore, move outward, and try things on their own. If accepted and supported in this desire the individual becomes self-assured. Adequate feelings about the self ensue. If hindered through too many restrictions and scoldings, the child will develop a sense of guilt, rather than initiative. That basic feeling of guilt about one's own actions is difficult to erase later.

Industry is the major goal of the stage that occurs between the ages of 6 and 12. It develops as individuals find success in productive, task-oriented activities. Success comes as a result of adult approval, as the child explores newer abilities that form an emerging sense of power for dealing with life. Failure in this stage produces a sense of inferiority. Failure comes when individuals are reprimanded, when they receive reproof, when they are frowned on for what they do. This feeling of inferiority is one of the most painful and lasting complexes that individuals can develop. Once established, it is almost impossible to eradicate, even though great successes may come later.

Identity is the third of Erickson's three I's. It is the major task for individuals between the ages of 12 and 18. This is the time when the individual is moving into adolescence and later into adulthood. The major task is to find a sense of self-identity. Success in this task comes from the opportunity to explore role models, from having suitable and adequate models available, and from adult support as individuals try out the traits and characteristics of models they admire. Failure produces a sense of identity confusion. The individual is belittled, even scorned. Conflict occurs between the individual and parents and other adults. This conflict should be seen as natural and necessary. While it is anything but pleasurable, it consititutes an essential step in normal personality development.

Maslow

Perhaps you recall Maslow's hierarchy of needs. Maslow believed that six levels of needs, some higher and some lower, described the prime motives that direct our lives. He believed that the lower-level needs had to be met before the higher levels could be considered. For Maslow, meeting those needs was equated with life success. Inability to meet them produced failure. Ultimate success meant reaching the highest need levels.

For higher-level needs to come into play one has to be successful in meeting the needs for belonging, love, and esteem. Meeting those needs releases the need for self-actualization, which for Maslow was the highest level of human functioning. In terms of general success and failure, success can be seen as meeting one's needs for belonging, love, and esteem. They permit one to function to the fullest, allowing as they do a general sense of comfort and acceptance. Failure can be seen as an inability to achieve belonging, love, and esteem. Without them, one cannot give attention to self-actualization.

Dreikurs

Rudolf Dreikurs believed that every person has a single, prime need in life. That prime need is for acceptance, by family, friends, colleagues, and social groups. Children in school, like everyone else, strive for acceptance. They want to belong more than they want to learn, more than they want to be best in the class, even more than they want to be naughty.

Dreikurs sees people as successful when they meet their need for acceptance. When they are unable to meet this need they see themselves as failures. The sense of failure then causes them to turn toward mistaken goals—attention, power, revenge, and isolation.

Dreikurs, then, believed that students become successful as they are accepted by their classmates and teachers. This acceptance, this success, sets the stage for all other achievement. (For a further discussion, see Chapter 5.)

Glasser

William Glasser says that schools offer youth their best opportunity for success and recognition. Schools are, he says, the only places where genuine succcess and recognition are available to many. This success is essential if students are to reach fundamental life goals, which include genuine esteem from others. Such esteem is essential before students can have a feeling of self-worth and take positive control of their lives.

Glasser emphasizes success and stresses that failure is the worst thing that can happen to people. By this, of course, he means not merely making errors, but acquiring a general sense of failure, incompetence, inability to deal with life. The worst failure of all is the failure to find acceptance from others. The desire for acceptance is the greatest motivating force in life.

Schools and teachers have great power to supply success. They can also supply a sense of failure. Glasser deplores factors such as grading that foster a sense of failure. He suggests many activities for helping students control their own behavior, in order that they can come to see themselves as successful.

In the final analysis, Glasser says, success is within the grasp of every student. Success comes from making good choices, from choosing behaviors that bring acceptance, recognition, and esteem. Failure comes from making bad choices, from choosing behaviors that bring hostile reactions and prevent acceptance. What teachers should do is help students make good choices. They do this by continually calling upon students to make choices, showing the results of those choices, and seeing that the natural consequences follow student choice, good or bad. (For a further discussion, see Chapter 4.)

Gordon

Thomas Gordon is the author of best-selling books entitled *Parent Effectiveness Training* (1970) and *Teacher Effectiveness Training* (1974). These books explain Gordon's ideas about how to communicate effectively with schoolage students. Among the tactics included is one that is especially related to school success: *the no-lose approach.*

The no-lose approach is especially helpful in resolving conflicts that occur among students. When disputes occur, as they inevitably do in the classroom, they must be resolved. Typically, that resolution casts one side as the winner and the other as the loser. This division is fine for the winner, but it is not healthy for the loser, who ends up hurt and debilitated.

Gordon describes his no-lose approach in which both sides are seen as winners in the following way. The disputants first clarify the nature of their differences. Next each suggests a few procedures that might resolve the dispute. They then look for common grounds, selecting one of the solutions that is acceptable to both parties. They implement the solution on a trial basis. If it does not work they go back to the drawing board, suggesting other solutions and selecting another that will be initiated. This procedure allows everyone to experience success; all are winners, none losers.

Skinner

The work spearheaded by B. F. Skinner has shown the power of reinforcement in shaping behavior. We can think of reinforcement as reward. When individuals behave in desirable ways, we reward them for it. This reward, this reinforcement, provides a sense of success. Skinner and the many researchers who have followed in his steps have shown that reinforcement is most effective when student responses are almost always correct. That is, students should be directed in ways that cause them to behave correctly almost all the time. When correct, they are reinforced. This procedure shapes desired behavior quickly and strongly. If too many errors occur, resulting in too little reinforcement, learning is slowed. It may even proceed in erroneous, undesired directions.

For Skinner, and indeed the mass of research evidence supports his position, effective learning depends on continued success. Failure should be eliminated to the greatest extent possible. Unlike other authorities whose views we have examined, Skinner did not deplore failure as damaging to the personality. He simply saw it as inefficient and as obstructive to rapid, strong learning. (For a further discussion, see Chapter 2.)

Rosenthal and Jacobson

Rosenthal and Jacobson (whose work was cited in Chapter 8) emphasized the importance of expectations as facilitators of success. They showed that students tended to be more successful when teachers expected them to be successful. Their view once again illustrates the importance of self-concept. When students truly believe they are capable and competent, they tend to behave in ways that bring more success. When they see themselves as incompetents and failures, they tend to behave in ways that reflect imcompetence and bring added failure. Teachers should expect all students to achieve. This expectation should be genuine, and it should be communicated in genuine, assertive ways to the students.

Block

James Block is one of the foremost proponents of mastery learning. Mastery learning holds at its core the notion that all students can achieve high levels of school learning called mastery levels. This view contrasts with the prevailing view in education, which holds that within any group of students some will achieve mastery, others will achieve acceptable levels, but a large percentage will be below average, dipping into levels of failure.

Block and others of similar persuasion feel it is morally wrong to allow large numbers of students to gain very little from their instruction, especially when it is technically feasible to promote high levels of learning in most students. This feasibility undergirds the viewpoint of mastery learning.

Block says that contrary to popular opinion, degree of learning is not related to intelligence. Rather, intelligence indicates speed of learning. People who have higher IQs learn faster than people who have lower IQs. That does not mean they learn with greater depth or permanence. That relationship between intelligence and speed of learning points to the factor of time in the classroom, time devoted to student learning. Block believes that all students can reach mastery levels in learning provided they are given sufficient time together with adequate instruction and support. This means that time should be made flexible in learning rather than being fixed into periods as is now done in school.

By making accommodations in the time allotments, all students can achieve success, all students can reach high levels of learning. Mastery learning can reduce the incidence of failure, reduce the number of students who see themselves as incompetent, and increase success for students who have been barely wetting their toes in the seas of information that comprise the school curriculum.

SUCCESS AND DISCIPLINE

When people think of discipline they rarely see it as the avenue to student success. Instead they think of controls as being necessary to stifle outbursts, shut down misbehavior, keep students orderly, and teach respect for adults.

In reality, however, discipline is the prime road to ensure student success in school. As elaborated earlier, discipline brings sanity to the classroom, promotes learning, and brings a sense of accomplishment and joy. Therefore, we should view discipline as the factor that contributes most toward student success.

This view has been reiterated time after time in the models of discipline examined earlier. The Kounin model (Chapter 1) showed how to use withitness, overlapping, and the ripple effect to help students keep on-task, to help them become successful. The neo-Skinnerian model (Chapter 2), emphasizing behavior modification, showed how rewards help students learn behavior that brings success. The Ginott model (Chapter 3) showed how teachers can protect students' egos while building a strong sense of success. The Glasser model (Chpater 4) showed that good choices reult in good behavior, and that good behavior is the only path to success in the classroom. The Dreikurs model (Chapter 5) showed how students continually aim at acceptance in the classroom, and how acceptance frees students to be successful, as opposed to the mistaken goals that bring failure.

The Jones model (Chapter 6), more powerful in its effects, showed how to use incentives, body language, and efficient help to move students toward greater accomplishments; and the Canter model (Chapter 7) perhaps the most powerful of all, showed how teachers can be assertively in charge of their classrooms, thus keeping down distractions, helping students stay on-task, and insisting on adequate behavior, all of which contribute to success.

Many teachers fear that forceful discipline produces bad results. They feel that if they set strong standards, stick by them, and do not take into account the moods and external forces affecting students, the students will be stifled, thwarted, and manipulated. They fear that students will not like them. Exactly the opposite is true. No one advocates harsh, abusive discipline. Firm, humane, consistent standards help students learn and experience success. They also cause students to like teachers better, like the school better, and think better about themselves. These desired effects do not occur in the absence of controls. Teachers need not fear that good systems of discipline will damage students or student–teacher relationships. If teachers want to be admired, respected, and ultimately liked, they must be fair, firm, consistent, and insistent in helping students make good choices.

HOW TO PROVIDE GENUINE SUCCESS

We have considered many opinions about the importance of success in school, about how it affects self-concept, and about how it affects achievement. These opinions unanimously placed highest importance on the value of success. Given this importance, the task for teachers becomes one of providing genuine success for students. Teachers need to know how to maximize student success efficiently and effectively.

Student success can be ensured by giving attention to the following: (1) objectives as targets; (2) curriculum that progresses; (3) materials that help; (4) teacher direction and urging; (5) group esprit de corps; (6) competition that improves; and (7) parental help. We will examine each of the factors to see how it contributes toward genuine success for all students.

Objectives as Targets

Objectives describe what we want to accomplish. They are the specific targets toward which instruction is aimed. They tell us what we hope students will be able to do as a result of instruction.

To be effective, these objectives must be clear. They must be public. They must be attainable. They must specify actions that are recognizable. To be clear means to be understandable. Teachers and students alike understand what the objectives say and mean. Vague terms, therefore, are not used. Simple, straightforward words are used to specify the observable actions.

The objectives must be public; that is, they should not be secrets kept by the teacher. They should be shared with students, sometimes with parents, to let everyone know what is being aimed at, what is expected. Ample evidence shows that clear knowledge of objectives is helpful in motivating and guiding student learning.

Objectives should be attainable, meaning that they should describe ends that students can reasonably expect to reach. They should not be too difficult or too easy.

Objectives should name behavior that is recognizable. Such behavior includes things we can see or hear people do, things such as talking, writing, demonstrating, explaining, drawing, computing, and so forth. We should avoid objectives that use vague, unobservable terms such as *know, understand,* and *appreciate,* not because they are worthless ends, but because we cannot recognize those acts when students perform them. If we want to use an objective such as understand, we are obliged to specify the behavior that tells us that students are understanding. Such behaviors might include explain, list, put into own words, or demonstrate.

Once objectives are made clear, public, attainable, and recognizable, we have a set of goals that will guide the efforts of teachers and students alike. They can be used as check points to indicate progress, as guidelines to direct further work, and as criteria for judging whether students have reached the intended instructional goals.

Curriculum That Progresses

Much of the curriculum that fills the school day comes from guides, textbooks, and other materials provided to the teacher. Besides that part of the curriculum there are numerous other activities that teachers provide for students. Teachers need to be sure that those activities always lead students forward. They do so when they are worthwhile, at the right level of difficulty, interesting, and in proper sequence.

Curriculum that leads students forward and provides new learning, attitudes, and abilities, enables students to make the progress that shows success. Time-fillers, regardless of how enjoyable they may be, do little toward providing student success. On occasion teachers need to fill awkward bits of time. They usually have fun activities to keep students occupied. Reliance on such activities may allow students to have a good time in class, but they provide little worthwhile learning.

Activities must be at the right level of difficulty. The tasks given to students must be suited to their levels of functional ability. They must be neither too hard nor too easy. When too difficult, they frustrate. When too easy, they do not pull students forward.

The curriculum should be as interesting as possible. Interest holds attention, and attention is necessary for learning. All curriculum is not exciting. It is difficult to find ways of making interesting the study of grammar, parts of speech, or punctuation. But even those activities can be enlivened through competition, humor, and application to real writing for display or publication.

Finally, the curriculum must be put into a sequence that allows students to build new learnings on top of prior learnings, to move from the familiar to the unknown, to progress from the concrete to the abstract, to move, in spiral fashion, to ever higher levels of knowledge and understanding. Such sequencing lets students see how knowledge is tied together. It lets them see they are making steady progress. It provides a means for achieving and for receiving recognition of that achievement.

Good curriculum, then, consists of worthwhile learnings, organized in such a way that students are led forward. Curriculum leads students forward when it is at the proper level of difficulty, when it is interesting, and when it is ordered into a sequence that allows learning to build in incremental fashion.

Materials That Help

Instructional materials enliven learning by making the subject more interesting, clearer, more understandable. They provide extensions, examples, illustrations, problems, and entertainment. They allow students to explore further afield, and they permit easier application of new learnings into realistic situations. These attributes of materials greatly extend and enhance the teacher's capabilities.

Materials are interesting when they deal with topics familiar to students or the mysterious and the unknown; when they are colorful, show movement, and include humor and novelty. Materials must be interesting if they are to hold students' attention. Otherwise, teachers will have to force students to use them.

Materials are useful when they clarify, when they provide explanations, examples, illustrations, and anecdotes. Clarity is necessary for helping students obtain meaning.

Good materials also allow students to practice what they have learned through repetition, drill, review, paraphrasing, rewording, and translating from one medium to another. These methods of practicing cause students to go over the material again and again, beyond the point of full learning.

Materials allow students to explore. There is no way most of us can visit the Amazon jungle, the Pyramids, Antarctica, or the Laplanders in Finland. There is no way we can see molecules, solar systems, or the inner workings of nuclear reactors. Materials help provide those experiences, allowing students to range far beyond the confines of the classroom.

Finally, helpful materials allow students to apply their new learnings going beyond practice and overlearning. Applications involve use of the new knowledge. Materials help by providing problems for students to solve through application of knowledge.

Teacher Direction and Urging

The teacher is the prime motivator in every classroom. Remember this point; it is the key. Like it or not, many students do not work well on their own for long periods of time. They are not self-directed when it comes to academic learning. They are not self-controlled. Meeting these needs depends on the teacher. This fact places the teacher continually on stage, guiding, exhorting, entertaining, monitoring, providing feedback, providing if nothing else simple physical presence that keeps students on task.

The importance of this function cannot be overemphasized. It is more important to student success than any other factor; more important, perhaps, than all other factors combined. We see an occasional person who learns without a teacher. Such people constitute a small minority. Most of us do not have sufficient motivation, neither do we have proper help and guidance. Too much learning must occur through trial and error, even when motivation is present. Most students require urging, direction, enthusiasm, spark, feedback, and someone to crack the whip, gently of course. These things enliven learning and greatly increase the likelihood that students will be successful in school activities.

Esprit de Corps

Success depends in large measure on morale. Morale is closely related to the phenomenon of esprit de corps—group spirit. Esprit de corps enlivens an entire group. It provides stimulation, direction, sense of purpose, sense of value. Every teacher hopes for good esprit de corps. It can be provided by getting across to students that they are special, that they have high potential, that excellence is within their grasp. Perhaps they will be the best learners, the best behaved students, the best models for others. Perhaps they will be the best representatives of the school. Once a reputation has been established for a group or teacher, the reputation feeds into esprit de corps. The groups has something to uphold. Every students strives to perpetuate the reputation, be it for excellence, innovation, creativity, good behavior, or responsibility.

Esprit de corps provides a strong feeling of group success. Even in situations without it, where poor morale exists, some students will find success, but many will not. Many will feel defeated. That's why a sense of group spirit is so important. Individuals identify with the group, are proud of the group, are motivated to do the best possible for the group.

Esprit de corps provides a sense of joy, of societal pleasure, that is important to most individuals. Teachers should use all devices at hand for establishing and maintaining strong esprit de corps.

Competition That Improves

Competition is known to bring success and recognition. It carries a certain joy of combat. For these reasons it is motivating to students, and it can be helpful in making learning more exciting. Competition has its drawbacks, however. If there are winners, there must be losers, and losing is not motivating. Unfortunately, the people in greatest need of success are those who seldom win. This fact has caused teachers to have second thoughts about using competition in learning. They judge that its bad effects, including failure, frustration, and sometimes overinflated egos, outweights its good effects. They have tended to replace it with cooperation, where students are caused to relate in ways considered more positive. Cooperation, unfortunately, is not nearly so exciting and motivating as competition.

Competition does not always have to be hurtful. It can be quite helpful. It is stimulating and exhilirating. When people compete against their own past performance, rather than against other individuals, competition is useful. When they compete as part of a group against past group performance, or against other groups, competition is good for all concerned.

Teachers can thus make competition helpful by allowing students to strive against independent goals and past performances. This sort of competition can be used for both individuals and groups. It allows individuals to remain rather anonymous, insulated within the group or kept private, as when competing against past performance. They do not show themselves in bad light, and they do not have a sense of failure when they do not do as well as the best in the group.

Competition against standards and against past performance is useful and highly motivating. Its value comes from the ability to see genuine progress. Teachers can help students keep graphs that show their individual performances against lists of objectives or against past performance. These graphs must be kept private so that students cannot be compared publicly against other students. Group efforts, however, can be displayed. Group averages on math or spelling tests, for example, can be charted. This can show comparative performance, and it provides motivation for the entire group to try to exceed former marks.

Parental Help

Parents can help make exceptional contributions to the feelings of success for students and teachers alike. They can be so helpful that Chapter 11 is devoted entirely to the contributions they can make and to how teachers can acquire their cooperation. For our purposes, it is sufficient to say that parents can make a great contribution toward genuine success for students. The burden is on teachers to initiate the understanding and cooperation that make parental contributions possible. The teacher must find ways to communicate extensively with parents allowing explanation of programs, information about goals, and information about activities and materials. Teachers should ask for parent support, both psychological and for direct instructional support at home. Often, parents cannot provide instruction. They can help, however, by providing a time and place for students to do homework, seeing that students complete the work, and communicating back to teachers any questions or difficulties encountered.

All parents want their children to learn. They want them to behave acceptably in school. Almost all are willing to help in the instructional process because they have such a stake in the education of their children. Since most do not know how to help, teachers must take the first steps in establishing working relationships. They do this by informing, explaining, and asking for help. A small amount of effort pays large dividends.

HOW TO RECOGNIZE AND PUBLICIZE SUCCESS

At the beginning of the chapter we saw that a major factor in acquiring a feeling of success is receiving attention and acknowledgment for one's efforts. That feeling of success is incredibly important. It behooves teachers to establish and maintain procedures that allow all students to be recognized for their efforts and accomplishments. The remainder of this chapter explains several ways for bringing such recognition to students.

Chart Group Gains

It was mentioned previously that competition can be motivating and can provide direction and interest for students. The kinds of competition provided must be in the form of group performance or in the form of personal gains against past performance. Group gains can best be shown by means of graphs, time lines, class diaries, and sometimes by class murals. Students can make these graphs and charts easily and quickly. They can be colorful, attractive, and informative. They can be posted and used as constant reminders.

Time lines can be placed high around the walls of the classroom, using either paper or cord. Paper can have events and dates written or drawn on it. The cord can be knotted, with tags or objects tied to it in chronological sequence. Examples of entries might be such things as finishing Unit 2 in the Spanish book, completing the 5s in the multiplication tables, having put on a science fair, and so forth. The advantage of a time line is that it shows class performance, progress, and a record of achievement.

Class diaries do much the same thing as time lines, except the records are kept in written form. Students can take turns making entires in the diary. The group can contribute. A good time is at the end of day or during the period when a rapid review is conducted. The diary provides documented history of class activities and accomplishments. Students will enjoy reading it later.

Some groups, particularly art classes and upper-elementary classrooms, can prepare murals that illustrate activities and accomplishments. The mural can be added to at regular intervals depicting significant events and accomplishments. Making the mural is enjoyable, it helps fix events in students' memories, and it provides a sense of accomplishment and success.

Chart Personal Gains

Individual student performance must not be charted publicly in the classroom, if unfavorable comparisons are shown among students. Individual efforts and accomplishments can be compared against stated objectives or past performances. They can be graphed to provide records that are instructive, rewarding, and motivating. They must be kept private, however. They can be kept in individual folders accessible only to the teacher, who uses them in conferencing with students and their parents.

Charting personal gains can be even more motivating than charting group gains. Within the group one remains anonymous, but as an individual one becomes the center of attention. Where individuals might show poorly when compared to the best students in the class, they can show significant progress against their past accomplishments. This progress reinforces and motivates further efforts.

Records of personal gain also serve well in conferencing with parents. Parents want to know as specifically as possible how their child is doing, how well he is reading, how well he is understanding American history, or how well he is performing in public speaking. They are pleased to see charts that show the child reaching objectives—improving in efficiency, in amount of work attempted, or in number of correct responses. These charts help present the teacher in a good light because they show that the teacher has a specific plan for the student and that results are being obtained.

Review Progress

One of the most helpful ways to publicize success is to review on a frequent basis the achievements and learnings that have occurred in the class. This may be done at the end of each period or day. Two to five minutes is all it takes. Review may also be done at the end of each week, the end of each unit of instruction, or other selected intervals. Such review reminds students what they have done, it gives them a sense of accomplishment, and it instructs them on how to report to their parents, who will want to know what they have been learning at school.

Review should remind students about the initial objectives and show the progress made toward those objectives. This clear marking of progress provides a genuine sense of success. Review can end with a brief notation of what is to come next.

Informing Parents

Parents should be informed regularly about experiences, activities, achievements, and future plans for their children. This information can be provided in three ways: (1) through student reports to parents; (2) through teacher communication with parents; and (3) through materials that show parents what their children are doing in class and for homework.

Student reports to parents are excellent. Students can be instructed on how to tell parents in a few minutes' time what they have done and what they have learned during the day. Parents can set a time for such reports, perhaps at dinner. A few sentences are enough to tell what the major activities of the day have been. Students become able to do this through the process of systematic review. This review prevents students' being speechless when parents ask them what they learned that day. The will be able to think of something more to say than "I don't know," or "Nothing."

Systematic communication from the teacher is also an excellent way to inform parents. This procedure requires effort and time, but pays good dividends. Teachers can send note, make telephone calls, and send newsletters. These things can tell parents what the teacher is attempting to accomplish and ways they can help at home. Parents usually hear from teachers only when something is going wrong, which causes them to be defensive and makes them dread to hear from school. When teachers take the time to inform parents about what is going right and about what their children are doing that is good, they create a bond of cooperation.

Samples of work sent to parents can be useful, too. Worksheets, reading assignments, sample questions, and an occasional test can be sent home as illustrative. Parents may want to do a few of the activities themselves. Such materials can present a clear idea of what is going on at school, especially when accompanied by brief explanatory notes from the teacher.

Sharing in the Classroom

Students need to receive attention from their peers, to have their classmates recognize their efforts and their accomplishments. They can get this attention through oral presentations, displays of work and bringing into the classroom some of their own handiwork. Individuals can do demonstrations. Small groups can put on skits. Displays of art, musical presentations, and reading stories and poems are good ways for individuals to share their accomplishments.

Some students are shy and reluctant. Some will not have much to share. Teachers should encourage all to share, if they can. Students should not be forced, if they are terrified. Shy students can often share better if they use puppets, hold an animal, or wear masks or costumes.

In classes where large-group activities are possible, such as project work in science, social studies, art, drama, and so on, provisions can be made for students to put on public exhibitions as culminating activities for their work. Aiming toward exhibitions provides motivation for completing work of high quality. If you know your parents and relatives are going to see what you have done, you put a little extra into it. Science fairs are popular. So are class plays, musical performances, readers' theatre, choric verse, and displays of arts and crafts. People who are invited to come to the exhibitions and performances can talk with the students, who can explain their work or performance. This is certain to bring attention and positive comments.

Class Newsletter

Many classes can produce a class newsletter on a monthly or quarterly basis. This newsletter can explain what is going on in the class, contain samples of student work, present announcements of displays and performances, and include anything else the class desires. To be most effective its tone should be businesslike, and it should leave an impression of good learning.

The newsletters can be delivered to parents, administrators, other teachers, and other students. Local newspapers are usually interested. Few avenues publicize so well the efforts and achievements of the class. Public relations are not the least of the benefits. Schools and teachers are targets for considerable criticism. Much of this criticism occurs because schools do a poor job of informing the public about the good things schools do. People simply do not hear about the significant learning that is provided. Newsletters can fill that void. They inform and they bring a sense of respect.

Genuine Compliments

As students inform parents, share with classmates, put on performances, or contribute to class newsletters, they put themselves in positions to receive recognition and genuine compliments. These compliments do much for self-esteem. They provide a sense of appreciation, competence, and success.

Other activities deserve equal attention but cannot be so easily shown outside the classroom. Examples are good manners, helping others, making the best effort, being friendly, and showing good sportsmanship. Students who exhibit these things deserve attention, too. To provide this attention, some teachers set up systems that encourage students to compliment each other. These compliments must be genuine and sincere. They should specify what it is that draws the compliment. To be sure that all students receive deserved compliments teachers may instruct students to look for someone who has been very helpful, been a good sport, worked hard, someone who is improving. They encourage students to spread the compliments around. They discuss how it makes them feel to receive compliments and how they feel when they give them.

The teacher will need to keep track, too. Some students will receive few compliments. The teacher should fill that lack by being alert to who needs compliments. Something good can be found about every student, even the laziest, most disruptive, most unlikeable. Those people, especially, can profit from genuine compliments given for small improvements.

Students should also be taught how to compliment themselves, how to recognize their own desirable behavior and reward themselves for it. They can be encouraged to state to themselves what it is they have done and tell themselves they are proud of it. This may sound silly, but it helps students focus on desirable behavior and self-control. Teachers can ask students to share from time to time what they have complimented themselves on. That draws attention to their efforts and gives other students a chance to compliment them, too.

Continual Teacher Reinforcement

Earlier we saw that the teacher is the prime motivator in the classroom, always on stage, always directing, always encouraging, always helping. The teacher is also the main source of reinforcement, providing rewards to students who behave in desirable ways, try harder, progress, relate well with others. Because the teacher is such a significant figure to students, rewards coming from the teacher have special power and cannot be matched by rewards from any other source. Recognizing the power of teacher rewards, we should be sure to provide them. These rewards should come mainly in the form of recognition, acknowledgment, compliments, and occasional praise. These statements should stipulate what the student has done right or well. They should thank the student for showing that behavior. Teachers need not use tangible rewards except in rare occasions when student behavior presents a problem so severe that verbal rewards do not improve it.

We must remember that teachers are among the two or three most important people in almost every student's life. While students may act as though they do not appreciate teachers, while they may even act disrespectfully toward them, they still see them as gigantic figures in their lives. Most students eagerly seek teachers' approval, dote on their recognition, and want their attention and acceptance. This fact reemphasizes the power that teachers have for providing feelings of belonging and success for students under their guidance.

REFERENCES

BLOCK, J. *Mastery Learning: Theory and Practice.* New York: Holt, Rinehart and Winston, 1971.

CAMPBELL, L. "Every Student a Success: Improving Self-Image to Increase Learning Potential." *NASSP Bulletin* 65 (January 1981) :76–78.

CHANDLER, T. "What's Wrong With Success and Praise?" *Arithmetic Teacher* 29 (December 1981) :10–12.

DREIKURS, R. *Psychology in the Classroom.* New York: Harper and Row, 1968.

ERIKSON, E. *Childhood and Society.* 2d ed. New York: Norton, 1963.

FREUD, S. *The Ego and Mechanisms of Defense.* London: Hogarth, 1937.

GLASSER, W. *Schools without Failure.* New York: Harper and Row, 1969.

GORDON, T. *Parent Effectiveness Training.* New York: Wyden, 1970.

————, *Teacher Effectiveness Training.* New York: Wyden, 1974.

MASLOW, A. *Toward a Psychology of Being.* New York: Van Nostrand, 1962.

ROSENTHAL, R., and L. JACOBSON. *Pygmalion in the Classroom.* New York: Holt, Rinehart and Winston, 1968.

SKINNER, B. F. *Science and Human Behavior.* New York: Macmillan, 1953.

·11·

PARENTS AS TEACHERS' BEST FRIENDS

BACKGROUND OF PARENT INVOLVEMENT

Since its inception, American education has had a noticeable difference from education provided elsewhere. The founding fathers determined that education should be controlled by the people, not by a national government. They did not mention education in the Constitution. They wrote in the Constitution that matters not included therein should be left to the individual states. This edict put education into the hands of state governments which made general laws to regulate it. Those laws, in turn, put matters of educational policy under the jurisdiction of local communities. The communities elect representatives to sit on boards of education that control what happens in American schools within the broad guidelines set down by state legislatures.

The tradition of local control was established long before the Declaration of Independence. Laws made in the colonies provided for the establishment of elementary and secondary schools, first intended to teach children how to read and write. Later the schools were seen as agents for democraticizing society and maintaining an educated citizenry that could govern itself. As immigrants began to pour into the country, the schools took on the added duty of forging a common bond among the multitudes of ethnics who became American citizens.

These forces for democratization, literacy, citizenship, and social unity supported keeping educational control in the hands of the populace. Such matters, especially in an age of great diversity, isolation, and slow communication could not be managed effectively from a single location in Washington, D.C. A factor even more powerful in maintaining local control of education was the pervasive spirit of individuality that characterized early America. People wanted to do things for themselves. They did not want unknown people hundreds or thousands of miles away telling them how they should educate their children.

This tradition of local involvement in education remains strong in the United States, although it has weakened somewhat because of federal regulations aimed at equality, the availability of funds from the federal level, and a burgeoning willingness in society to let someone else do things for us. Still, all citizens, parents of schoolage children or not, pay attention to education in this country. Everyone feels a direct stake in education of the young. We have kept at full blaze the belief that we have a right to be involved in public education, whether we choose to exercise that right or not.

That feeling of legal and moral right to participate has kept parents closely involved in education. They maintain their right to criticize policy, curricula, teaching, and everything else that schools represent. While criticism is vexing to educators who seldom see it as justified, it is needed to keep education effective as a democratizing agent. Active parental involvement is equally important. It ensures a balance, a stability, a compromise between lofty educational goals and social, political, and economic reality.

This involvement unnerves many teachers. They wish parents would leave education to the professionals. They feel they know best what should be taught and how it should be taught. They see parental involvement as a hindrance to their efforts, a nuisance that cuts deeply into their time and energy. Other teachers see parental involvement differently. They know it takes up time, interferes with schedules, and diminishes efficiency, but they have learned that small investments of time can pay huge dividends. They know they can rally parents to their side and count on them for support and help. They know that simply having parents support their efforts will forestall two-thirds of the battles they would normally expect to encounter with students. Those teachers will tell you it is worth the effort to cultivate parents. They will tell you that in these times of educational adversity, parents can be teachers' best friends.

PARENTS AND SCHOOL DISCIPLINE

All parents want their children to learn and behave acceptably in school. Some of them may not act as though they do, but you cannot find one in a thousand who will say, "Nah, I don't care if my kid learns or not," or, "Behave? Heck no. I hope he misbehaves." Of course there is a difference between saying you care and really caring. But if we assume that parents really do care even when they do not seem to, we will be correct most of the time.

It is easy for teachers to get a one-sided view of parents' concerns about schooling. There are occasional students whose parents cause difficulty, either because they will not support the teacher or because they continually interfere in negative ways. A few such cases can camouflage the value of the vast majority. It is that large majority of caring parents that teachers can count on. Parents will support and they will help; teachers have only to say the word.

The Gallup poll on attitudes toward education points out, year after year, that parents of school children give good marks to education, schools, and teachers. They think education is doing a good job. They point out some things they think need shaping up such as lack of discipline, increased use of drugs, and inadequate citizenship training. However, they are very supportive of what teachers and schools are doing.

WHAT PARENTS EXPECT FROM TEACHERS

Parents do not expect teachers to promise the moon or turn every dull Jack into a budding Einstein. But they do have a few clear expectations that teachers should heed:

1.   They expect teachers to *care* about their child, to give attention to his or her interests, joys, fears, and personality.
2.   They expect them to *teach* their child. They want their child to learn the basics, become literate, and know and appreciate something of art and music.
3.   They expect teachers to *excite* their child about learning, make her or him want to learn and enjoy school.
4.   They expect teachers to *encourage and support* their child's efforts; to urge, prod, and nurture the process of growth.
5.   They expect teachers to *discipline* their child. They know that order and self-control are necessary not only in school but in life outside school.
6.   They expect teachers to *inform* them about their child's educational program and progress. They want to know about successes, difficulties, failures, and problems that require attention.
7.   They expect teachers to make a *strong effort* in teaching, to be serious and dedicated, and to do the best they can.

WHAT PARENTS NEED TO KNOW

When it comes to schooling and discipline, parents need to know four things: (1) *what*, exactly, is expected of the students; (2) *how* those expectations are going to be enforced; (3) *how* their child is doing, generally and specifically; and (4) *what* they can do to help.

Expectations in discipline come from two sources. The first is the school behavior code. Most schools have established such codes or are in the process of doing so. Those codes tell generally how students must behave and how they will be treated if they violate provisions of the code. The second source is individual teachers who have their own standards, expectations, and enforcement procedures. Teachers seldom communicate their discipline programs to parents. They should do so, because their programs are much more specific in terms of standards and enforcement than is a school code.

These expectations should be as few in number as necessary to cover the territory. They should be stated briefly, in simple language. They should be clear and easily understood. Both the school code and the individual teacher expectations should be distributed to all parents. At conferences and open house, they should be repeated. Parents need and want to know these expectations.

Enforcement must be coupled with the expectations. Parents need to know what the enforcement procedures will be. The school code will probably explain enforcement from the school level. Teacher enforcement should not run contrary to the school code. It may augment it, and it will be formulated to match the age of students and the personality and philosophy of the teacher. An outline of enforcement procedures should be composed by every teacher and sent to the parents. It should tell what will happen for the first offense, the second, and the third. There should be no surprises for parents when it comes to enforcing the proper behavior of their children in school.

Knowledge of how their child is behaving is information that every parent wants and has a right to expect. This information should be both general and specific, and it should be communicated regularly. General information comes in the form of statements such as "a good citizen," "needs to get along better with others," "usually works up to capacity," or "not making best effort." Specific information comes in the form of statements such as "engaged in name calling three times last week," "did not disrupt class at all this week," or "shows courtesy and manners to adults and other students."

This knowledge can be sent by means of notes and telephone calls. The notes can be written personally or entered on forms made for the purpose. Two telephone calls made each afternoon after school reaches parents of an entire elementary class in only three weeks. Secondary teachers have to make selective calls. There are too many students to reach personally on a regular basis. When students required special attention, the information communicated to parents should be quite specific.

Help from parents is always appreciated by teachers. Most parents are more than willing to support the teacher's efforts with their child at home. They will seldom ask to help, especially as their children progress beyond the primary grades, but that does not mean they have lost interest. Parents can support teachers by backing their policies, reinforcing procedures at home, providing special places and times for students to do homework, insisting that homework be done as assigned, reporting back to teachers on problems and successes, and continually emphasizing that school is a place for serious learning.

Parents usually collaborate with teachers if teachers ask for their help. They have a stake in the education of their child and will do what they can. They need, however, to be asked, and they need to be instructed about how they can help.

WHY PARENTS DO NOT PARTICIPATE

Parents are vitally interested in their children's education, yet most of them take a hands-off approach to what goes on at school. That seems paradoxical, but the reasons they are reluctant to participate are easily understood.

One reason parents do not come forward is an unwillingness to interfere. They feel that education is the job of the school, and parents should not meddle. They should only back what the school is trying to do. They see a clear division of effort: teaching is for schools and upbringing is for parents. Neither should short-circuit the other.

Another reason why parents do not participate is because they feel insecure about what to do and how to do it. It takes some nerve to make overtures to a teacher, and parents feel uneasy, embarrassed, out of their medium when they do so. They want to be involved, maybe just a little bit, maybe a great deal. But they are timid and need to be encouraged.

A third reason why parents do not participate is simple ignorance. Ignorance does not mean stupidity; it means not knowing. They do not know how to help. They do not know what to do at home, how to reinforce what the teacher is doing, how to arrange study places and times, or how to instruct their children when difficulties in schoolwork arise. Parents want to help but they need some instruction from teachers. This instruction can be communicated by way of notes and newsletters that ask for parents' help, tell them in simple terms how to provide it, and indicate how parents can follow through on a routine basis.

WHAT PARENTS WILL GIVE

Teachers are amazed at how much parents will give, how much they will put into the education of their child, and how much they will contribute to the education and enjoyment of the entire class. Most kindergarten teachers rely on parent collaboration. It comes naturally there. Parents are torn by their child's entering school. It is difficult, indeed, to sever the bonds, so parents hover around protectively, hoping to be involved somehow in the kindergarten program. This involvement continues in declining fashion through the first grade, then fades away. Still, parents rally to classroom needs through the upper grades and into secondary levels when they are needed and called on.

Help from parents comes in varied forms. The most important of these forms is backing. If parents support teachers and schools, if they convey that idea to their children in no uncertain terms, if teachers know they have support and backing, the entire educational enterprise can move forward with vigor. Parents back school programs almost without exception if they believe that the teacher has a specific plan for their child and is truly trying to help the child learn. Teachers who reassure parents of these facts draw strong support.

Parents can help with home study. They will, when asked and informed, set aside a time and place for students to do uninterrupted homework, without distractions. This time can be sandwiched in, through, and around favorite television programs. Seldom must there be a family fight over missed programs. Rarely does the child need to do more than an hour's homework, which can be fitted around the normal family schedule.

Parents can provide simple instruction at home. To make this feasible, teachers can send brief, direct instruction sheets home with the child. Those sheets tell what is being taught and how, and they tell how the parents can help the child. They should make it plain that parents should only help when students encounter obstacles to progress and should not do the work for the child.

Teachers at all levels can count on parents for donations of time, services, goods, transportation, and even money. Teachers often hesitate to ask parents to make contributions, but many parents are more than happy to become involved. They enjoy feeling a part of the educational process. They like to be around schools and will usually come through bountifully when help is needed.

Many parents are eager to volunteer to help in the classroom. They may be hesitant to do so, because they feel presumptive or are afraid they might not be wanted. If teachers open the door, they can almost always secure volunteer parent help. This help can be used for in-class work with students; for producing plays and other performances, including costuming, making sets, providing musical assistance, and arranging transportation; for going on class outings where drivers, supervisors, and chaperones are needed; and for preparing and working in class carnivals and festivities surrounding athletic events.

COMMUNICATION IS THE KEY

There is a vast deposit of parental support and help available to teachers that is locked up by apathy, insecurity, ignorance, timidity, and a hands-off view of education. The key that opens the lock is communication, and that communication must first come from the teacher.

A masters degree study conducted by Janet Mulder at San Diego State University in 1978 investigated the effects of teacher communication on parental attitude toward teachers at the elementary and junior high levels. Before becoming a teacher, Mulder had worked for several years in business as a buyer for a chain of department stores. She knew from that experience how important good communication was in establishing ties between merchants and consumers. She suspected that the same thing was true for teachers and parents. She went to several different public schools and asked the principal of each school to identify a teacher that the public considered especially outstanding. She interviewed each of those teachers to determine to what extent they attempted to communicate with parents

Mulder found that outstanding teachers without exception maintained elaborate systems of communication with parents. They used a variety of techniques and devices, but they were consistent in advising parents of their educational intents, how they were attempting to accomplish them, how the parent's child was doing, and what they could do to help. Mulder did not seek any objective data to indicate whether the teachers were, in fact, superior when it came to student learning. She did not even presume that they were. But parents fully believed that the teachers were exceptional. This belief rallied parents strongly behind the teachers' efforts.

A more elaborate research project was later conducted at San Diego State University. Entitled "Education for Dignity and Rapid Achievement" (EDRA), it involved many teachers and hundreds of school students. EDRA (Charles, 1981) had three thrusts: (1) academic achievement, (2) self-concept, and (3) exemplary personal relations. Teachers in EDRA used a small number of strategies to keep students on task, progressing, feeling good about themselves, and seeing that learning was serious though enjoyable business.

One of the strategies that EDRA teachers used was an organized system of communicating with parents. This communication was intended to show that the teachers were serious about teaching and learning, bent on doing the very best for every student. EDRA teachers informed parents, told them how they could help, and asked for their support. This resulted in an extremely positive attitude from parents and excellent support for their children's learning.

The Mulder and EDRA studies merely illustrate a fact that is known to many teachers. A small but significant number of teachers capitalize on a fact that bears repeating: Parental support and help have immense value in the educational process. The key to securing that help is good communication from the teacher.

HOW TO COMMUNICATE WITH PARENTS

Since communication is essential, how does one go about arranging an effective communication system? Experience has shown that two elements are important in communication with parents—content and style of communication. In other words, the things you say and how you say it. Let us examine these two elements, beginning with style and then considering content. In the subsequent section we will then explore suitable vehicles through which the content can be disseminated.

Style

Parents expect teachers to be professional. They expect them to be knowledgeable, communicative, and friendly. They expect them to have the best interests of their child in mind. They do not expect teachers to be their pals or buddies. They do not want them to be silly, wishy-washy, or disorganized. The first consideration in style is to be professional—to know what you are doing, to say what you mean in simple terms, to maintain your poise, and to be willing to listen.

Along with being professional, teachers should be disarming. Remember that most parents are very sensitive about hearing from a teacher, at least at first. Tradition has it that parents hear from teachers only when their child has upset the apple cart. In this situation, parents are going to get blamed, scolded, and made to feel bad. Teachers can disarm these fears by being friendly (but not silly) and straightforward, indicating they are pleased to have the opportunity to work with the child and parents for the year. They disarm by showing they are optimistic, have high expectations, and feel sure that by working together both parents and teacher can help the child make good progress.

Teachers should be frank. They should tell it like it is, no shading facts, no hemming and hawing. However, this frankness must be combined with a positive attitude about further growth. This principle applies for both positive and negative comments. If students have been excellent, emphasis should be put on their potentials for continued advancement. If they have been below par, a positive plan should be stated for improvement.

Frankness must also be linked to a feeling of support. Remember that parents' egos and feelings are on the line. A supportive attitude from the teacher engenders a supportive attitude from the parent. Support is shown through genuine interest in providing quality education for the student, describing the plan for providing that education, soliciting parental feedback regarding the plan, and stressing the positive advantages accruing to the student when teacher and parents work together.

Within the aura of frankness and support, teachers should do their best to be brief, plain, and businesslike. Whether in written communiques sent home or verbal messages delivered personally, short, concise messages are always preferable to long, wordy messages. They should always be written in plain English. Jargon and special terminology are familiar and comfortable to teachers, but indecipherable to parents. To be businesslike is to state the information in a brief and plain way, matter of factly, showing that the teacher's professional judgment has been brought to bear and this is the result. Brevity must be maintained. Teachers tend to be overly wordy. Parents do, too. They often need someone with whom to talk. Communication with parents cannot serve a therapeutic function—it takes too much time. It should serve nothing more than the basic function of exchanging information that bears directly on the education, progress, and well-being of the student.

Content

The content of communication with parents, to the extent possible, must be confined to educational matters. Those matters fit into five categories: (1) learning, (2) discipline, (3) self-concept, (4) how parents can help, and (5) class news.

Learning. Learning as content of communication directs attention to objectives, activities, and homework. Objectives are the specific goals toward which education is directed. Parents and students should be informed of those objectives. In this way, everyone will strive for the same result. For parental information, the specific objectives may be grouped into larger goals, such as mastering the multiplication tables, learning the classification of animal and plant kingdoms, or being able to describe the interrelations of the legislative, executive, and judicial systems in American government.

Activities describe the means that will enable students to achieve the goals and objectives. They tell what should go on inside and outside of class. When described to parents, the activities should be summarized. One can say that the textbook will be used in combination with lectures, tests, and student reports; or that 20 minutes of instruction will be provided each day, followed by 20 minutes of practice, requiring about 15 minutes of homework three times a week; or that group project work will occur in class, culminating with a fair in which student work will be displayed for viewing by parents, visitors, other teachers, and students.

Homework should be described fairly explicitly: five problems each night, outline a part of the chapter, write five paragraphs, correct errors made in work done during class. It should also indicate what the parents can do to help. Examples might include providing a quiet place at a regular time, so that the student develops the habit of doing homework at a set time and place, free from distractions; reading a nursery rhyme to the child each evening; discussing with the child the day's learnings by having the child report verbally, explain what the information means, and discuss its importance and applications; providing needed instructional help in simpler processes of mathematics, phonics, outlining, finding the main idea, and so forth.

Discipline. Discipline describes the methods of control that will be used. Communication should spell out rules, enforcement procedures, and necessary backing from home. The tone should be entirely positive. Parents should see clearly that discipline helps their child to make good choices, behave responsibly, and remain open to learning. They should see that good discipline promotes good learning.

Communication about discipline should solicit parental support. Parents should be asked to support the system in the following ways:

1. Impress on their child the importance of proper behavior.
2. Show their agreement with the discipline approach being used.
3. Indicate that they will back up teachers' efforts at positive control.
4. Attempt to practice some of the same disciplinary techniques being used at school.

The fourth point requires understanding of the control system being used. If it is behavior modification, parents should be informed in simple terms that the procedure involves supplying rewards after the child behaves appropriately. If it is informed choice followed by natural consequences, parents should understand that rules must be laid down, together with consequences that will invariably follow student compliance or noncompliance. The consequences must be within reason, but they must be enforced. Parents learn that they no longer need to use threats or bullying, but they must have the fortitude to enforce the choices that their child makes. They need not feel guilty about it. The child, after being fully informed, has chosen the consequences that follow.

Self-concept. Self-concept is closely related to discipline. It grows out of behavior that produces learning, followed by attention given to the progress that the student has made. Disruptive behavior hinders learning. For students to progress in ways that bring success and recognition, they must attend to the educational tasks at hand.

Students must have regular attention drawn to their successes. That attention comes from teacher, parents, and other students. Teachers and students can provide recognition in a systematic way within the classroom. Parents need information about their child's progress and about how to acknowledge it. Progress can be reported through notes, samples of work, graphs that show attainment of objectives, graphs that show improvement over past performance, and oral reports given by the student to parents every evening. Parents can respond with shows of pleasure, moderate praise, and moderate rewards. Praise should be limited to statements such as: "You should be really proud of yourself." "This speaks awfully well for you." "Good going—it makes me feel good to see you trying so hard."

Rewards should be moderate, too. They should be given in the form of desired activities rather than in money or gifts. Those activities can be discussed in advance. Good progress can be rewarded by such activities as going to a motion picture, getting to stay up late on Friday or Saturday night, getting to go to the park or to lunch with dad, or getting to spend the night with a friend. Praise and rewards of the types mentioned draw attention to accomplishment. They are directed at the student: *"You* should feel proud of yourself." *"You* get to go with dad because you have done so well." They should not be directed at other people or things. They should not say: *"I* am really proud of your work. Here is five dollars. Keep it up and there will be another five next month." These things make other people and other things the focus of attention. For self-concept, the focus must be on the student who is achieving.

How Parents Can Help.   How parents can help is an indispensable ingredient in communication. Parents give increased support when they feel a part of things, when they feel they are contributing directly to the child's learning and behavior. We have already seen that parents can help through backing, support, donations, volunteering, providing simple instruction, and practicing some of the same control techniques that are used in school. But we have to realize that parents do not automatically know how they can help. Nor are they sure that help is wanted. Teachers have to solicit parents' help and have to inform parents how help can be provided. The solicitation must be genuine, and the information must be explicit. In discipline, for example, the teacher can say:

> We have a plan that will help all the students learn more and behave better. These benefits will be seen at home as well as school. I must have your help in order to make the plan work, and I am sincerely asking you for that help.

After describing the plan briefly and plainly, the communication indicates what the parents can do.

> Together, we can help your child greatly. For your part, I hope you will support what I am doing at school by discussing it with your child. Ask your child regularly how class behavior has been. Please use as much of this plan as you can in disciplining your child. Try to set up two or three rules about homework, chores, and polite talk at home. Decide on positive consequences (mild rewards) that will come to the child for compliance with the rules. Decide on negative consequences (mild punishments such as missing a favorite television program or going to bed a half-hour early) that will come if the child breaks the rules. Help your children see that they are *choosing* the consequences that follow, good or bad. Then be sure that the consequences are applied. Do not worry that

this will harm the child or the relations between you. This plan builds responsibility and it helps children understand that learning and good behavior are important. Together we can help your child learn in a way that will make all of us proud.

When asking for other kinds of help the explanations, while explicit, need not be so lengthy. An example might be:

We have decided to have a class bake sale on Saturday, November 24, to help raise money for our trip to the zoo. We need cakes, cookies, pies, and brownies. May I count on you to contribute something for the sale? If so, please check the blanks below and have your child return the form to me. Thank you very much for you continued support.

Class News.   Class news items serve as a very valuable function. They keep parents apprised of what is going on in school and remind them that significant learning is occurring through interesting activities. These news items, best conveyed through a class newsletter, should report on activities associated with school curriculum. They should never be gossip items. They should describe specific activities in the class, name students who received best citizen and other awards, report on favorite class books, tell how many students got perfect spelling, math, or grammar papers, describe individual and class projects in science, social science, and creative writing, report on class productions in drama and music, report on special visitors to the class, and report interviews, opinion polls, and aspirations of various class members, being sure that each student is included once in a while.

These items have special interest for parents. They furnish topics for discussions with children about what is going on in school. They show that activities of academic importance are occurring in abundance. They keep parents' attention attuned to the important life that their child is leading in school, and they show that the teacher cares about students and parents.

Vehicles for Communication

Style and content of communication have to be transmitted in some coherent form. Some vehicle, some avenue, some technique must be employed to convey messages to the parents. Many such vehicles have been mentioned already. They will be repeated and elaborated, along with vehicles not previously mentioned, in the sections that follow.

Open House.   Open house is a time when parents and other interested people in the community are invited to visit the school and various classrooms. Most elementary and junior high schools have open houses. Many high schools have them, too. They are usually held in the fall of the year, after teachers have had a chance to get their programs established, but before the school year has progressed too far.

Open house gives teachers an opportunity to explain their programs directly to parents. Usually teachers outline what they are attempting to accomplish, the course of study, homework, grading procedures, typical activities, and discipline requirements.

Parents have the opportunity to see the facilities, ask questions of the teachers, and examine samples of work done by students. Often there is a general meeting, too, where the school principal gives an overview of school programs and policies. Open house provides one of the best vehicles for communicating with parents because parents and teachers can see each other in a friendly, nonthreatening atmosphere. The main difficulty with open house is that not all of the parents attend.

Newsletters.   Newsletters get to all parents. They, too, can outline goals, programs, procedures, activities, and discipline methods. They can include many other things of interest to parents. They indicate that the teacher has a strong interest in the students and that parents are seen as important parts of the educational process.

Newsletters for primary grades should be written by the teacher. Students can give input. Content should be limited to aspects of the educational program plus notes about field trips, parent conferences, performances, feast days, holidays, and special events.

The primary-grade newsletter should be limited to one page. It should be sent home at least once a month. Each issue should remind parents of how much their help is needed and appreciated. Upper-elementary and secondary newsletters can be larger. Students can do much of the work in writing and producing them. Production of the newsletters can be done as part of the language arts program. Illustrations can be added by students skilled in graphic arts.

The contents of the upper-grade newsletters should also revolve around the educational program. They should not be gossip columns. Activities, special events, and outstanding student work can be featured. Book, motion picture, television, and music critiques can be included. The teacher should write a teacher's column. This newsletter, too, should communicate directly to parents, showing interest in their involvement in school and appreciation for their contributions.

Notes.   Teachers should send notes home to parents on a regular basis. Canter's model of assertive discipline calls on teachers to send notes home with two students every day. These notes inform the parents about something good that the student has done. The intention is that each student will be motivated to do something laudable. These notes should be quite personal. They should be handwritten. They may be written on duplicated forms which saves time, but the personal touch given by the teacher's own handwriting has strong effect.

Notes can be used to remind parents of performances, trips, special snacks, money for lunches and admissions, and so forth. They should always mention the teacher's appreciation for the parents' cooperation.

Phone Calls.   When students get into serious trouble at school, parents get a call from the teacher or principal. This makes calls from school an unnerving event for parents. Wise teachers work early to forestall the unpleasantness associated with telephone calls from school. Some elementary teachers try to call the home of each child early in the year. They set aside time to make five or six calls each evening. Within a week they make contact with the parents of most of the children. They speak in a friendly tone, saying they just wanted to call and let the parent know how pleased they are to have the opportunity to work with their child. They name the two or three things they intend to work hardest on, and they say that with "both of us working together, we can make this a very good learning year for Sally." They indicate that notes and other information will be sent home occasionally and end by thanking the parents for their attention.

Homework Assignments.   Homework assignments serve better than anything else to inform parents of the objectives and activities stressed at school. Some of the homework is self-explanatory. The student has to read a chapter or complete a worksheet. Parents can easily tell what it is about. Other assignments are not so easily understood. Perhaps the student is to prepare an outline of a chapter, correct mistakes on work done at school, or do a summary and analysis of national news presented on television. Parents may not understand exactly what is expected and will not know how to help.

When assignments are not quite clear, teachers can prepare brief notes that explain the assignment. The notes can be used by students and parents to keep the work on target. For instance, they can remind that outlining is done by finding the main idea in each paragraph, together with smaller ideas that support the main idea. The main ideas are numbered with Roman numerals. The smaller ideas are numbered with capital letters beneath the Roman numeral. These reminders help parents know what students are supposed to do, enabling them to help the student when necessary.

Discussions.   To remain informed of daily activities, parents should be encouraged to ask their child to tell briefly what happened in classes that day. Teachers should prime students with brief reviews to help them know what to tell parents. These reports require little effort and they have large advantages. They help the student remain aware of learning and progress. They help parents understand and support the instructional activities at school. They provide an entry for better academic communication between parents and child.

Conferences.   Most elementary schools schedule conferences between the teacher and the parents of each child individually, usually during January or February. Some schools have them twice a year, once in the fall and again in the spring. Junior high and high schools seldom have regularly scheduled conferences. Those teachers have so many students it would not be feasible to conference with the parents of each. They call parents for conferences when difficulties arise with the student.

Conferences between teacher and parents can be very productive and enlightening. But they are delicate and require tact. Parents are on unfamiliar turf at school. They are nervous, apprehensive, wondering what is going to happen. It is the teacher's responsibility to put parents at ease, to set a positive, friendly, businesslike tone for the conference. Teachers are nervous, too, but they have to be poised and take the lead. Because these conferences are delicate yet so important in establishing positive relationships, teachers must put a good deal of thought and preparation into them. Here is advice provided by an elementary teacher who has been widely recognized for her ability to conference profitably with parents:

1. Reponsibility for the success or failure of the conference rests with the teacher. Plan each conference well.

2. Greet the parent in a friendly, relaxed manner.

3. Do not sit behind a desk. Sit side-by-side with the parent at a table. This helps establish a cooperative relationship.

4. Begin by chatting about the student as a worthwhile person. Mention good traits. This reassures the parent.

5. Guide the parent through the student's file, commenting on samples of work included there.

6. Encourage the parent to talk. Listen carefully. Be accepting. Do not argue or criticize. Parents cannot be objective about their own child. Arguing and criticizing cause resentment.

7. Keep in mind at all times that PARENTS ARE YOUR BEST ALLIES. Let the parent know you feel this way. Show that you both want the best possible education for their child.

8. End the conference by describing your plans for the student's future progress. Earnestly request the parent's help in supporting your efforts. Thank the parent for talking with you about the child.

9. When preparing for conferences, keep these things in mind:

    a. Have a folder for each child, with the child's name written on it in an attractive, impressive manner.

    b. Include a profile of skills covered, skills mastered, and skills to be introduced later.

    c. Include samples of the student's work, with tests that back up your evaluation.

    d. Make notes that remind you of anecdotes that provide insight into the child's behavior and progress.

    e. Think of yourself in the parent's place. Always be tactful and polite.

List courtesy of Ruth Charles.

Parent and Teacher Organizations.   Most schools have an organization of parents and teachers. These organizations are active in some schools, but relatively inactive in most. Schools that have good participation provide excellent opportunities to communicate goals, activities, efforts, and progress. They offer a good place to present skits and other performances that show what the students are learning. Such performances are fruitful for dawing attention and providing a forum for students to show something of their accomplishments.

Some teachers are very active in having their classes put on performances and displays for the public. These activities draw favorable attention to the teacher, the class, and the school.

Typical examples of these activities include musical productions, plays, choric verse, readers' theatre, science fairs, art exhibitions, and athletic events. Parents eagerly turn out to see their child perform and to see work displayed. The whole affair presents a most positive picture. Parents are enthusiastic; students are proud and excited. Teachers are shown as truly wanting to help students and give them a chance to shine. This attitude rallies parents to strong support of school and the teacher's entire program.

REFERENCES

CHARLES, C. "Education for Dignity and Rapid Achievement." Washington, D.C.: *ERIC Reports*, 1981. Document 170. SP 016751.

FABER, A., and E. MAZLISH. *Liberated Parents, Liberated Children.* New York: Grosset and Dunlap, 1974.

KROTH, R., and R. SIMPSON. *Parent Conferences as a Teaching Strategy* Denver: Love, 1977.

BUILDING CLASSROOM DISCIPLINE

·12·

BUILDING A PERSONAL
SYSTEM OF DISCIPLINE

The purpose of this book, as suggested by its title, is to assist classroom teachers in building and implementing an effective system of discipline—one that takes into account the realities of school and classroom, the ages and personalities of the students, and the philosophy and personal preferences of individual teachers. Ultimately all teachers construct such systems for themselves, but until recently they had to do so with only vague notions of how to proceed. Beginning with imitations of their own teachers and proceeding through trial and error, they usually settled in on a system that relied on force of teacher personality and some measure of intimidation. These systems usually worked to a degree, but left much to be desired. Students took advantage of teachers who tried to be friendly, gentle, and understanding. They feared and reviled teachers who had to be sternly harsh. Rarely did students behave well just to be nice to the teacher, or for that matter even when they knew it was for their own good. With few exceptions, teachers who finally achieved adequate discipline did so by threat, punishment, and continual willingness to confront misbehaving students sternly or angrily, which resulted in loss of considerable teaching time.

That uneasy picture still holds true in a great many classrooms, although the previous chapters show that much progress has occurred in school discipline during the past few years. Teachers need no longer rule by threat. There is no need to waste psychic energy and precious instructional time attempting to correct students bent on misbehavior. There exist proven methods of helping students behave in ways that are beneficial, not detrimental, to their personal and educational growth. Moreover, there exist well-established complete systems of discipline, with records of proven effectiveness, that teachers may adopt as they are and implement overnight in their classrooms. With the knowledge and training that are available, teachers need no longer fear that their personal and professional lives will be ruined by misbehaving students.

The major discipline question for teachers today is not how to maintain discipline, but rather how to combine proven elements of discipline into a balanced system, one that is personal in the sense that it is consistent with the personality and philosophy of the teacher; effective for the age and behavior characteristics of the students in the class; understood and supported by administrators, parents, and other teachers; and easily implemented without robbing students and teachers of their energies and time for teaching and learning. One might think that teachers need only compare the existing systems and select one that seems most effective. Unfortunately, the picture is not quite so simple. Behavior modification, for example, may work wonderfully well with young and some handicapped children, but not so well with older students or those inclined to rowdiness. Assertive discipline, while effective in controlling misbehavior at all levels, may be too cumbersome for early primary students, and many teachers feel that it does little to guide and mold desired behavior. And so it is with discipline systems based on good communication, efficient lesson management, or counseling students who seem compelled to defy the teacher. All the existing models described in earlier chapters have their special strengths for certain situations and points of view, while they may also have glaring weaknesses in light of other situations and points of view. Thus, despite having at hand so much information and technique, teachers still have the obligation (and opportunity) to build their own personal systems of discipline that they believe most useful for their particular situations. They can do this by selecting from among the numerous elements that comprise the models and supplements presented earlier and by recombining them into their own special system—one that for their situation gives greatest promise of controlling student misbehavior, encouraging positive behavior, building stronger teacher–student relationships, enlisting parental support, and ultimately moving toward the elusive but highly prized student self-discipline.

The remaining pages of this chapter provide reminders and guides to assist teachers in building their personal systems of discipline. The material is organized as follows:

1. Certain themes that repeatedly appear in the literature on discipline are presented as reminders.
2. Four facts of life regarding student behavior are reemphasized.
3. Rights to which students and teacher are entitled are listed.
4. Twenty major strategies of discipline, taken from the various models, are repeated.
5. Three facets that are essential to the effectiveness of any overall system of discipline are described.
6. A 20-step process for building a personal system of discipline is presented as a guide.

ELEVEN RECURRING THEMES

Certain ideas appear often enough in the literature on discipline to be considered themes that cross different views and approaches. Eleven are presented here that should be kept in mind as one begins to develop a personal system of discipline.

THEME 1 *All students seek acceptance, belongingness, and success.* Most social behavior in the classroom is related to the student's desire to attain acceptance, gain a feeling of belonging, and enjoy a measure of success.

Students tend to behave in socially acceptable ways when appropriate avenues toward those ends remain open to them. When the avenues are closed off they turn to unsuitable means for reaching the goals. This results in unacceptable behavior, that is, in discipline problems. For that reason, teachers should be mindful of helping students reach their prime goals in acceptable ways.

THEME 2 *All students can behave acceptably; it is a matter of choice, and students make their own decisions.* There is no excuse for bad behavior. All students, except for some with known brain dysfunction, can behave acceptably. Behavior is a matter of choice. Students choose to behave the way they do, usually because of rewards they receive or hope to receive from others.

THEME 3 *Discipline helps bring success, which is a powerful motivator with a snowballing effect.* When students grow in learning and desirable behavior, and when they are recognized for that growth, they experience a feeling of genuine success. That feeling spurs them on toward greater growth and helps produce a strong positive self-concept. Some students can achieve success in classrooms with poor discipline, but they are few in number. The majority cannot transcend or remove themselves from the destructiveness of poor classroom behavior. Discipline guides behavior and suppresses destructiveness, in turn allowing students to make progress and gain recognition.

THEME 4 *The teacher is the most important figure in establishing class discipline.* Wise teachers involve students and parents in the process of establishing rules of discipline. But it is the individual teacher that sets the tone, establishes the expectations, enforces those expectations, and continually strives to help students avoid self-destructive behavior.

THEME 5 *Teacher persistence and genuine caring are essential.* Teachers cannot love all their students, but they can care genuinely about their behavior, for the sake of everyone concerned. Teachers who truly care never give up in attempting to shape student behavior in directions that bring success rather that self-defeat.

THEME 6 *Effective school discipline requires the collaboration of many different people.* The individual teacher is certainly the most powerful figure in classroom discipline, but even the most competent teacher requires the collaboration of others. It is very important that students begin to play a collaborative role in maintaining a healthy atmosphere in the classroom. Parents play essential roles in supporting and expecting discipline, as do school administrators and the entire instructional and support staff. Everyone has a stake in good behavior and should support each other in its maintenance.

THEME 7 *Discipline depends on consistency and follow up.* As nearly as possible, teachers must react the same way every time to student misbehavior. They must not appear exasperated or angry when invoking consequences, although it is fine to show anger at other times. They must always follow up on student behavior, never ignoring violations of class rules, and be sure consistently to invoke the established consequences for student behavior whether good or bad.

THEME 8 *Seriousness, rules, and high expectations underlie effective systems of discipline.* It is essential that in developing a personal system of discipline teachers be serious about teaching and learning, that they work with students to develop a good workable set of class rules, and that they then genuinely expect students to abide by the rules. This produces a sense of purposefulness that students tend to acquire, expect, and appreciate.

THEME 9 *Students who choose to break rules must endure the consequences that accompany the rules.* Consequences are not arbitrary punishments. They are results that students choose just as they choose their behavior. Teachers must explain in detail the consequences and their linkage to the rules. When students choose to break the rules teachers invoke the consequences. The entire process is depicted as students' choosing the consequences.

THEME 10 *The correction of misbehavior should involve redirecting the student.* "Correcting is directing," Ginott said. Teachers must remember that students do not always know how to behave correctly. They may need to be shown proper behavior, reminded of it, and reinforced when they do what is expected.

THEME 11 *One of the best ways to teach good behavior is through example.* Students imitate teachers. If teachers are kind and respectful, students tend to be kind and respectful. Because imitation learning is so powerful, teachers should endeavor to provide the best possible examples through their own personal behavior.

FOUR FACTS OF CLASSROOM LIFE

Teachers enter practice with a variety of views about human nature and how young learners are likely to act. Some believe that students are angels and never willingly misbehave, that if misbehavior does occur it is not the fault of the student but of conditions or bad teaching. Others think that students will all misbehave unless thwarted, that the devil is in their blood. Some know that students misbehave, but believe that a caring attitude by the teacher will erase the bad and bring out only good behavior. Since teachers have so many different beliefs about students—and most of the beliefs are at least partly true—it is important in planning a personal system of discipline that teachers understand and accept four basic facts about student behavior in the classroom.

FACT 1 *Students are going to misbehave in school.* Students are not always angels. Sometimes they act up, misbehave, and disrupt. Some do it a little bit and others do it a lot. Even the best have their bad moments. Therefore, teachers should not be so naive as to think that given a nurturing atmosphere students will always do what is right and good. They will frequently display behavior that works against their ultimate well-being. That is when discipline is needed.

FACT 2 *Students need discipline.* Although some students misbehave a great deal and even the best misbehave occasionally, teachers should not conclude that something uncontrollable makes them do it. All students can behave appropriately if they wish to do so. The pursuit of mistaken goals (attention, power, revenge, withdrawal) that occurs when students do not readily find the desired sense of acceptance and belonging may result in misbehavior. Sometimes students just feel a little bit naughty and do some things they know they should not do. And at other times, they may be trying out a variety of behaviors, as they must do in the process of socialization, and some of those behaviors are not acceptable. Discipline helps students learn what they may and may not do, and its shows them that someone cares enough about them to restrict their erroneous behavior. Discipline makes better people of us all, students and adults alike.

FACT 3 *Teachers cannot teach well without discipline.* Many teachers see teaching and discipline as entirely separate realms. In actuality, they are very much the same: *Both* are processes for bringing about a lasting change in behavior. But even if considered separate tasks, good teaching cannot occur without discipline. If no attempt is made to discipline, chaos is almost certain to result, and students are severely hampered in learning in such an environment. If attempts are made to discipline, but they are not successful, much teaching time is lost. Without discipline teachers cannot fill their prime function, which is to teach.

FACT 4 *Teachers can learn to discipline well.* Teachers used to say you either had it or you did not. They meant that discipline was instinctive; you could not learn it. We know now that discipline is a skill, a procedure, and a set of techniques that all teachers can acquire and implement effectively. That of course is what this book is about.

BASIC RIGHTS IN THE CLASSROOM

The Canter model of discipline, more than any of the others, clarified certain basic rights to which students and teachers are entitled in the classroom. These rights do not reflect idealized, hoped-for conditions but rather conditions that all classroom participants have a right to expect. Students, administrators, and parents all have parts to play in securing these rights, but it is the primary responsibility of the teacher to see to it that they are obtained, for these rights form the infrastructure on which discipline is built. Without that structure, discipline is but a facade that falls away as soon as it is tested. Let us review certain of the basic rights of student and teacher.

Student Rights

Students may be considered to have several basic rights in the classroom. These are rights to which they are entitled and which they should expect, but which unfortunately they often do not enjoy. Three such rights are:

1. The right to a learning environment that is appropriately well ordered, peaceful, safe, nonthreatening, and conducive to learning.
2. The right to have a caring, well-prepared teacher who instructs well and who limits students' inappropriate self-destructive behavior.
3. The right to choose how to behave, with full understanding of the consequences that automatically follow their choices.

Teacher Rights

Teachers like students are entitled to certain conditions that are so crucial to teaching and learning that they are to be considered basic rights. Teachers should insist, for the good of everyone concerned, that these rights be established and easily afforded. Such rights include the following:

1. The right to establish optimal learning environments that are consonant with the teacher's individual strengths and weaknesses.
2. The right to teach in ways that meet the learning needs of the students in the class.
3. The right to expect behavior from students that contributes to their optimal growth, while also meeting the reasonable needs of the teacher.
4. The right to teach in a climate that is free from disruptions.
5. The right to ask and receive help and backing from administrators and parents.

Guaranteeing the rights of students and teachers does not of course automatically ensure the best educational experiences, but those rights do form the essential basis from which excellence can proceed. Without them, quality instruction cannot be maintained over the long run. With them, teachers are freed to instruct in accord with their talents, and students are freed to concentrate on learning in accord with their individual potentials.

TWENTY STRATEGIES IN DISCIPLINE

To this point several realities of student and teacher behavior in the classroom have been established: Students will misbehave; their misbehavior is self-defeating; behavior is a matter of choice—students can always choose to behave properly rather than improperly; students have a basic right to a calm, threat-free classroom in which to learn; teachers have a basic right to teach without disruptions from misbehaving students, and they have a right to expect strong support from administrators and parents. Given these rights and realities, little question remains about whether teachers should use discipline techniques to maintain a quality learning atmosphere, limit student self-defeating behavior, and meet their own needs to teach without disruptions. What remains is for teachers to construct systems of discipline that assure basic rights, maintain quality learning environments, are consistent with the realities of the situations in which they find themselves, and that are consonant with their personal philosophies of working with students.

To begin that construction, let us consider 20 strategies of discipline that have been given much emphasis in literature and classroom practice.

STRATEGY 1 *Take charge in the classroom.* Every authority on discipline agrees: teachers must take charge firmly in their classes, and there should be no doubt about it. They can be pleasant, but they must at the same time be forceful. They usually call for some student input, but they make the final decisions.

STRATEGY 2 *Make good rules for class conduct.* Rules should be short and clear, five or six in number. Students should be involved in establishing them. The rules should be stated positively, if possible, and posted in the room. They should be explained so that all students understand. Consequences for abiding by the rules and for breaking them should be explained also. The rules should be reviewed periodically.

STRATEGY 3 *Expect the best of students; say it and show it.* Rules are made and posted to inform students and remind them of expectations. Every student can abide by them and every student is expected to do so voluntarily because they are in students' best interest.

STRATEGY 4 *Enforce the rules consistently.* Rules are worthless if not enforced. Students understand them and the consequences that entail from breaking the rules plainly. When they choose to break the rules, they choose the consequences. Teachers should without hesitation invoke the consequences that are chosen.

STRATEGY 5 *Allow no destructive behavior.* Never allow students to behave in ways that disrupt teaching or learning. Such behavior is destructive. Good discipline assists constructive behavior, permitting good instruction and promoting good learning.

STRATEGY 6 *Manage groups and lessons efficiently.* Pace lessons so that boredom does not become a problem. Move from one lesson to another smoothly, without wasting time. Boredom and rough transitions provide fertile grounds in which undesired behavior can grow.

STRATEGY 7 *Teach students how to choose good behavior.* Show students that they can choose between good and bad behavior. Show them that good choices lead to success, acceptance, and esteem. Help them to decide whether their choices are good or bad. Reinforce them when they make good choices.

STRATEGY 8 *Use effective styles of talk with students.* Ginott stressed effective communication that addressed the situation rather than attacking the student. Glasser described how to confront misbehaving students in productive ways as did Canter and Dreikurs. Hostile talk and wish-washy talk are both ineffective. Speak plainly and matter of factly. Be calm, but forceful and insistent.

STRATEGY 9 *Provide an abundance of genuine success.* Every student longs for success and recognition. Provide genuine success through progress and acknowledgment. Reinforce students in ways most effective for the group and individual. Help students keep charts that show graphic evidence of progress. Call this progress to the attention of their parents.

STRATEGY 10 *Reduce failure to a very low level.* Failure and errors are not synonymous. One can make errors and still be successful. Failure results from lack of growth. Even with growth, lack of recognition can cause the feeling of failure. Failure should be kept to a minimum because it tends to feed on itself. When people see themselves as failures, they tend to behave more often as failures.

STRATEGY 11 *Shape behavior through systematic reinforcement.* Implement a system of behavior modification. Be sure it is in keeping with the maturity level of the students. Systematic reinforcement motivates and shapes behavior for all types of students at all age levels. It is the single most effective techinque for building the kind of behavior you want to see in your students.

STRATEGY 12 *Confront misbehavior forcefully but positively.* Some misbehavior can be ignored, but when it becomes disruptive to teaching and learning it must be dealt with. Teachers must have the fortitude to confront students who are disruptive. Skills of confrontation have been described by several authorities, including Ginott, Glasser, Jones, Dreikurs, and Canter.

STRATEGY 13 *Invoke the logical consequences of good and bad behavior.* When students comply with rules, they should be rewarded. When they break rules, they should be punished. In either case they are aware of the consequences prior to their actions. When students choose to behave or misbehave; at the same time they are choosing rewards or punishments. This principle must be made absolutely clear to the students. The teacher in turn must apply it consistently and dispassionately.

STRATEGY 14 *Do all you can to support good behavior.* Discipline tends to focus on misbehavior, since that is a major source of problems for teachers. However, good behavior should continually be supported, as one of the ounces of prevention that save pounds of cure. How to support good behavior was explained in the works of several authorities, including Skinner, Canter, Ginott, and Jones.

STRATEGY 15 *Teach good behavior though good example.* Be the best model you can be for your students. Show concern, manners, and courtesy. Be polite and helpful. Have students practice the behaviors modeled for them. Reinforce them when they repeat desired behaviors that have been modeled.

STRATEGY 16 *Stress good manners and living by the golden rule.* Make it plain from the outset that you have high standards of student conduct. You expect students to use good manners. You expect them to live by the golden rule. Forbid their use of sarcasm or cruelty. Reward them when they show kindness and consideration.

STRATEGY 17 *Establish a good support system for your program of discipline.* It is very difficult for teachers to work in isolation from other teachers. Cooperation is often needed in discipline. At times students may refuse to obey rules. On those occasions a teacher must be able to count on immediate positive support from principal, other teachers, and parents. Means of establishing such a support system were described in the Canter model. (See Chapter 7.)

STRATEGY 18 *Set up a production communication system with parents.* Parental support is very important. You can secure it if you inform parents of your program, acitivities, and expectations regarding student behavior. Rules, consequences and enforcement procedures should be described in writing and furnished to parents. Stress that your control system is necessary for maximum learning and that it teaches students to relate to each other in positive ways.

STRATEGY 19 *Communicate regularly and clearly with students.* By talking with students formally and informally you show that you are concerned about them, that you care about their learning and behavior. One way to maintain good communication is through the use of classroom meetings conducted as suggested by Glasser. Students feel involved when kept informed about their learning, behavior, problems, and future activities. They are then more likely to support the teacher and other class members, causing fewer behavior problems.

STRATEGY 20 *Be persistent; never give up.* Do not quit; do not excuse misbehavior; do not cave in before student hostility. Keep your poise. Keep trying. The essence of discipline is caring enough that you will let nothing interfere with teaching and learning. This caring is one of the best contributions you can make to the welfare of your students.

THREE FACES OF DISCIPLINE

An examination of the 20 strategies of discipline reveals that all of them are not for the purpose of correcting misbehavior once it occurs. Some of them are intended to prevent misbehavior from occurring, and others are intended to support desirable student behavior. Thus, we see that discipline has three facets, all large and powerful. A good system of classroom discipline must give attention to all three.

Preventive Discipline

Preventive discipline is the face that has to do with forestalling misbehavior, with preventing it from occurring in the first place. Teachers have long been told that good curriculum and teaching prevent discipline problems, or that good management does the trick, or scowling, or getting in one's bluff from the first day. These factors do not take care of all the problems. If they did we would have no behavior problems. Each, however, contains a kernel of truth. Good curriculum, teaching, and management are positive and productive, and they will be discussed further in this chapter. Scowling and bluffing may work to some extent, but they tend to turn students against the teacher. Good preventive discipline should rally students to you, not against you.

Supportive Discipline

Supportive discipline consists of the application of a number of gentle though effective techniques that assist students in maintaining their own self-discipline. Essentially, they are techniques that constantly remind students that the teacher is aware of their activities, is willing to help, and will not allow misbehavior to get started. These techniques allow the teacher to keep students on track without nervousness or distress. Feelings remain positive. Specific supportive techniques will be discussed later in this chapter.

Corrective Discipline

Corrective discipline consists of the moves teachers make to suppress, correct, and rechannel misbehavior. Despite teachers' best efforts in preventive and supportive discipline, a certain amount of misbehavior is bound to occur in the classroom. Corrective discipline stops the misbehavior and puts the students back on a productive line of work without undue waste of teaching and learning time. At its best, it minimizes negative feelings and attitudes while helping foster positive work and improved self-discipline.

BALANCED DISCIPLINE

When we attend to all three faces of discipline—preventive, supportive, and corrective—we begin building a system of balanced discipline. This term refers to a complete approach to discipline that utilizes in a coordinated way all the best techniques known for controlling student behavior. In order to see specifically how each of the three faces of discipline contributes to the balanced approach, we return here to a detailed examination of each of the three faces.

Preventive Discipline: Power-Packed Ounces

You cannot prevent all behavior problems, but you can prevent many of them, and each occurrence prevented adds to the quality of educational life for students and teacher. The most effective steps that one can take in prevention are not difficult ones, and they offer a high payoff. Here we consider 10 things teachers should do in preventive discipline. Of them, 6 are done during preparation for teaching, and 4 are done during the actual teaching performance.

Preparation.   Before teaching ever starts there are six areas teachers can adjust to prevent misbehavior and they are discussed in the following paragraphs.

SETTING

The *setting* refers to the physical aspects of the classroom. The room should provide physical comfort, advantageous seating, and efficient traffic patterns. Physical comfort depends on adequate ventilation, heat, lighting, and furniture. Ventilation is important to keep a supply of fresh air to students. Stuffiness produces lethargy and inattentiveness. Adequate heat, around 70° is necessary for good concentration. If students get too cold, they become tense; they cannot sit still or keep their minds fully on their work. Lighting should be such that work space is clearly illuminated. Light sources should be overhead or to the backs of students. Students should never be seated so that they must look into direct light from windows. Eye distress produces nervousness, tension, anxiety, and frustration. Furniture should match the physical sizes of students and should encourage postures that reduce fatigue. Feet should reach the floor and knees should fit comfortably under tables. If furniture makes students stretch, slump, or crouch, they will soon seek relief.

Students should not be seated too closely together. Physical closeness furnishes a hotbed for misbehavior, encouraging talk, laughter, and inattention. Students in pairs reinforce each other's misbehavior. Allow students to sit close together only after they have proven they can and will control themselves.

Traffic patterns should be established so students are allowed to move most efficiently from one place to another, without congestion that encourages misbehavior. Routines for movement should be established and modified to support student self-control.

CURRICULUM

The *curriculum* has to do with objectives, activities, and materials for learning. If improper, it can produce student apathy, boredom, fatigue, and frustration, with strong potential for misbehavior. Teachers should provide activities that are as interesting and enjoyable as possible. Those activities should provide challenge but remain within reach of student ability. Novelty and variety should be added frequently. When we hold student attention and interest, we remove many of the conditions that encourage misbehavior.

ATTITUDE

The *attitude* of the teacher should be established before teaching begins. Teachers must determine that they will be in charge, that they will be at the helm in making the decisions. They do well to consult students and ask their opinions, but teachers must have the final say.

EXPECTATIONS AND LIMITS

Expectations and limits can be decided on before teaching begins. Every teacher needs to perform a realistic self-appraisal to establish what can and cannot be accepted. This allows one to identify thresholds of tolerance for noise, movement, and talk. It links expectations, in the form of class rules, to good learning and behavior. Such a self-appraisal recognizes that teachers have needs and rights just as students do.

Out of these limits and expectations grows a specific set of rules. Teachers should decide in advance on five or six rules they want students to follow. These rules are nonnegotiable. They must be explained to students clearly, in terms of real behavior. Reasons must be given that show how rules contribute to learning and enjoyment. The rules can be written out on a chart, then used as a basis for discussion. The chart is posted in the room for periodic reference.

Linked directly to the set of rules should be a system of positive and negative consequences. The positive consequences are pleasant things that happen to students when they comply with the rules. These should be discussed first. The negative consequences are undesirable things that happen to students who break rules. These consequences must be humane, but they must be things that the students do not like or want.

It must be emphasized that students choose the consequences, good or bad, through their behavior. Good behavior means the student chooses good consequences. Bad behavior means the student chooses undesired consequences. The teacher does not reward or punish; students reward or punish themselves by how they behave. The teacher simply administers what the students choose to have happen to them.

The teacher should also decide on the method to be used for enforcement of rules and invocation of consequences. Specific means of rewarding, confronting students, correcting misbehavior, and following through with consequences were discussed in several different models in earlier chapters.

SUPPORT SYSTEMS

The support systems must be identified and established before the discipline system is put into effect. It is essential that the principal approve and support the program and be willing to follow through when the teacher needs help. It is highly desirable that parents understand and support the program, too. They have follow-through responsibilities when the student refuses to comply with demands of teacher and principal. It is desirable as well that other teachers be brought into the plan. Teachers working together can reinforce each other, and they can use each other's classrooms as isolation for students who misbehave in their rooms.

SPECIAL AND UNEXPECTED EVENTS

One final preparation must be made in preventive discipline, that is, to prepare for *special and unexpected events*. You know such events will occur although you do not always know when or what they will be. Examples are visitors to the room, animals in the room, substitute teachers, injured students, fights, and emergencies such as fires, ill students, and sudden teacher illness. Find out in advance how these matters are handled in your school and how you want your students to deal with them. Prepare to discuss such events and to train students about how to behave when they occur. Discussions should be held with students following the introduction to expectations, limits, and rules of behavior.

Performance.   Many discipline problems can be prevented by what the teacher routinely does in teaching. The way of talking, sense of humor, ability to manage, charisma, attention to every student—all these things can forestall behavior problems. Four elements of performance merit attention and are discussed in the following paragraphs.

MANAGEMENT OF TEACHING

Management of teaching refers to the conduct of routines and the delivery of lessons. Routines are very important in management. They establish how students are to enter and leave the room, sharpen pencils, obtain materials, replace materials, ask to go to the restroom, and so forth.

The delivery of lessons should be done in ways that highlight suspense and interest, maintain flow, end at the right time, prevent flat spots, and provide smooth transitions. Materials associated with the lessons must be distributed and collected efficiently. Attending to these details eliminates the rough spots in lessons that encourage misbehavior.

TEACHER ON STAGE

Teacher on stage refers to the mannerisms and speech the teacher uses while directing lessons. Teachers cannot discount their roles as entertainers. They have unique powers to attract and hold student attention. They should use gestures and voice control to further their entertainment power. From that basis, they should concentrate on teaching through example using the techniques of modeling, which is the best way to teach correct behavior, manners, courtesy, and living by the golden rule. Do not think of entertainment only as making students laugh and having a good time. Entertainment includes drama, mystery, and suspense. It includes excitement and helps students enter into a spirit of good learning. There is nothing wrong with cracking a joke now and then. Student appreciate it, but they do not need a stand-up comic for a teacher. They do better to have teachers skilled in dramatic techniques who can hold attention, instill a sense of mystery, and portray the best in human relations.

THE GOLDEN TONGUE

The golden tongue refers to language teachers use in talking with students and to the way they speak sincerely and humanely. Much has been written in this book about good communication. Authorities have stressed using sane messages, attaining congruent communication, and being a genuine person. Teachers should decide how they want to speak with their students so as to remain genuine without using cutting tones, sarcasm, or attacking students' character. Teachers may want to practice polite speech, saying "thank you" and "please." Teachers may want to practice a variety of comments that show mild praise, approval, and acceptance.

ACCEPTANCE FOR EVERYONE

Accepting for everyone is a technique that does much to prevent behavior problems. Various authorities stress that students' prime objective is to be accepted, feel wanted, feel that they belong in the class. One way to foster a sense of belonging is to give regular attention to every student. Canter says that elementary teachers should praise every single student every day and that secondary teachers should praise each student as often as possible. Other authorities say to speak directly to every student individually sometime during the day. Some teachers set up systems where students acknowledge each other, through greetings, participation, and genuine compliments.

Teachers have the main responsibility for providing a sense of acceptance, but students have their responsibilities, too. These should be discussed with the students, who can give their input on how they want to be acknowledged and how they want to acknowledge each other.

Supportive Discipline: Calling on the Superego

Teachers want to do what they can to prevent misbehavior. That is a priority item. However, not all misbehavior can be prevented. Despite teachers' best efforts, there are times when students become restive, have difficulties, are seduced by attractive objects, fall under the spell of intriguing classmates, or for myriad untold reasons just feel like kicking up their heels.

At the first signs of incipient misbehavior, teachers should implement techniques of supportive discipline. This type of discipline simply helps students maintain self-control. The techniques are subtle. Unnoticed by others, they get students back on track.

Teachers can do many things to assist self-discipline. Some of those things are described in the following paragraphs.

Supporting self-control.   When teachers catch first glimpse of incipient misbehavior they can apply any of eight techniques that help the student get back on course without trouble. Following is a discussion of those techniques.

SIGNALS

Signals can be sent in a private way to a student needing support. The teacher catches the student's eye, holds eye contact for a moment, frowns, shakes the head, or gives a hand signal.

If signals fail, the teacher can use *proximity*. This is simply moving closer to the student, showing awareness and willingness to help. Nearness is usually enough. Sometimes a light touch on head or shoulder helps.

SHOWING INTEREST

Showing interest is an effective way to help students who are beginning to lose interest in their work. The teacher moves alongside, looks at the work, and comments favorably on it or on the student's efforts. Sometimes a light challenge helps, as when the teacher says, "You have gotten a lot of this done already. I bet you will get at least five more done before we have to stop. What do you think?"

HUMOR

Humor is an effective device when students begin to get restive. Students enjoy humor. It gives them a change from the routine and a brief respite from tension. A momentary break is all that is needed. You must be careful, though, that the humor does not provoke joking and horseplay, which will put an end to the lesson at hand.

HURDLE HELP

Hurdle help is assisting students who have come up against a problem on which they are stuck. Most students stop work, begin asking others for help, or sit and do nothing. When it is evident that a student is stuck the teacher gives a hint or corrects an error that allows the student to move ahead.

RESTRUCTURING

Restructuring means changing an activity in midstream to add excitement or reduce difficulty. When students get bored or when the work is too hard they have a tendency to misbehave. A change in the activity can solve the problem. Changes in schedules are important, too, to add variety, provide reward, and accommodate instruction to special events.

ESTABLISHING ROUTINES

Establishing routines reduces confusion. Students may be unsure about how to go to the reading area, get their laboratory equipment, or request special help. When confusion is evident, teachers can take a few moments to say, "Here's how we do that," and proceed to demonstrate the routine.

REMOVING SEDUCTIVE OBJECTS

Removing seductive objects assists student self-control. Toys, books, rubber bands, animals, notes—a great variety of such things appear regularly in the classroom. They intrigue students and draw attention away from the lesson. Teachers can remove the object without fuss and return it to its owner at the end of the period or day.

Reinforcing Good Behavior.   One of the very best techniques for supportive discipline is providing ongoing reinforcement. This is done in an informal way with nods, smiles, and pats; and words such as "Thanks," "Good," and "Keep it up." This procedure shows students that the teacher is aware of them, their work, and their behavior. It shows that the teacher cares and appreciates. Often that is all it takes to keep students working hard.

Requesting Behavior.   As students begin to drift away from the lesson teachers must draw them back. They may do this by demanding better behavior or by requesting it. For mild misbehavior requests are preferable because they produce no resentment or hostility. Teachers have three ways of requesting correct behavior: hints, I-messages, and questions.

HINTS, I-MESSAGES, AND QUESTIONS

Hints remind students of what they are supposed to be doing. Some examples are: "Remember, we are trying to finish early today." "All of you are supposed to be using your encyclopedias." "The reward for best manners will be given at the end of this period."

I-messages inform students about the teacher's needs. "It is so noisy I can't talk with Jack." "I am feeling very nervous about the behavior I am seeing." "I'm afraid we are not getting as far as I hoped we would."

Questions are like hints, but they are presented as interrogations. "Do you remember our two rules about talking?" "Are we getting our 15 problems completed before lunch?" "Do you suppose I can count on your cleaning the work area quickly?" There is simply no intention that these questions be answered. They are simply reminders.

Making good choices.   Much has been said in this book about behavior as student choice. Glasser, the Canters, and Dreikurs base their models on the premise that students choose to be good or bad, and in so doing choose the consequences that logically accompany their behavior.

The Canters and Dreikurs say that all students can behave adequately; they choose to act in a good way or to act in a bad way. At the same time they choose to receive positive consequences or negative consequences. Glasser emphasizes this point even more vividly. He says that schools provide the best place in most students' lives for making the choices that bring success and belonging, effects that are necessary for adequate functioning in society. He advises teachers to force students to make value judgements about their choices. In so doing, they learn how to make better choices, choices that lead to success.

Teachers can help students make better choices by stressing behavior as choice, providing suitable alternatives to bad behavior, and having students make value judgments about their misbehavior. Students must see that they do, in truth, have the right to choose how they will behave. They must see at the same time that all behavior has its consequences and that teachers will always invoke those consequences.

Alternatives to bad behavior must be clarified. This can be done in group discussions using anecdotes to describe student misbehavior and to show what they could have chosen to do differently. Suitable alternatives can be found for tattling, fighting, arguing, stealing, talking out, and speaking sarcastically and cruelly. Alternatives might include writing the messages out to hand to the teacher, writing out the arguments for teacher and class to consider, setting up a system for loaning books and materials rather than stealing them, and practicing statements that acknowledge and compliment.

Value judgments provide the avenue toward students' making responsible decisions on their own. Students can be caused to respond when they misbehave in the manner suggested by Glasser. They are asked to state what they are doing. They are then asked if their behavior is helping either themselves or the class. Finally, they are asked to name a behavior that would help themselves or the class. If unable to think of any, the teacher suggests two or more alternatives from which the student selects. The teacher insists that the student follow through on his commitment to the behavior he has chosen.

Resolving conflicts. People disagree. They argue and they fight, especially during childhood and adolescence. Piaget says that arguing is good for kids. It builds their thought processes and their self-confidence. However, conflict is not good for the classroom; it disrupts and hinders teaching and learning. Conflicts can be resolved without producing disruptions. Hurt feelings can be avoided. Three techniques make this possible and they are described below.

Verbot is when the teacher says, "We don't do that. It is forbidden. Stop it now." If teachers see students move toward dispute, fight, or name calling, they use the verbot. That stops the behavior at once. They do not discuss it or call for value judgments. They say, "That's all," and they separate the disputants if necessary.

Write it out is a way of dealing with conflict that serves two purposes. First, it lets disputants cool off, since it takes a bit of time to complete. As they write out their points of view, the whole conflict begins to look silly. The combatants drop the incident. Second, it eliminates disruption. If two students get into an argument or fight, the class grinds to an immediate halt. Everybody is caught in a turmoil of emotion. If the disputants are nabbed immediately and directed to write, nobody pays attention. Classroom goes on as usual.

The *no-lose approach*, popularized by Thomas Gordon, is used when disputants have strong differences even after a cooling-off period. With this approach, each person names or writes two or three suggestions that would correct the situation. They consider their suggestions together, helped by the teacher or another intermediary. They look for a suggestion acceptable to both. When they agree on one, they implement it. If it works, fine. If it does not, they repeat the process. The result is that both parties are satisfied with the result. There is no winner, no loser. Good feelings result, rather than hostility and hurt.

Communicating and counseling.   Communication and counseling provide excellent assists to supportive discipline. They are furnished in various ways, including the following.

VERBAL REINFORCEMENT

Verbal reinforcement consists of words and tone of voice that students find rewarding. It includes words and expressions such as "good," "wow," "fine," "thanks," "good going, " and "keep up the fine work." Verbal reinforcement becomes more powerful when it describes exactly what is being rewarded: Thank you, Jimmy, for raising your hand before speaking." "I surely appreciate the way everyone came into the room and got to work immediately." "Since you all completed your work without interruptions, there will be no homework tonight."

ACTIVE LISTENING

Active listenting is a way of helping students express themselves, without value responses to what they say. The teacher (active listener) nods, says, "Uh huh," "Go on," "I think I understand what you mean." The teacher reflects back feelings and opinions expressed by the student: "I can see that you are upset." "You feel that you haven't been given a fair chance." This technique is used during group discussions or individual conferences. It is not used for dealing quickly with misbehavior during class time because it requires too much time and it interferes with the work of other students.

CONGRUENT COMMUNICATION

Congruent communication is a process of matching teacher talk with the demands of the situation. It includes using sane messages, in which the teacher addresses the situation rather than the character of the student. It involves laconic language, short and succinct, when student misbehavior must be suppressed immediately. It instructs students on how to behave correctly. It is to the point and can be used during class time.

POSITIVE PROBLEM SOLVING

Positive problem solving is used during group discussions. It is especially effective as a part of classroom meetings. A problem is identified. Students contribute comments, always positive, for helping solve the problem. No blaming and backbiting are allowed. The teacher contributes little, but does help direct the discussion. Positive steps are taken to solve the problem.

MAKING VALUE JUDGMENTS

Making value judgments causes students to decide whether their behaviors are worthwhile or not. The intent is to cause the students to make better choices that lead to success. Glaser advocates this technique for confronting student misbehavior during class time. Most teachers find it too time-consuming and too disruptive. They prefer using it during discussions or private conferences.

TELLING IT LIKE IT IS

Telling it like it is has a place in communication, but it should be used infrequently. It consists of the teacher stating the reality of the situation, in no uncertain terms. Distasteful and hurtful language are not used. An example is: "We have something here that is forbidden in this room. Cruel language was used. James, I will not tolerate cruelty. Never, ever, do that again."

Providing Success.   Time and again these pages have mentioned the value of success. It motivates, builds self-concept, and removes many of the causes of misbehavior. For those reasons, it is a powerful factor in supportive discipline. Success does not correct misbehavior, but it does support good behavior. Students hope for continued success and recognition from others. Self-assurance grows. Students realize that good behavior has worthwhile payoffs.

Corrective Discipline: Pounds of Cure

Teachers do their best to prevent misbehavior by organizing teaching well and establishing a tone of seriousness. They do their best to support self-control through attention, communication, and success. It would seem that misbehavior would be unable to slip through those filters. Still, misbehavior does occur. Students violate established rules. They choose bad behavior. When they do so, they must be corrected.

Corrective discipline is what most teachers, students, and parent think of when they hear the word discipline. The student acts and the teacher reacts. The teacher has a frightful look on her face. Blue blazes leap from her tongue. She brandishes a willow rod. Students quiver in puddles of sweat.

Enlightened corrective discipline falls well short of that shocking stereotype. In a relatively inconspicuous way, corrective discipline stops misbehavior, redirects it, and reteaches correct behavior. This is done by squelching grossly inappropriate behavior, confronting students who misbehave, redirecting their behavior, invoking logical consequences, following through consistently, and insisting assertively that teaching and learning rights be met.

Squelching misbehavior must be done if the behavior is a gross violation of rules, such as fighting, cruelty, and cursing. The teacher stops it immediately, either through emphatic verbot or through banishing the offenders to the principal's office. Misbehavior can be stifled more gently when it does not fall into the emergency category. A good example is the Canters' suggestion of putting students' names on the board as a warning. Later, checks call for punishment.

Confronting students who misbehave received much attention in the models proposed by Glasser, Dreikurs, and Jones. Students must be called to task. Confrontation during class time, however, disrupts and stops the normal teaching and learning process. It may pit teacher against student in a power struggle in which one or the other is bound to lose, but it is disastrous for teachers to lose. Confrontation is best done in two steps: First, deal with misbehavior in a way similar to that suggested by Canter. Later, talk with the student in private to establish judgments and positive courses of future action.

Redirecting student behavior is a primary aim of corrective discipline. We want bad behavior changed to good behavior. Ginott tells us to correct students by directing them, by telling them how to do it right. Canter and Glasser get at redirection through invoking consequences and insisting that students choose behavior that leads to success. Redirection is one point on which all experts in discipline agree. The purpose of discipline is first to stop the disruption and second to teach students how to behave correctly.

Invoking logical consequences lies at the heart of both the Glasser and Canter models. Consequences are linked to rules. Everyone knows in advance what the rules are. When students choose to misbehave, teachers invoke the consequences immediately. The understanding is that teachers do not punish. Students choose consequences through their behavior.

Consistent follow-through is absolutely essential in any system of discipline. Students must know that rule violations bring negative consequences, every time. No getting out of it. Teachers who do not follow through invite more serious misbehavior, and they will surely get it. Follow-through applies also to plans for positive behavior that teachers and students develop jointly. The teacher monitors student adherence to agreements, providing reinforcement or additional negative consequences when necessary.

Assertive insistence on teaching and learning rights is the great contribution made in the Canter model. Teachers have a right to teach. Students have a right to learn. No one has a right to interfere through disruption. Teachers have a right to apply firm, humane discipline. They have a right to receive support from administrators and parents. They must insist that students abide by the consequences of their behavior. Teachers must not back down.

BALANCED DISCIPLINE YOUR WAY: TWENTY STEPS

Balanced discipline provides a complete approach to classroom control. It attends equally to preventive, supportive, and corrective measures. It allows teachers to select just the right amount and style of discipline to meet learning and teaching needs in accord with ages of students and personalities of class and teacher.

The following 20 steps show how to construct your own system of balanced discipline.

1. Determine that you will have discipline, and have it your way.

2. Set your limits. Think about what you will and will not allow students to do regarding talk, movement, noise, self-control, getting to work, finishing work, good manners, and so forth.

3. Write out your rules. State them positively. Limit the list to no more than five or six. Put them on a chart that can be displayed in the room.

4. Establish your support system. Explain your rules and system to the principal and as soon as possible to parents. Indicate that you need their approval and must have their support. Enlist the support of a fellow teacher, if possible.

5. Arrange your classroom environment to enhance discipline. Be sure students are comfortable, not distracted by the surroundings, and not seated too closely together.

6. Discuss rules and consequences with students on the very first day. Be sure they understand what the rules mean, in terms of overt behaviors, and what the consequences will be for both compliance and noncompliance.

7. Assert your rights to teach, to discipline, and to ensure student learning. Make sure students understand that you will let nothing interfere with your right to teach and their right to learn.

8. Work to enliven and smooth out your curriculum. Try to provide work that is worthwhile and interesting. Establish routines and procedures that contribute to efficient flow while eliminating dead spots and confusion.

9. Be the best example possible for your students. Always act in the very ways you want them to act. Speak in the ways you want them to speak. Think what those are. Practice them. Make a checklist and keep it in the room as a reminder.

10. Interact with your students on a personal level. Talk with them. Help with individual difficulties. Conference with them individually while the class is at work. Show personal attention to every single student as often as possible.

11. Help students choose good behavior. Be sure they understand that good behavior comes from making good choices. When they choose good behavior they choose pleasant consequences. Help them identify alternatives to bad choice, bad behavior, and bad consequences.

12. Confront misbehavior. Do not let rule violations go unnoticed or unenforced. Try to confront misbehavior in a way that does not disrupt teaching and learning, but do not ignore it, excuse it, or accept it.

13. Follow through consistently. Always apply positive consequences. Always invoke negative consequences. Every time, without fail. Show students that you never give up in trying to help them.

14. Reinforce good behavior. Set up a system so you will be sure to reward students for behaving acceptably. Positive reinforcement is the most powerful technique at your disposal for establishing good behavior.

15. Use sane messages when talking with students about misbehavior. Talk about a situation and about how to correct it. Do not tell students they are awful, inconsiderate, beastly, or moronic.

16. Develop a system for conflict resolution. Do not allow student fights or arguments to disrupt class. Do, however, help students resolve their conflict, if it is serious. Have them write out their complaints or use the no-lose approach.

17. Communicate regularly with students and parents. Use classroom meetings to talk with students about education, school problems, upcoming activities, and so forth. Use newsletters, notes, phone calls, and guided homework to keep parents informed and secure their support.

18. Provide acceptance and success for all students. Acknowledge every student, every day. Ensure and graph academic progress. Be sure others recognize it, together with other contributions any student makes. Be sure parents know about it.

19. Stick by the principle of "least necessary discipline." This means avoiding overkill, using only the amount of discipline necessary to protect teaching and learning rights. For some classes, the amount and type of discipline will be light; for others, it will be heavy. Do not use too little or too much.

20. Never give up. Never give up. Never give up.

·13·

TOWARD SCHOOLWIDE DISCIPLINE

Prior to 1970, discipline was an instructional variable that rested almost entirely with individual teachers. Some teachers were able to control their classes under almost all conditions, so that order and productive student output resulted. Others were unable to maintain order in their classrooms even under the best conditions. This ability (or lack thereof) to control, manage, and guide student acitivity seemed to result more because of the individual personality than any set of organized procedures. Most people believed, therefore, that a given teacher either "had it" (the ability to discipline) or did not, and those who did not have it to begin with were unlikely ever to get it.

For the most part, the conventional wisdom held true. Teachers with good discipline seemed to come by their ability naturally, possibly through good perceptions, ability to interface with students, and force of persuasive personality. There did exist a body of folklore about discipline, such as the familiar: "Don't smile before Christmas," "Get your bluff in early," "Don't be friendly with the students." Yet many teachers most successful in control violated those adages—they smiled, they did not bluff, and they related quite well with students on a personal basis. This fact made it even more difficult to sort out any *behavioral* differences between teachers who were adept in discipline and those who were inept.

In the late sixties and early seventies, this picture changed rapidly and dramatically. All seven models of discipline described earlier were put forth in a scant 10 years (1969–1979). Each of the models added behavioral skills, actions teachers could perform rather easily, that were shown by evidence to improved student behavior. A few new attitudes came along with them—students have a real need for discipline; teachers have a right to have discipline and be able to teach; and students have a right to have good teaching within an atmosphere conducive to learning, with severe restrictions placed on self-defeating behaviors. Today, teachers have at their disposal a powerful array of management skills that when implemented properly reduce misbehavior, produce orderly learning environments, and channel student energies toward productive ends.

These techniques and skills appeared at a propitious time. The decade of the sixties showed what many considered a serious decline in respect for authority, combined with a view toward immediate self-gratification. This view spread through the schools, so that students no longer deferred readily to teacher authority. When confrontations with students occurred, teachers felt powerless to deal with the situation and to maintain the upper hand, so to speak. Needless to say, the powerful control techniques that appeared with discipline systems such as assertive discipline seemed a godsend to teachers.

But as surely as the tides ebb and flow, public opinion about schools, education, and discipline began to reverse direction. Parent concern about discipline had remained constantly strong, as evidenced year after year in the Gallup poll on attitudes toward education, but with the decade of the eighties parents and communities at large began to show increased willingness to take positive steps toward school improvement. This occurred on many fronts—curriculum, teaching effectiveness, and support for education, as well as discipline. The public became appalled at the incidence of physical attacks on teachers, which though relatively rare still grabbed the headlines. Much was written and said about teacher burnout and the effect that discipline problems had on it. The public became greatly concerned about the flight of quality teachers into other lines of work. Schools that somehow managed to maintain discipline and quality instruction captured public attention, especially when located in areas of economic deprivation. Parents began to see that high expectations for children could be maintained and quality learning could be provided if they gave support to teachers and schools.

These factors combined to produce broad support for teachers and schools that adhered to high standards of discipline, achievement, and quality instruction. Therefore, in the mid-1970s, when teacher morale was approaching its lowest ebb, renewed public support came together with newly developed systems of discipline so that teachers became empowered, once again, to establish the kinds of learning climates that brought a sense of purpose and joy to the classroom.

This resurgence at first homed in on individual teacher and classroom. As teachers began to sense renewed support, and as they gained exposure to the new systems of discipline, they began individually to reformulate better approaches to classroom control, finding elements and techniques that seemed consonant with their own personalities and at the same time effective for the students with whom they worked. The positive effects were immediately obvious to many teachers, but it is accurate to say that even highly beneficial ideas such as effective discipline did not sweep through teaching like wildfire. The movement was more akin to a snail's pace, with large percentages of teachers failing even to this day to make use of the powerful techniques available to them. But those who have done so provide abundant testimonials about their newly found leases on teaching life.

Because this movement occurred piecemeal, individual teachers adopted, adapted, and developed individualistic systems of classroom discipline—One teacher making use of assertive discipline while the teacher next door made use of behavior modification and the teacher down the hall using something else. Each of the teachers effectively controlled and channeled student behavior, but the student body had no consistent structure. From teacher to teacher, rules differed as did the procedures of enforcement. As students changed classrooms so did they change discipline systems. What might be acceptable behavior in one room could be a gross violation of the rules in another. In the halls and on the grounds, students often functioned without structured discipline at all. This lack of consistency resulted in confusion and behavior problems for many students.

THE PUSH FOR SCHOOLWIDE DISCIPLINE

The early 1980s saw a growth of interest in discipline systems for use by all the teachers and students within a given school. This interest grew only in part from the realization that classroom-specific programs allowed inconsistency and student confusion. This fact alone might sooner or later have generated interest in adopting a unified discipline system, but it did not do so immediately. Most progress occurs in small steps. Teachers were at first concerned with making an immediate improvement in their own classrooms. Only after that was accomplished were they ready to consider that their efforts might be more effective through a unified approach in the school. Discipline, like that infant, had to learn to crawl before it learned to walk.

It was, rather, another development that fueled interest in schoolwide discipline. This development was the growing concern about what appeared to be a pervasive decline in school effectiveness, as indicated by falling SAT and other achievement test scores. That concern fostered considerable research into how teachers and schools could more effectively promote learning and thereby reverse the prolonged decline. The research identified several factors that when applied or corrected served to promote higher levels of student learning, at least in the basic areas of reading, language, and mathematics. The identified factors have been grouped under the rubric of "school effectiveness," and one reads much about it in the literature.

Most of the factors within school effectiveness can be attained poorly, if at all, without sound discipline. Examples of such factors are:

1. A safe and orderly environment for learning;
2. High standards and expectations;
3. Opportunities for student responsibility and involvement;
4. Maximum use of time;
5. Focus on student success;
6. Focus on dealing with causes rather than symptoms of problems;
7. Emphasis on positive behaviors and preventive measures.

Several other factors are included in school effectiveness, such as rigorous academic content, strong administrative leadership, and a coordinated curriculum. It is evident, however, that the seven factors listed above cannot be implemented effectively without a sound system of discipline. Since the effectiveness factors are the same for all grades and classes within the school, a unified system of discipline used by all teachers and staff in the school could be very helpful. That realization probably did more than anything else to spur the growing movement toward establishing unified discipline programs for use by all personnel in a given school.

SCHOOLWIDE DISCIPLINE PROGRAMS

Today a great many schools across the country have put schoolwide discipline programs into place or are in the process of doing so. These programs for the most part fall into three types: (1) a single established power system, such as assertive discipline, used by all teachers in the school; (2) a power system for Grades 3 and up, combined with a persuasive system such as behavior modification for primary grades; or (3) an eclectic system, comprised of elements familiar to teachers whose long-established effectiveness provides comfort and confidence. Eclectic approaches are familiar enough; the single power and the combination systems are explained in the following paragraphs.

Single Power System (Secondary Level)

A single system of discipline to be used by all administrators, teachers, and staff (secretaries, custodians, cafeteria workers, librarians, bus drivers, and so forth) is often favored at the secondary level. The program has three parts: (1) policy established by the board of education and disseminated to the public; (2) rules of student conduct; and (3) enforcement procedures, consequences, and means of follow-through.

The discipline policy adopted by the board of education provides broad limits and guidelines within which any specific discipline program is to function. The policy addresses such issues as the district's philosophy; responsibilities of the student, parent, teacher and administrator; prohibited behaviors; and disciplinary actions. The *philosophy* includes the right of all students to have access to quality education within a safe and orderly environment and explains that ensuring this right requires the close cooperation of all members of the school and community. The *student responsibilities* include respect for authority, behaving in ways that do not infringe on the rights of other students, and attending classes regularly and on time. *Parent responsibilities* include cooperating with school officials, accepting the school's right to require consistent behavior standards for all students, and supporting and assisting the school's efforts to provide quality education. *Teacher responsibilities* include clear explanation of standards, rules, and consequences, consistent and fair enforcement of standards and communication with parents concerning student behavior. *Administrator responsibilities* include assisting students, parents, teachers and staff; communicating policy and procedures clearly to the community; and maintaining a total-school environment that is orderly and safe. *Prohibited behaviors* include such things as defiance of authority, fighting, use of drugs and alcohol, destruction of property, and so forth, and *disciplinary actions* indicate what will be done in the event of both ordinary and serious violations of the established regulations.

Rules of student conduct are established that apply to all students in all parts of the school. This system calls on students to adhere to the following five rules.

1.   Always be on time and ready to work.
2.   Treat all people and property with respect.
3.   Cooperate with those in positions of authority.
4.   Leave nuisance items at home.
5.   Do not disrupt the teaching-learning process.

All school personnel in positions of authority are empowered to enforce these rules.

Rules can be enforced in the following way. First, all students are made thoroughly aware of the rules and what they mean. Charts are posted in every room displaying the five rules. When a student violates a rule, a verbal warning is given. That warning carries no penalty, but puts the student on notice that consequences will result from the next violation. If a violation reoccurs, the person in authority makes a notation on special forms in triplicate—one copy goes to the student, a second to the office, and the third is kept by the person initiating the complaint. School counselors keep a conduct card for all students assigned to them. Violations of the rules of discipline are reported by note to the counselor who in turn enters the notation on the student's conduct card. Consequences are then imposed on the student, in a way similar to that advocated by Canter, progressing through restitutions, teacher conference, calling the parent, referral to the counselor, referral to principal or vice-principal, and loss of normal privileges such as attendance at dances, taking a class trip, or participation in athletic events. Always in effect is a "severe clause," which allows immediate referral to the principal or suspension from school for acts such as fighting and using drugs.

Combination System (Elementary Level)

The combination of a power system (one that immediately suppresses misbehavior) with a persuasive system (one that guides behavior through example and reinforcement) is often favored in elementary schools. This is due to the fact that very young children in primary grades are still in the process of learning what are and are not acceptable behaviors. This learning occurs best through good example combined with reinforcement, both of which are very effective in shaping the behavior of young children

After the primary grades students have become fully aware of the difference between acceptable and unacceptable behavior and do not require nearly so much teaching in that regard. Social reinforcement supplied by teachers begins to lose effectiveness as students grow older and fall under the influence of reinforcement from their peers. Therefore, a stronger system of discipline is often advocated for them.

This system of schoolwide discipline can be understood in terms specifying school policy, schoolwide acceptable and unacceptable behaviors, classroom rules, and procedures used to enforce the established rules. As contrasted with the single power system (secondary level) the elementary plan places less emphasis on defining broad policy while placing more on specifying in detail what children may and may not do at school

Policy in this plan is established by the school staff, with representative parent advice and consent. It can be communicated to the childrens' parents by means of informative letters from the principal to the parents' homes. The letter can mention the school's intent to provide warmth and support for appropriate productive behavior while taking benign steps to discourage inappropriate behavior. Strong emphasis is placed on positive reinforcement of good behavior, as a means of providing a calm, happy, supportive place for children to learn, while at the same time teaching them the social behaviors that lead to successful interpersonal relations in all aspects of life.

At the bottom of the first page of the letter is a place where parents are asked to indicate with their signatures that they have read, understood, and accepted the discipline plan used by the school. They send this part of the communication back to the school where it is kept on file.

The next section of the letter specifies in detail behaviors expected of students. Included are sections having to do with school standards, how to enter and leave the school grounds and buildings, rules of the playgrounds, rules of the cafeteria, bicycle regulations, personal property concerns (such as labeling items with names), clothing concerns (safe, nondistracting), bringing pets, rules of the lunch area, rainy day regulations, use of restrooms, use of multipurpose room, use of library–media center, what to do when dismissed, and regulations concerning buses. There may also be discussion of the responsibilities of students, parents, teachers, and administrators, and there is a listing of the behaviors that will not be tolerated and that call for immediate suspension.

The third section of the letter describes steps that will be followed in enforcing the regulations. Primary grade students will to the extent possible be corrected through redirection and positive reinforcement. The teacher will model and discuss correct behavior and apply positive reinforcement when students exhibit that behavior. Inappropriate behavior (such as talking without raising one's hand) will be discouraged by giving attention to students who abide by the rule. Very inappropriate behavior (such as fighting or throwing tantrums) will be suppressed by removing the child from the group to sit alone.

Older students, beginning with the third grade, can be corrected using a system that immediately suppresses behavior that violates rules. Care will be taken to be sure that students understand the rules and what constitutes compliance and violations. They then receive consequences such as those suggested by Canter: first violation is a warning, and each successive violation that day calls for a more severe consequence. Violations do not accumulate over days; each day begins with a clean slate. Along with this system of consequences, large measures of positive reinforcement and counseling are used to reemphasize the importance of living by rules and not infringing on others' rights.

Single Power System (Elementary Level)

When used at the elementary level, the single power system is something of a cross between the two systems previously presented. Policy, expectations, and detailing of behaviors are expressed as was done for the elementary example, while a single system of enforcement and consequences is used as illustrated in the secondary example. A favored plan for this approach is Canter's "assertive discipline," which is very effective in suppressing misbehavior even at the kindergarten level. Many primary teachers do not approve of the use of a power system with very young children, considering it too harsh and not sufficiently concerned with teaching children how they *should* behave instead of how they should not. This feeling accounts for the interest in combination systems, as illustrated in the previous example. Nevertheless, there are many primary teachers who strongly support assertive discipline in the primary grades. They argue that it need not be harsh, that teachers can teach good behavior along with its use, and that it gives all students a feeling of consistency in the discipline system used at school.

PROBLEMS OF IMPLEMENTING
A SCHOOLWIDE DISCIPLINE SYSTEM

Problems arise when any change of consequence is made in the school program, even when the change is universally acknowledged as desirable. Advance planning that identifies potential problems is useful in circumventing them. Problem areas requiring attention when a school attempts to implement a single discipline system include faculty and staff agreement, feasibility, parental support, and faculty ability to perform roles required of them. This section indicates how these typical problems can be reduced, so that a school-wide system can be installed and made operational within a short time.

Faculty and Staff Agreement

As with almost any human endeavor that involves more than one person, disagreement on problems, issues, solutions, and procedures is bound to occur. In the case of discipline, areas of disagreement often include rationale, solutions, extra work, and new procedures. The role of the site administrator is pivotal in resolving these kinds of disagreements, and that person must be a strong, informed leader who is adept in human relations and positive persuasion.

Rationale.   Rationale refers to the reason for putting a new operation in place. Teachers are certain to disagree to some extent about the desirability in change and usually to a greater extent about whether a schoolwide system is better than an individual classroom system in which teachers use what is already comfortable, convenient, and effective for them. Those teachers who do not feel discipline problems quite so keenly (usually primary teachers) may balk at giving up what they know works for them in favor of something about which they are unsure.

Solutions.   Many teachers have become weary over the years of having administrators press for single solutions to school problems, only to see that after much work and effort the problem remains or else the solution produces yet another problem. This has led to a reluctance to invest time and energy into new schemes whose effectiveness remains to be proven. This reluctance should be considered when attempting to get the faculty and staff to agree on a single, or at most a dual approach to dealing with discipline in school. If this resistance is to be set aside, the administrator must furnish evidence that schoolwide discipline approaches do in fact increase the quality of the total school program while adding no new burdens for the teacher. The solutions proposed should include two or three options that allow teachers some discretion; this provides an avenue for decision making that can help them find a personal stake in the system that is finally adopted.

Extra Work.   It should be taken as a given that teachers automatically balk at anything new that adds to existing workloads. This is not because teachers are lazy. It is well documented that teachers on the average put into their jobs well in excess of 40 hours per week. Their inability to leave their work at school and free their minds in the evenings for other things has produced a level of stress matched by few other occupations, and when the stress level becomes high enough, a person attempts to avoid anything that seems to add to the load.

Teachers do, nevertheless, have a remarkable record of willingness to work on new projects when they see that benefits accrue to students. Teachers will invest time and effort into organizing a schoolwide discipline system if they believe that students will be the better for it and if they see that their professional lives will not suffer. The site administrator must provide compelling evidence that such will be the case, evidence that is readily available.

New Procedures.   There are many ways to skin a cat and many different roads to the mountaintop, and because teachers have found so many different ways to produce effective results, they are likely to disagree about the exact steps that should be incorporated in a new discipline system. At this point, it is helpful for school faculty and staff to hear brief descriptions made by teachers whose schools use a single discipline system. Teachers listen to other teachers because they have confidence that they speak from experience on the firing line. If possible, teachers should be invited from schools that use different systems or ways of implementing them. This provides alternative views as well as increased input for use in deciding on the approach to be adopted.

Feasibility

Many innovations that sound good at the abstract level never bear fruit at the practical level. Good examples are seen in the extensive rhetoric about matching teaching to students' diverse learning styles and reorganizing curriculum to match more closely the way the human brain functions. Who would argue that such ideas are poor ones? The trouble in both cases has been that while the idea seems true and workable, teachers have found in practice that far too little is known about learning styles and human brain function. Even experts who devote much of their time to those matters have not furnished compelling models, including detailed procedures, that enable teachers to put the ideas into practice. There is also a dearth of evidence that supports the contention that such approaches produce the results for which they are intended.

Curriculum workers have discovered that any idea, however noble and correct it might appear to be, has little chance of becoming a part of classroom instruction unless it: (1) is clearly defined and detailed; (2) is "classroom friendly"; and (3) has evidence of effectiveness (Loucks and Zacchei, 1983). These three criteria are descriptions given in plain language of what Doyle and Ponder (1977) call instrumentality, congruence, and cost.

Definition and Detail. Definition and detail are necessary so that everyone—teachers, staff, administrators, and parents—knows what the program looks like; what its key components are; what teachers and students do in the classroom; what administrators and parents do; and what the results are expected to be.

Classroom Friendly. "Classroom friendly" means that the new program fits into what is already going on in the classroom. Ideas that can be integrated into or superimposed over existing programs can be managed and are thus acceptable to teachers. Ideas that require a substantial reorganization of the existing program are usually rejected.

Evidence of Effectiveness. Evidence of effectiveness is becoming more and more a requirement before teachers will invest effort into new projects. As mentioned previously, teachers have grown weary and leery of panaceas that turned out after much time and effort to be ineffective and, in some cases, even detrimental to student growth.

The site adminsitrator who hopes to assist teachers in bringing about a schoolwide system of discipline must be able to attend to these matters of psychological feasibility. Programs to be considered by teachers must be presented in detail that is understandable, must be congruent with existing classroom practice, and must have a record of proven effectiveness. If these criteria are met, the innovation is feasible in the eyes of teachers and staff.

Parental Support

While parents like teachers disagree on almost any matter, their disagreement over discipline will focus on detail rather than substance. Few parents argue against the need for better discipline in the schools, and most eagerly support it. They may not agree with some of the specific details of a given program, such as sending home the severely misbehaving student or suspending him from school. They many not welcome being called for conferences about misbehavior. Yet most will agree to the necessity of effective programs. Lack of parent support for positive nonpunitive discipline comes more from ignorance of the program than from a reluctance to see discipline made stronger at school. The school must, therefore, take pains to see that parents have representative involvement on committees that deliberate the school discipline plan and that all are kept informed through meetings, newsletters, and community media.

Faculty Ability to Fill Roles

Instructional innovation cannot occur if teachers lack the skills for new approaches required. Teachers cannot implement assertive discipline, for example, if they have only scanty information about how it is organized and conducted. Some informative or light training sessions must, therefore, be built early into the deliberations. These sessions need not be extensive, but they must be sufficient to ensure understanding of programs and needed skills. Fortunately, no highly specialized training is required in any of the established systems of discipline, with the possible exception of Dreikurs's system. The steps required in Jones's classroom management program, for example, can be learned easily by teachers and nonteachers alike. There is nothing esoteric about them. The Dreikurs's system does call for more extensive interpretation and counseling and, therefore, is not a highly attractive option for a school-wide system.

The point then is that teachers must be able to fill the roles expected of them and carry out the details of the program adopted. Otherwise their inability will severely hinder success of the program. Teachers must either already possess the required skills or else be able to acquire them with a minimum of training.

POSITIVE STEPS FOR IMPLEMENTATION

Schools that wish to adopt a standard discipline program should attend to five positive steps, which when achieved provide high likelihood of program success. These five steps are:

1. Provide quality rationale and options.
2. Forsee and forestall problems.
3. Involve all concerned and communicate fully.
4. Provide for "buy-in" by all groups at all phases.
5. Conduct trial implementation, with evaluation and revision.

Let us consider each of the following steps.

Provide Quality Rationale and Options. Some type of needs assessment must show first that there is a clear concern among teachers and parents about school discipline. If there is no concern, there is no need for a schoolwide plan. If the concern is evident, two or three quality programs that have been used effectively in other schools can be described and made available to discussion groups. These programs should be known to improve student behavior, improve school climate, and facilitate the process of dealing with student misbehavior.

Foresee and Forestall Problems.   The preceeding section detailed problems that are most likely to occur as schools attempt to implement single systems of discipline. Means for avoiding and reducing the severity of those problems were mentioned.

Involve All Concerned and Communicate Fully.   All people who are to be involved in and concerned with the new discipline plan should be informed and consulted to the greatest extent feasible. The one exception is the elementary school students, who need not be consulted or involved in the deliberations. Secondary schools students, however, should be consulted and input sought from them. All should understand the rationale of the project, ends sought, and steps being taken toward those ends.

Teachers, staff members, parents, and administators should be represented extensively on committees selected to work on the new system, and each of these groups should receive full communication about all aspects of the project. The board of education, through the superintendent or designate, should also be kept fully apprised. Board approval of the idea would have been secured in advance.

Provide for "Buy-in" by All Groups at All Phases.   To *buy-in* means to acquire a personal stake in the project. This is accomplished through enabling people to explore the specific advantages that accrue to them, their children, or students, and through enabling them to make suggestions or other contributions that are incorporated into the project. The personal stake that results causes each person to become more supportive of the project and more willing to cooperate and invest further effort.

Conduct Trial Implementation with Evaluation and Revision.   It is important that everyone concerned understand that the new plan when implemented has trial status—that is, it is not cast in stone but rather is being tried out with the understanding that modifications will be made as necessary. People concerned with development and implementation should continue to serve as monitors of the program for at least the first few months of its existence. The monitor and review function should be made an integral part of the plan, not one carried out as an afterthought or done on a hit-and-miss basis. A process for this function should be put in place for dealing with modifications as the need becomes evident.

TRAINING FOR IMPLEMENTATION

Virtually any plan selected or formulated by the school committee will require some in-service teacher training. If an existing program is adopted, such as Canter's assertive discipline, Jones's classroom management program, or Glasser's reality approach, certain specific techniques peculiar to that program are required. Many or most of the teachers will not be adequately familiar with them to be able to implement the program without at least some refresher work. The same situation is likely to exist if the school modifies existing programs or composes its own. Even in the unlikely case that most teachers are familiar with the essential contents and techniques of a given plan, it is necessary to arrive at consensus about what constitutes misbehavior and how the agreed-upon consequences are to be invoked.

This training should not be imposed from outside. The teacher and staff groups themselves should be charged with the responsibility of identifying needed training. An effective administrator can then help find the resources to provide that training. The training might consist of nothing more than an exposure to the elements and procedures in the program. To be most effective, however, training should involve teachers and staff in the actual practice of intervening and following through on student misbehavior.

Training sessions seem to be considerably more effective when done in a series of short sessions rather than in longer one-shot presentations (Berman and McLaughlin, 1978). The reason for this may be that when sessions are spaced over time teachers have more opportunity to do mental practice with the techniques, applying them to imagined occurrences. This reflection or mental rehearsal has long been recognized as an important factor in learning.

Stallings, Needels, and Stayrook (1978) have concluded that staff development seems to occur best when scheduled in a series of 4 to 6 workshops, each of about 3 hours in length, spaced 1 or 2 weeks apart. In the case of a new discipline system, probably no more than 4 training sessions would be needed, each of 2 hours in length and spaced over 2 or 3 weeks' time. This schedule allows for mental rehearsal and seems to assist in a gradual change in teacher attitude and skill that results in more lasting results.

Some of the most important recent work in staff development has been done by Joyce and Showers (1982) who have popularized the concept and practice of "coaching" in teacher training. Like other people interested in teaching new skills to teachers, they stress the four steps of presentation, demonstration, participant practice, and corrective feedback. Their special contribution is the element of coaching, a practice designed to increase dramatically the transfer (application) of skills learned during training to actual practice in the classroom. The amount of transfer in most training programs is incredibly small, but Joyce and Showers have found that if teachers work together in pairs, with some opportunity to observe and critique each other, the amount of transfer of the new skill is dramatically increased.

DISSEMINATION OF THE SCHOOLWIDE PROGRAM

It was indicated earlier in this chapter that full communication among all parties concerned is an essential consideration in the formulation and implementation of new school programs. Without such communication, problems of disagreement, protection of territory, and withdrawal from the process are likely to hinder the program seriously. Good communication, though it often causes initial slowdown while people discuss and come to understandings, results in vested interest and consensus, which in turn increase markedly the program's chances for success.

The new schoolwide discipline program, once adopted, should be disseminated to all people and agencies that might have interest. Included are teachers and staff, not only in the individual school but throughout the district, students in the school, parents of students in school, the community at large, and possibly the educational community nationwide.

Most of the teachers and staff members will have been closely involved or fully informed throughout the process of developing the school plan. When the plan is completed, it should be described briefly and clearly in writing (preferably in nice print on good paper) with a copy furnished to every teacher, staff member, administrator, and family associated with the school.

Students in the school should have the plan described to them fully and carefully. At the secondary level, student input would have been obtained. Dissemination there includes discussions in class, presentations in assemblies, and rules and reminders posted throughout the school. Students also have access to printed descriptions that are sent home to parents.

Parents will have been informed to some extent during formulation of the plan. When the plan is completed, they are further informed through the printed descriptions, at open house at school, in PTA meetings, and in other meetings and conferences called for purposes of information and discussion. Along with the printed description of the school plan should be a form for parents to sign and return to school indicating that they understand the program and support its implementation.

The community at large will show a surprising amount of interest in discipline programs developed for schools. Newspapers will want to mention the efforts and results, and some will wish to do feature stories on the program. Community service organizations are usually pleased to hear brief reports on such efforts.

Schools that develop especially effective programs, with documentation of significant improvement in student behavior, or those that have found especially fruitful or efficient procedures for developing and communicating their discipline system, will have an interested audience nationwide. They may wish to report their efforts in the form of journal articles submitted for publication in any one of a large number of journals concerned with teaching, research, administration, teacher taining, in-service education, or support services, Schools and agencies are continually on the lookout for exemplary programs that they might be able to adopt or modify to their use. Phi Delta Kappa has compiled a listing of schools recognized across the country for having outstanding discipline. Schools that have developed plans of which they are proud might wish to contact Phi Delta Kappa (PDK Commission on Discipline, Eighth and Union, Box 789, Bloomington, Ind. 47402) for consideration for future inclusion in their listing.

REFERENCES

BERMAN, P., and M. MCLAUGHLIN. *Federal Programs Supporting Educational Change, Vol. VIII: Implementing and Sustaining Innovations.* Santa Monica, Calif.: Rand, 1978.

DOYLE, W., and G. PONDER. "The Practicality Ethic and Teacher Decision-Making." *Interchange*8 (1977) :1–12.

JOYCE, B., and B. SHOWERS. "The Coaching of Teaching." *Educational Leadership*40 (October 1982) : 4–10.

LOUCKS, S., and D. ZACCHEI. "Applying our Findings to Today's Innovations." *Educational Leadership*41 (November 1983) :28–31.

PINNELL, G. et al. *Directory of Schools Reported to Have Exemplary Discipline.* Bloomington, Ind.: Phi Delta Kappa, 1982.

STALLINGS, J., M. NEEDELS, and N. STAYROOK. *How to Change the Process of Teaching Basic Reading Skills in Secondary Schools: Phase II and Phase III Final Report.* Menlo Park, Calif.: SRI International, 1978.

INDEX